INTIMATE VIOLENCE

INTIMATE VIOLENCE

Anti-Jewish Pogroms on the
Eve of the Holocaust

**Jeffrey S. Kopstein and
Jason Wittenberg**

CORNELL UNIVERSITY PRESS   ITHACA AND LONDON

Copyright © 2018 by Cornell University

All rights reserved. Except for brief quotations in a review, this book, or parts thereof, must not be reproduced in any form without permission in writing from the publisher. For information, address Cornell University Press, Sage House, 512 East State Street, Ithaca, New York 14850.

First published 2018 by Cornell University Press

Printed in the United States of America

Library of Congress Cataloging-in-Publication Data

Names: Kopstein, Jeffrey, author. | Wittenberg, Jason, 1963– author.
Title: Intimate violence : anti-Jewish pogroms on the eve of the
  Holocaust / Jeffrey S. Kopstein and Jason Wittenberg.
Description: Ithaca : Cornell University Press, 2018. | Includes bibliographical
  references and index.
Identifiers: LCCN 2017048064 (print) | LCCN 2017051368 (ebook) |
  ISBN 9781501715266 (epub/mobi) | ISBN 9781501715273 (pdf) |
  ISBN 9781501715259 | ISBN 9781501715259 (cloth : alk. paper)
Subjects: LCSH: Jews—Persecutions—Poland—History—20th century. |
  Pogroms—Poland—History—20th century. | Antisemitism—Poland—
  History—20th century. | Holocaust, Jewish (1939–1945)—Poland. |
  Poland—Ethnic relations.
Classification: LCC DS134.55 (ebook) | LCC DS134.55 .K68 2018 (print) |
  DDC 305.892/4043809041—dc23
LC record available at https://lccn.loc.gov/2017048064

ISBN: 978-1-5017-8502-3 (pbk.)

For Max and Isaac
—J.K.

For Dahlia
—J.W.

Contents

Preface ix

1. Why Neighbors Kill Neighbors 1
2. Ethnic Politics in the Borderlands 22
3. Measuring Threat and Violence 43
4. Beyond Jedwabne 57
5. Ukrainian Galicia and Volhynia 84
6. Pogroms outside the Eastern Borderlands 114
7. Intimate Violence and Ethnic Diversity 127

Appendix: Pogroms in the Eastern Borderlands, Summer 1941 137
Notes 143
References 153
Index 167

Preface

This book grew out of an invitation to a conference on the Holocaust and its local contexts. Jan Gross's *Neighbors* had been published several years earlier and debates continued (and still continue) to rage about who had committed the Jedwabne pogrom and why. It was an unexpected opportunity to bring together two important streams of scholarship that had never adequately been integrated: the large social scientific literature on intercommunal violence and a new generation of Holocaust historiography that situated the violence in specific communities, each with its own backstory. Could the theories and approaches used to explain ethnic violence in other contexts help explain the neighbor-on-neighbor violence that broke out in hundreds of communities in the eastern Polish borderlands as the Germans passed through in summer 1941?

Our intuition was that the roots of more than two hundred 1941 pogroms were located in the ethnic demographics and political behavior of the interwar era, information that we had already been collecting for a project on the ethnic origins of dictatorship and democracy. The historical literature focuses on anti-Semitism and beliefs about Jewish support for communism. The social science literature, which does not analyze these pogroms in any detail, suggests the answer lies in the economic and political threat to pogrom perpetrators by those who would become their victims. Our data could speak to these arguments. We discovered a connection between interwar political behavior and the occurrence of pogroms that centered on the local political milieu and, in particular, non-Jewish rejection of Jewish efforts to achieve national rights within Poland.

We were not working in a vacuum. Other scholars before and during our research had already started the slow and painstaking job of documenting pogrom occurrence and nonoccurrence; we supplemented this work with our own archival and secondary research across multiple languages. To this we added our interwar census, electoral, and other data. We sought out the expertise of many historians who specialize in Poland and the Holocaust, and the following deserve special mention: Doris Bergen, John Connelly, Sol Goldberg, Antony Polonsky, Anna Shternshis, and Timothy Snyder. We have presented this research at many institutions and conferences and have benefited tremendously from the feedback of our colleagues in political science, history, and Jewish studies.

Data collection is not only tedious, but expensive. We could not have completed this project without generous funding from the National Science Foundation, the

National Council for East European and Eurasian Research, the Social Sciences and Humanities Research Council of Canada, the University of Toronto, the University of Wisconsin–Madison, the University of California–Berkeley, and the University of California–Irvine. We owe a great debt of gratitude to our many undergraduate and graduate research assistants, who performed the crucial but often unglamorous task of keying in and checking the accuracy of entered data. Special thanks go to Sarah Cramsey for her help with the Polish literature and comments on the entire manuscript, and to Laura Jákli for her technical expertise.

We are particularly grateful to Roger Haydon at Cornell University Press for his patience, professionalism, and good judgment and to two readers who offered very important advice for revision. Finally, to our spouses, we apologize for spending so long on such a depressing topic and appreciate the sacrifices you have made that allowed us to finish what we hope will be a lasting contribution to the social scientific study of ethnic violence and the Holocaust.

A note on language: we use the pre–World War II Polish version of place names except where the English spelling is internationally recognized. Therefore, we use "Warsaw" and "Volhynia" rather than "Warszawa" and "Wołyn." In eastern Poland, many of these place names also have Ukrainian, Yiddish, German, and/or Belarusian variants. We remain with the Polish versions for clarity of presentation and to avoid ambiguities introduced by transliteration.

INTIMATE VIOLENCE

1
WHY NEIGHBORS KILL NEIGHBORS

Two tragedies befell the Jews of Eastern Europe after the outbreak of World War II. The first and by far the best known and exhaustively researched is the Holocaust, the Nazi extermination effort. The second is "the violent explosion of the latent hatred and hostility of local communities" (Żbikowski 1993, 174). With the Soviet army retreating, the German army advancing, and government authority collapsing, civilian populations across hundreds of villages and towns stretching from the Baltic states in the north to Romania in the south committed atrocities against their Jewish neighbors. These often gruesome and sadistic crimes ranged from looting and beatings to public humiliation, rape, torture, and murder. One of the most widely known such incidents occurred in the town of Jedwabne, Poland, on July 10, 1941. In a day-long rampage under the approving eyes of the Germans, Poles committed mass murder. The Jews were ordered to gather in the town square, where among other humiliations they were forced to clean the pavement, smash the monument to Lenin, and hold a mock "religious" funeral on his behalf. Those who attempted to flee were hunted down and clubbed, stoned, knifed, and drowned, their bloodied corpses often left in pits. Apparently dissatisfied with such inefficient methods of murder, the perpetrators herded hundreds of remaining Jews—women, children, the old, and the sick—into a barn that was doused with kerosene and set alight (Gross 2001). Ethnic violence is never easy to comprehend, but it is especially puzzling when the perpetrators are civilians and the victims are their neighbors (Fujii 2009; Straus 2006; Kalyvas 2006).

This book investigates the reasons for such "intimate" violence. The 1941 pogroms are a particularly interesting instance of such violence for two reasons.

First, they happened under conditions of state collapse. Many who study ethnic violence emphasize the key role of state elites in orchestrating conflict (e.g., Brass 2003; Gagnon 2004; Lambroza 1992; Wilkinson 2004). But state actions cannot explain the 1941 pogroms because state institutions in the areas of Poland under Soviet control had all but collapsed by the time they occurred. The Germans invaded the Soviet Union on June 22, 1941, but did not establish full political authority on Polish territory that had been annexed to the Soviet Union until at least September (Żbikowski 2007, 315; Snyder 2008, 96). In the period between Soviet and German rule, there was no central government in this region. To the extent anyone was in control, it would have been the Germans, but, as we argue later in this chapter, they did not yet function as a de facto state elite. Although the Germans did try to incite pogroms, they met with only limited success. Pogroms occurred both with and without the Germans being present. Like Kalyvas (2006) and Petersen (2002), we seek to understand ethnic violence under conditions of state collapse such as can occur during periods of war, civil war, regime change, and the collapse of empire.

Second, the scale of the attacks demonstrates that ethnic violence is not an inherent feature of intergroup life under anarchic conditions, even with relationships as long-standing and conflictual as those between Jews and non-Jews. Given the long history of restrictions, attacks, and expulsions directed against Jews in Eastern Europe, it is easy to believe that non-Jews must have eagerly assaulted their Jewish neighbors when the Nazi onslaught on the Soviet Union presented an opportunity. After all, the Germans were, if anything, sympathetic to those who wanted to attack Jews, and in the absence of a state the "clouding features of legal restraint" (Petersen 2002, 12) disappeared and people were freer to act on their desires. As Kalyvas (2006, 389) notes in regard to civil wars, chaotic and uncertain circumstances offer "irresistible opportunities to harm everyday enemies." Where violence did occur it was often quite gruesome and could include beheading, the chopping off of limbs, rape, and the ripping of fetuses from the wombs of pregnant women.[1]

Yet pogroms were relatively rare events. According to our data, in the six regions composing most of the eastern Polish borderlands that had been occupied by the Soviet Union in 1939 and by Germany following the outbreak of war in 1941—Białystok, Lwów, Polesie, Stanisławów, Tarnopol, and Volhynia—pogroms occurred in 219 localities, making up just 9 percent of all localities in the region where Jews and non-Jews dwelled together. Most communities never experienced a pogrom and most ordinary non-Jews never attacked Jews. Such a pattern is not limited to Poland. Tolnay and Beck (1995, 45), for example, report that more than one-third of counties in the U.S. South never experienced a lynching. Varshney (2002, 6–7) notes that only eight cities in India accounted for just over 45 percent of all deaths in Hindu-Muslim violence. Our data show that ethnic violence is situational rather than inherent. The task for researchers, one we undertake in this book, is to identify and characterize the local contexts that stimulate or inhibit ethnic violence in societies with long histories of animosity.

Our central question is, Why did pogroms occur in some localities but not others? Our results demonstrate the limitations of some of the most commonly believed explanations for pogroms. The 1941 pogroms were not orchestrated by the state, and in general did not occur where economic competition between Jews and non-Jews was fiercest or where Jews were the most sympathetic to communism. None of these accounts explain the relative rarity of the violence. Anti-Semitism may have been a necessary background condition, but the more robust explanation is that pogroms were rooted in competing nationalisms. We contend that the pogroms represented a strategy whereby non-Jews attempted to rid themselves of those whom they thought would be future political rivals. Pogroms were most likely to occur where there were lots of Jews, where those Jews advocated national equality with non-Jews, and where parties advocating national equality were popular. In the following section, we review existing explanations for municipality-level variation in ethnic violence and then expand on our own explanation that focuses on political threat.

Explanations for Pogroms
Revenge

As a consequence of secret protocols to the 1939 Molotov-Ribbentrop Pact concluded between Germany and the Soviet Union, the two countries divided Poland between them. Germany invaded Poland on September 1, 1939, and after a two-week period of confusion, pulled back to its allotted territories in the west. The Soviet Union invaded Poland on September 17, 1939, and occupied the eastern borderlands, or *kresy*, with the intention of incorporating this territory into the Soviet state. During the roughly two years between the Red Army's arrival and its retreat in the wake of the June 1941 Nazi invasion, the Soviets ran a brutal occupation regime. The Jewish collaboration hypothesis (e.g., Musiał 2004) posits that pogroms served as revenge for Jewish support of the Soviet occupation.

This hypothesis is both logically plausible and consistent with some aspects of the historical record. First, although it is impossible to know the entire distribution of attitudes toward Soviet rule on the eve of the occupation, most scholars agree that a common Jewish reaction to the arrival of Soviet soldiers was one of relief. Having experienced open discrimination and many pogroms in interwar Poland, Soviet rule, harsh as it might have been expected to be, offered at least the prospect of civic equality. It was certainly preferable to the Nazi rule in western Poland. In the words of Moshe Levin, it was "the lesser of two evils," a sentiment some Jews were known to have voiced openly. For example, according to Henryk Szyper, whose memoir was written just after the war, a Jewish director of a store would say to a Pole who complained, "There is no more free Poland, your time is over. It is our time" (AŻIH 301-4654). Such attitudes, however rarely expressed, could only have inflamed Poles, for whom the occupation meant the end of national sovereignty.

Second, although all national groups suffered under Soviet rule (collectivization, nationalization, and deportation, for example, touched all corners of society), the de jure removal of barriers that had impeded Jewish integration in interwar Poland meant that the status of Jews increased relative to that of Poles, who were no longer the ruling *Staatsnation*; and also to that of Ukrainians, whose nationalist aspirations, already frustrated by Poland, the Soviets brutally repressed. Positions within the Soviet apparatus were in theory as open to Jews as they were to Poles or Ukrainians and, at the lower levels of the administration, the regime found many Jews willing to serve. As Brakel (2007) reports in his study of the Baranowicze region in northeast Poland, Jews worked in the Soviet administration, ran for office, were members of the newly created communist youth organization, and were even among those more trusted *vostochniki* (easterners) brought in from other parts of the Soviet Union to help administer the new territories. The fact that low-level state bureaucrats would have had the most contact with the local non-Jewish populations meant that Jews were visibly associated with the Soviet regime. According to one observer, "Offices and institutions that never saw a Jew on their premises abound now with Jewish personnel of all kinds" (cited in Pinchuk 1990, 50). In the words of Szyper (AŻIH 301-4654), an unquestionable achievement of Soviet rule was "factual emancipation and equalization of political citizenship." For Petersen (2002), Polish and Ukrainian resentment at their relative loss of status was a prime driver of pogrom violence, regardless of whether the Jews actively had a hand in the reversal of Polish and Ukrainian fortunes.

Third, there is ample anecdotal evidence that local non-Jewish populations blamed the Jews for the Soviet occupation. We agree with Żbikowski (2007) that no "uniform pogrom scenario" existed, but eyewitness accounts of how pogroms actually occurred do reveal some recurring themes. One of these is the ritual humiliation of the Jewish victims in ways that clearly associate them with the Soviet regime. For example, in the towns of Kolno and Jedwabne, locals forced the Jews to remove the statue of Lenin and bury it in the ground. In Kolno, the Jews then had to sing and pray for the buried monument; in Jedwabne, the Jews were subsequently beaten to death and thrown into the same grave.[2] In Siematycze, the Jews had to dismantle the Lenin statue with hammers and sickles.[3] In Radziłow,

Poles made the Jews sing a Soviet song, *Moskva Moia*, and in Kościelne, as the Lenin statue was being thrown in the water, the Polish police forced a local Jew to give a dictated speech in which, among other things, he said, "Lenin, you gave us your life and you give us death, you'll never rise again."[4] We also know that the perpetrators of many pogroms had previously been incarcerated in Soviet Secret Police (NKVD) prisons.[5]

Chapters 4 and 5 will investigate the consistency of the connection between local perceptions of Jewish collaboration and the distribution of pogroms. Although we have no systematic data by locality on Jewish presence in the Soviet administration, it stands to reason that sympathy for the Soviet regime would be highest where support for communist parties was strongest. Therefore, if pogroms constituted punishment for collaboration with the Soviet occupation, then the probability of a pogrom should be positively related to prewar communist support. We find no such systematic relationship between pogrom outbreaks and the vote given to communist parties during the interwar period.

We can also challenge the degree to which the locals' beliefs were warranted given actual evidence of collaboration. Such a challenge is important because it provides leverage on the crucial issue of perpetrator culpability. The pogroms were barbarous and unlawful, but there is still a difference between punishing those who are guilty of traitorous acts and scapegoating a vulnerable minority for acts it either did not commit or were also committed by members of other groups. In the former case, we might condemn the perpetrators for the manner in which punishment was delivered but concur with the principle that treachery deserves punishment. In the latter case, the perpetrators are guilty of both inhumane punishment and persecuting the innocent. In fact, a balanced consideration of the historical record casts significant doubt on the Jewish collaboration hypothesis.

First, if one component of the humiliation ritual during a pogrom involved having Jews dispose of a Soviet statue, another had them assume "Jewish" roles while doing it. In Kolno, for example, the blacksmiths who broke up the Lenin monument had to sing *Hatikvah*, a song associated with the Zionist movement that would later become the national anthem of Israel. The broken monument was placed on a cart, and other Jews, dressed in prayer shawls, had to pull the cart to the Jewish cemetery for "burial."[6] In Kościelne, it was *Hatikvah*-singing Jews that carried the Lenin statue from the center of town to the river.[7] In Siematycze, all the Jews had to wear prayer shawls while they dismantled the symbols of Soviet rule.[8]

Second, although some Jews certainly collaborated, so did some non-Jews. Indeed, as many have noted, the common non-Jewish perception—that most Jews were sympathetic to communism and supported the Soviet occupation and that most of the collaborators were Jews—is not borne out by actual facts. We do not have numbers to prove this for the kresy as a whole, but regional studies clearly bear this out. Consider, for example, the Białystok voivodship (province) in northeast Poland, which according to the 1931 census was roughly 67 percent Polish, 16 percent Belarusian, and 12 percent Jewish (just over 150,000 Jews). According to Jasiewicz (2001, tables 7–16, 1119–1134), in 1940 Jews composed 1.2 percent of 238 chairpersons of rural committees, 9 percent of 297 people in communist youth organization (Komsomol) management, 5.4 percent of 10,045 government candidates, and 4 percent of 8,885 (Communist Party) cadres. Not only are these rates of participation well under the Jewish proportion of the population, but in absolute terms represent a miniscule proportion of even the working adult Jewish population. Only among "local careerists" (*wydwiżency*) was there disproportionate Jewish presence, with Jews constituting just over 19 percent of 5,404 people. Brakel (2007) reports similar findings for the Baranowicze region. Moreover, to the extent there was a Jewish presence, it was more pronounced at the lower rather than the upper levels of Soviet administration. For example, in the March 1940 elections to the Supreme Soviet, not a single Jew was among the representatives of the newly incorporated provinces of eastern Poland. The Galician city of Lwów was roughly 30 percent Jewish, yet Jews made up a far lower percentage of its soviet. Some other towns with Jewish majorities nonetheless had non-Jewish mayors (Pinchuk 1990, 49; Yones 2004, 48).

In short, although the face of the Soviet regime may have had more Jews than non-Jews were accustomed to seeing, on the whole it would appear Jews were underrepresented in the administration both in absolute and relative terms. Those in more influential positions, who thus bore greater responsibility for Soviet crimes, were overwhelmingly non-Jewish. We can conclude two things from these observations. First, if pogroms were really about collaboration, then there ought to have been retaliation against non-Jewish collaborators. Yet there are exceedingly few such instances. Żbikowski (2007, 348) writes of the "discount" generally applied to Polish and Belarusian collaborators. According to one eyewitness, in July 1941, soldiers returning to Bolechów (in Galicia) wearing Soviet uniforms after the departure of the Red Army were killed only if they were Jews (Mendelsohn 2006, 195).[9] Similarly, regarding the city of Lwów, Syzper observes that "somewhat tacitly all Ukrainians agreed to peace. Nobody [i.e., no Ukrainians] was attacked for participating in the Soviet administration" (AŻIH 301-4654). If there were pogroms against communities of non-Jews in retaliation for collaboration, no one ever reported them. Anti-Jewish sentiments outweighed the anti-Soviet ones when it came to retaliation. Second, given the tenuous relationship between non-Jewish perceptions of Jewish collaboration and actual Jewish collaboration, it is difficult not to conclude, along with Mick (2007) and Brakel

(2007), that these perceptions have more to do with anti-Semitic stereotypes that predate the Soviet occupation than with the occupation itself. This brings us to another important proposed explanation for the pogroms, anti-Semitism.

Anti-Semitic Hatred

Among those who see the 1941 pogroms as simply yet another manifestation of a long history of anti-Jewish discrimination and violence, anti-Semitic hatred is an obvious explanation. How else to explain the brutality, the humiliation, the desecration of religious objects, and the victimization of children who could not possibly have collaborated? After all, these were hardly the first pogroms to have struck Poland, even in the twentieth century. There were a few scattered pogroms during the period when the Soviet Union invaded eastern Poland in September 1939 (Himka 1997, 182) and a major wave of anti-Jewish violence between 1935 and 1937. For example, in 1936 there were 21 pogroms and 348 "outbreaks" in the Białystok region (Tolisch 1937). In August 1937 alone, Jews in 80 different localities suffered attacks (Melzer 1997, 66). Less widespread violence occurred in the early 1930s in universities, where some students hoped to pressure the government to limit the number of Jewish pupils (Michlic-Coren 2000, 35). Hundreds of pogroms occurred between 1918 and 1920 in Polish- and Ukrainian-inhabited areas in the southeast, where Jews were caught in the middle of a Polish-Ukrainian struggle for political supremacy. During the November 1918 Lwów pogrom, Polish perpetrators destroyed Torah scrolls and humiliated religious Jews, foreshadowing the widespread ritualized violence of 1941 (Hagen 2005, 137–138). Other pogroms, resulting in hundreds of deaths, occurred in the Russian part of Poland between 1903 and 1906 (Lambroza 1992).

Nor were pogroms the only means by which Jews were attacked. Although Jews participated in most aspects of interwar Poland's economic, social, and political life, they also suffered discrimination, both formal and informal. As detailed by Rudnicki (2005), the last legal restrictions against Jews left over from the partition era (before World War I) were lifted only in 1931, a decade after the establishment of independent Poland. But Jews still had to contend with the efforts of right-wing Polish nationalists to curb Jewish rights and circumscribe Jewish influence. In the 1930s, for example, nationalists organized boycotts of Jewish businesses and portrayed the Jews as an "alien element" that was incompatible with Polish national life (Rudnicki 2005, 160). They made numerous political proposals, such as to deny Jews equal political rights, to prevent them from entering military service, and to bar them from employment across a range of professions. Though these proposals never made it very far politically, both Jews and non-Jews who wanted to protect equal rights were forced into a position of having to argue against them.

Other measures, less overtly discriminatory against Jews but with barely disguised (and sometimes undisguised) anti-Jewish intent, were popular enough to become law. These included a ban on "inhumane" (read: kosher) animal slaughter, a more restrictive citizenship law, and various measures empowering state officials to regulate their spheres of activity in ways that ultimately resulted in a reduced Jewish presence (Melzer 1997, 81–94). Among the better known of these measures pertained to higher education. Under pressure from nationalist students and their allies, in 1937 the Ministry of Education issued regulations that segregated seating areas for Christians and Jews across higher education, with punishment for those who failed to comply. These "ghetto benches," as they were known, resulted in a drastic decline in Jewish enrollment (Rudnicki 2005, 166; Melzer 1997, 71).

To these we can add what authors have referred to as non-Jewish "folk culture" or "folk prejudice." Generalizations are hazardous given the dearth of systematic evidence, but there is some consensus that ordinary non-Jews viewed Jews as something of an alien element in their midst, not necessarily mortal enemies but certainly not as one of their own. Before the advent of modern political anti-Semitism, Jewish difference was construed primarily in religious terms, with Jews cast as Christ-killers and enemies of the church. For Gross (2001, 122–124), this image of the Jews lay behind the 1941 pogroms in Radziłow and Jedwabne, where "peasant mobs," imbued with deeply ingrained beliefs about the Jewish need for the blood of Christian children to prepare the Passover matzo, swooped in for primitive slaughter and plunder. Over time, especially as religious anti-Semitism evolved into modern Jew hatred, other stereotypes were added to the religious one: Jews as swindlers, as atheists, as archcapitalists, as communists. In the case of Ukrainians, Himka (1997, 182) argues that within the Galician peasantry there existed a belief that "a day of reckoning was coming when all the Jews would be slaughtered." Whatever the particular stereotype, Jewish "otherness" meant that, however cordial the relationship might be between Jews and non-Jews at times, in the end non-Jews would not feel the same solidarity with Jews that they felt toward one another (Struve 2012, 271–272; Weeks 2005, 29–30).

Neither successive Polish governments nor the Roman Catholic Church condoned physical violence against Jews, and, indeed, at the highest levels both explicitly condemned such violence. At the same time, however, many influential political and religious leaders sympathized with the idea of defending Polish interests against a perceived Jewish threat. A full accounting of either the evolving state attitude toward or Roman Catholic views of the Jews is beyond the scope of this study. Instead we provide only some illustrative examples. In June 1936, Prime Minister Sławoj-Składkowski all but expressed support for the nationalist boycotts, stating that "[If you want] an economic struggle, then by all means go ahead."[10] By 1938, acting as minister of internal affairs, he was less equivocal, claiming that the struggle against the Jews was "a struggle of economic necessity."[11] In 1936 both Roman Catholic Primate August Hlond and Archbishop of Cracow Adam Sapieha issued pastoral letters that condemned violence but also endorsed the boycotts and accused Jews of a host of other threats to Poland, such as atheism, bolshevism, and corruption (Michlic 2006, 122–123). The portrayal of the Jews as what Michlic (2006) refers to as a "threatening other" was also visible in the Catholic press (Landau-Czajka 1994, 146–175) and in the attitudes of portions of the lower Catholic clergy (Libionka 2005, 234–237).

There is no question that antagonism toward Jews has had a long history in Polish lands; that during the interwar period the atmosphere became increasingly hostile and, indeed, violent toward Jews; and that in summer 1941, many pogrom perpetrators were animated by hatred or rage (or both). Nonetheless, we should not be too quick to infer that the wave of pogroms in summer 1941 can be reduced to anti-Semitism. First, the number of pogroms that occurred is not consistent with a one-sided portrayal of interwar Poland as uniformly hazardous for Jews. As noted earlier, pogroms occurred in roughly 9 percent of localities where Jews and non-Jews dwelled together. Even one pogrom is one too many, but over 90 percent of the places where a pogrom *could* have occurred experienced no pogrom at all. Despite the increased opportunity offered by the German invasion and the collapse of state authority, the vast majority of Poles and Ukrainians did not perpetrate pogroms, and the vast majority of Jews were not victims of them. If interwar Poland were as riven with anti-Semitism as the "pessimistic" view would have it and anti-Semitism were indeed the primary motive behind pogroms, then we would expect far more pogroms than we actually observe.[12] The relative rarity of pogroms thus implies one of two things: either violent anti-Semitism was not as widespread or deeply held as in the pessimistic view, in which case its more limited distribution might (or might not) account for the pogroms that we observe; or violent anti-Semitism was widespread and therefore could not have accounted for the pogroms.

We dissent from the pessimistic view, which tells only part of the story, though no doubt an important one. Although Jews in interwar Poland certainly experienced discrimination and violence, their story is not one of unremitting doom, even in the 1930s. For example, Jewish commerce survived and, in the case of large enterprises, may have even thrived, despite nationalist boycotts and acts of violence (Marcus 1983, 243–245). Although small traders suffered far more, even at the end of 1938 half of such traders were still Jews. Moreover, for all of interwar Poland's faults, Jews enjoyed many freedoms permitted under the Polish system (Mendelsohn 1986, 138). They formed their own political parties that competed and won seats in elections and served as representatives of other parties. They had a lively cultural and civic life, including Hebrew, Polish, and Yiddish presses, a system of schools, and sundry religious and other volunteer organizations. Jews were free to be Hasidic or Zionist or Socialist or Marxist or even Polish. Mendelsohn (1986, 139) lauds "the extraordinary creativity of Polish Jewry."

Although more radical Polish nationalist views of Jews spread among the elite as the 1930s wore on, not all non-Jewish leaders were hostile, and some, albeit a distinct minority, actively promoted joint cooperation between Jews and non-Jews. For example, the Polish Socialist Party (PPS) and (Jewish) Bund organized various joint actions in protest against anti-Jewish initiatives. The PPS stood alone in the late 1930s as the only major (non-Jewish) political party that did not openly advocate a Poland free of Jews, and some of the leadership explicitly condemned the rising anti-Jewish tide (Brumberg 1989, 82–89; see also Holzer 1994, 202; Melzer 1997, 24–25). There were similar liberal currents within the Catholic Church, though before the war they never influenced church policy (Polonsky 1997, 209; Connelly 2002, 653). Michlic (2006, 77–78) lists a number of other prominent non-Jewish political and intellectual elites who denounced the violence and the idea that Jews were the enemy of Poles.

Moreover, notwithstanding a prevailing folk prejudice with its stereotypical image of Jews, there is little actual evidence that the nationalists' more sinister views were even close to universal at the mass level. Consider the boycott of Jewish businesses, a key nationalist demand that by the late 1930s was being encouraged even in pastoral letters of the Catholic Church. According to Marcus (1983, 244–245), the vast majority of peasants nonetheless patronized Jewish traders because their prices were lower. That decision hardly implies a love for the Jews, but it is consistent with Weeks (2005, 29), who notes that the most important anti-Semites were middle class that did not effectively sell their program to the peasants even in the interwar period. The overview of memoirs in Bronsztejn (1994) illustrates that there were many non-Jews who had sympathy for Jews or judged them as individuals by the same standards that they judged other non-Jews. Jolluck (2005) analyzes the testimonies of thousands of Polish women who during the Soviet occupation were considered "harmful" by the authorities and thus deported to the Soviet Union. Even among this sample, which was almost certainly more nationalist in orientation than Polish society as a whole, roughly one-third expressed either positive or neutral views of Jews. Therefore, the baseline assumption of ubiquitous hatred toward Jews does not capture the truth.

The second reason for caution in prematurely reducing the 1941 pogroms to anti-Semitism concerns what gets counted as anti-Semitic acts. At risk of oversimplification, we can identify both broad and narrow understandings. In the broad understanding, anti-Semitism is something of a grab bag of different kinds of hostility (e.g., Brustein 2003; Gross 2006; Michlic 2006). It includes cases in which the primary target happens to be Jews for incidental reasons, as for example, the economic boycott organized by the National Democrats' party, also known as Endecja. Given the Jews' position in the Polish economy (to be discussed further in this chapter), the nationalists' desire to claim a commanding position for Poles in commerce was bound to have the largest effect on Jews because of their proportionally large commercial role in comparison with other minority groups. It includes cases where the primary target could well have been other groups, but the Jews were singled out, as in beliefs that Jews were uniquely enthusiastic in their support for the Soviet occupation. Poles might well have pinned the accusation on Belarusians but did not. It includes cases in which the target could only be Jews, as in accusations of deicide or the ritual murder of Christian children.

The narrow understanding of anti-Semitism, by contrast, excludes scenarios in which Jews are targeted in their role as prosperous traders, sympathizers with communism, or supporters of the Soviet occupation. In the narrow view, anti-Semitism refers only to instances in which Jews are targeted for being Jews. For example, Blobaum (2005, 4) contrasts the anti-Semitic 1918 Lwów pogrom, where, as noted previously, religious Jews were humiliated and religious objects desecrated, with the 1898 Galician pogroms (Stauter-Halsted 2005), where the victims were Jews but were targeted "as owners of inns, taverns, and distilleries." In the former case, the pious could have avoided injury only by ceasing to be Jews; in the latter, the victims' Jewish identity was seen to be ancillary.

We take no position on whether anti-Semitism *ought* to have the broad or narrow interpretation except to say that for our purposes it is better to "split" rather than "lump." We would like to know which purported motive for the 1941 pogroms best accords with the observed distribution of those pogroms. Were the pogroms revenge for alleged Jewish support of the Soviet occupation? Were they about robbery and the opportunity to get rid of economic rivals? Were they about ridding the nation of an alien and fundamentally unassimilable group? For analytic clarity, we refer only to the last question as implying anti-Semitism. We make local-level anti-Semitism operational by using the interwar vote for nationalist parties that espoused the narrow view of anti-Semitism. These parties are described in more detail in chapter 2. Chapters 4 and 5 demonstrate that at best there is a middling relationship between the distribution of mass anti-Semitic attitudes and pogrom occurrence.

Avarice

Another family of explanations relates to economic rivalry and hardship. The study of the economic roots of ethnic violence has a long pedigree in comparative politics (Bonacich 1972; Horowitz 1985; Forbes 1997). Three kinds of arguments get made. One focuses on the deleterious effects of economic downturns, which lead to the scapegoating of vulnerable minorities. Jews would be particularly targeted in times of crisis because non-Jews associate them with markets and capitalism (Rogger 1992; Rohrbacher 1993). We do not doubt the applicability of this hypothesis under more settled political conditions, but even the most creative conspiracy-mongers were not blaming the Jews for the Nazi invasion and concomitant economic collapse. The economic scapegoating hypothesis lacks prima facie validity.

A second and related economic explanation focuses on competition in ethnically segmented labor markets and economic production. In this view, Jews constitute a quintessential "middleman minority" (Blalock 1967). As summarized by Olzak (1992, 40), such minorities are distinguished by their dwelling in enclaves, sojourner status, and "concentration in finance, commerce, and other jobs that mediate between producers and consumers." Of these characteristics only sojourner status does not clearly characterize Polish Jews. At just under 10 percent of the population, as late as the early 1930s, Jews composed more than a significantly disproportionate share of university graduates (Marcus 1983, 67), over 70 percent of those employed in commerce, and controlled 39 of 137 registered joint-stock companies (Tomaszewski 1989, 147). Particularly sensitive were the small market towns, the *shtetlach*, where Jews were demographically weighty and tended to be notably wealthier and more influential than their peasant neighbors. Jews were not sojourners in Poland in the literal sense, having dwelled in Poland for hundreds of years. Nonetheless, as noted earlier, many non-Jews, particularly on the right of the political spectrum, considered them a foreign element. In the middleman minority view, Jews are most vulnerable to pogroms where they are most segregated from non-Jewish populations and where they have excessive influence over important economic sectors, such as commerce. Adapting Olzak (1992, 40), in these areas Jewish success is likely to be seen as a threat both to non-Jewish elites who seek to maintain power and to those in lower-status positions who resent their economic reliance on Jews.

Ethnic economic competition ought to be a compelling explanation. Having regained their own state after well over a century of submersion in other empires, many Polish leaders were keen to take ownership of the new state. As we have discussed, the idea of "polonizing" the economy—ensuring that ethnic Poles dominated—originated with right-wing nationalist elites. But by the latter half of the 1930s, it had become more broadly accepted and led to calls for an economic boycott of all Jewish businesses and scattered pogroms. Unfortunately, we lack good local-level indicators of economic competition between ethnic groups. As an admittedly inadequate proxy we use a dummy variable identifying the shtetls, where we know that such competition was most bitter. A shtetl was basically a small town that had lots of Jews, so this indicator will unfortunately capture both demographic and economic dynamics. We find that in the Polish-dominated northeastern voivodships, a shtetl was not more likely to experience a pogrom (conditional on levels of nationalism and other factors), whereas in the Ukrainian-dominated southeastern voivodships, the opposite was true.

A third and closely related economic explanation argues that the 1941 pogroms occurred where non-Jews sought to rob Jews of their wealth. Looting during the pogroms is well documented (see, e.g., Żbikowski 2007, 343–345). In the case of the Jedwabne pogrom, for example, we know that peasants from surrounding villages brought carts to carry away Jewish property. In other cases Jews were able to buy their way out of trouble, at least temporarily. But we should not confuse looting that might occur incidental to a pogrom with looting as the motive for a pogrom. It is hard to reconcile anti-Semitic and anticommunist pogrom rituals with the claim that the motives were economic. If robbery or extortion were the driving force, we would expect pogroms to occur where the difference in wealth between Jews and non-Jews is the largest. One way we proxy for this is with data from the American Jewish Joint Distribution Committee on the location of free loan associations. These associations were established to assist Jews in economic distress by offering no-interest loans for economic development. According to the wealth hypothesis, pogroms should take place in localities where Jews were too prosperous to warrant a free loan association. We find no evidence of an economic effect in ethnically Polish regions, but a strong one for economic competition in Ukrainian Galicia.

Political Threat

Our explanation focuses on dueling nationalisms and is broadly consistent with the "power-threat" model initially developed to understand the dynamics of U.S. race relations (Blalock 1967). Power-threat theory argues that where minority groups threaten the dominance of the majority, the majority will take actions to suppress minority power.[13] In the postbellum U.S. South, for example, this view holds that whites saw two sources of threat to their continued racial dominance.

One was the sheer number of liberated blacks, which led to white fear of being outnumbered. Another was the influence of political parties such as the Republicans and later the Progressives, who were more sympathetic than the Democrats to black civil rights. The theory maintains that where the perceived black threat was most acute—where blacks constituted a substantial minority and racially inclusive parties were popular—whites intent on preserving the racial status quo were most likely to implement measures of social control such as electoral disenfranchisement, Jim Crow legislation, and lynching (Tolnay and Beck 1995, 57).

We argue that a similar dynamic accounts for the difference between violent and nonviolent localities in Poland. Pogroms were most likely to break out where non-Jews perceived a Jewish threat to their political dominance. There are three important explanatory factors, each of which can be measured at the local level and can independently influence the probability of a pogrom: the popularity of Polish parties advocating ethnic tolerance, the demographic weight of Jews, and the degree to which Jews advocated national equality with Poles and Ukrainians. Let us first address the effect of ethnically tolerant parties. One of the most important divisions within mass opinion in interwar Poland pitted nationalists who advocated imposing a homogeneous culture throughout the territory against others who preferred more inclusive nationality policies. Although this conflict is sometimes reduced to one between majority and minority groups, in actuality both majorities and, to a lesser extent, minorities were internally divided on these issues.

For Poles, this conflict played itself out in the political struggle between two blocs of parties: the National Democrats and their allies, who sought a "Polish" Poland with minimal minority rights; and the party of the dictator Marshal Józef Piłsudski, the Non-Party Bloc for Cooperation with the Government (Bezpartyjny Blok Współpracy z Rządem, or BBWR), which favored an accommodation with the minorities in exchange for allegiance to a multinational state led by Poles. Ukrainians were a minority in Poland but constituted a majority in the southeastern region of Galicia. They were basically united in their desire for autonomy (from Poles) but, like Poles, were divided on the extent to which Jews could be included in their national project. According to power-threat theory, pogroms would be more likely to occur where the popularity of tolerant parties indicated a population supportive of pluralistic nationality policies. In these areas the nationalists would have felt the most threatened and attacked Jews in the hopes of forestalling the need to acknowledge Jewish national rights. Of course, this theory is only true up to a point: there would be no perpetrators in localities where all the non-Jews respected Jewish rights. Sadly, such a situation appears to be exceedingly rare. We show that, in accordance with power-threat theory, the probability of a pogrom increases with support for both the ethnically pluralist BBWR party and Jewish nationalist parties.

The second factor correlated with the likelihood of a pogrom is the size of the Jewish population relative to that of non-Jews. Where Jews were few in number they posed little danger to Polish and Ukrainian authority, and there were correspondingly few pogroms in those localities. But the likelihood of a pogrom went up in tandem with the proportion of Jews in a given settlement. Part of this was probably about increased Jewish visibility, which made Jews easier targets. But a more important aspect was the potential threat substantial Jewish numbers posed to non-Jewish dominance. Polish and Ukrainian nationalism had never been sympathetic to Jewish difference, and attitudes hardened after the Nazi seizure of power and the 1935 death of the dictator Marshal Piłsudski. These circumstances put the Jews in a difficult situation. Allying with the Polish or Ukrainian nationalists might have allayed nationalist fear, but at the unacceptably high cost of forsaking Jewish culture. Any other option left the Jews open to suspicion of disloyalty to the national cause. For nationalists, then, Jews were inherently suspect. We illustrate the positive correlation between the Jewish population proportion and the occurrence of a pogrom using interwar census data on ethnic and religious affiliation.

The third factor associated with pogroms is the proportion of Jews who sought national equality with the Poles or Ukrainians. Among the political options that significant numbers of Jews actually pursued in interwar Poland, Jewish nationalism had arguably the least sympathy among non-Jews. (We do not count communism. Contrary to popular belief both then and now, Jewish support for communism was miniscule at the mass level. See Kopstein and Wittenberg 2003, 2011.) Jews who identified with nonethnic parties that acknowledged at least some minority rights might well have been seen by Polish and Ukrainian nationalists as a threat, but at least they would have gotten some credit from those non-Jews who saw in that identification a reasonable attempt to fully participate in political life as Jews. But even nonnationalist Poles and Ukrainians balked at the idea of Jewish self-government, comprehensive Hebrew and Yiddish education, and other rights the Jewish nationalists were hoping to acquire. Localities where Jews supported national equality with the majority group proved particularly vulnerable to pogroms. In these areas, where non-Jews felt the least solidarity with their Jewish neighbors, Jews were doubly cursed: they contained a greater number of both potential perpetrators and non-Jews who did not feel enough solidarity with the Jews to intervene on the Jews' behalf. Our indicator of Jewish nationalism is the proportion of Jews who supported parties advocating national rights. We compute this quantity from interwar census data on the number of Jews and the electoral results obtained by the Bloc of National Minorities and the east Galician

Zionists, two of the leading parties promoting Jewish national rights. We show that the greater the proportion of Jews voting for these parties, the more likely a pogrom.[14]

The role of the non-Jews who do not participate directly in the violence is crucial. First, they may, of course, warn Jews of the impending attack or rescue them if it is imminent. There are many documented cases of violence having been averted, frequently at great risk to the lives of the rescuers. Second, and more commonly, they contribute to what Horowitz (2001, 326–373) calls "the social environment for killing." Would-be perpetrators may refrain from acting if they do not sense broader popular support for violent activity. Fujii (2009, 30) describes a range of responses to genocide between rescuing on the one hand and perpetrating on the other. It is the bystanders, who neither rescue nor kill, that often set the tone of community expectation for or against violence independent of any state instigation. The most important of these bystanders are authoritative figures such as priests or teachers, whose statements and actions will be interpreted to signal approval or disapproval. But even where these authoritative figures were inclined to help Jews, they often found themselves constrained by communal sentiments. Pogroms occur when there are both perpetrators motivated to act and others who either implicitly or explicitly are willing to condone the violence.

It might appear puzzling that in the midst of the Nazi offensive against the Soviet Union ordinary non-Jews could even think that attacking Jews would improve their national prospects. But this is because we have the benefit of knowledge of the horrors that were to come. In summer 1941, most civilians, Jewish or not, could not have known what ultimate fate awaited the Jews or even how bleak Polish or Ukrainian national prospects were. The Germans did murder thousands of Jewish and non-Jewish civilians during summer 1941, and often in the most brutal manner, but the ghettos had yet to be fully operational, plans for total extermination of the Jews had yet to be implemented, and many non-Jews were still being lulled by the Germans into believing they would be treated leniently if they joined the fight against the Soviet Union. Consequently, non-Jewish civilian populations could have seen the lawless atmosphere as an ideal and perhaps their only opportunity to rid themselves of competitors in anticipation of a future autonomous national life. This was certainly the message the Germans wanted to telegraph as they strove to incite local populations to attack their Jewish neighbors.

We summarize the alternative and main hypotheses in table 1.1. The broader historical context in which these factors took shape will be discussed more fully in chapter 2. We test these hypotheses in chapters 4 and 5. In the remainder of the present chapter, we discuss our research design and provide a roadmap of the book.

TABLE 1.1. Why do pogroms occur in some localities and not others?

HYPOTHESIS	INDICATOR	STRENGTH OF EVIDENCE
Political threat	Strength of Jewish nationalism	High
Political threat	Strength of ethnically tolerant parties	Medium
Economic competition	Shtetl/Free loan association	Medium
Anti-Semitism	Vote for anti-Semitic parties	Medium
Revenge for communism	Vote for communist parties	Low

Note: Columns represent the leading hypotheses, the indicators we use to test them, and the strength of the evidence in their favor.

Research Design

As noted at the beginning of this chapter, we choose to focus on the summer 1941 pogrom wave in Poland's eastern borderlands because of the peculiar conditions under which those pogroms took place. With the collapse of the Soviet administration in the wake of the German invasion of the Soviet Union in June 1941, the eastern borderlands were for a short period thrown into chaos and uncertainty. The retreat of Soviet personnel meant there was no functioning state capable of reigning in anti-Jewish violence. The presence of the Germans and their local allies meant that local civilian populations were permitted and even encouraged to attack Jews. These are ideal circumstances under which to examine the structural characteristics of localities where pogroms occur because the absence of restraint meant that perpetrators could act on their desires without fear of punishment.

All research on the spatial distribution of violence must grapple with an inevitable tension between the level of aggregation at which violence takes place and the ecological units for which there are data to test competing explanations. Brass (2003, 28) notes that in India and the United States ethnic riots never take place across entire cities, but instead occur in neighborhoods or even on specific streets. Much the same could, of course, be said for other countries. Yet at the same time, systematic economic, political, and social data to test competing explanations for such violence are usually available only for municipalities or larger geographic units. Important microcomparative data collection exceptions such as Kalyvas (2006) notwithstanding, researchers usually address this mismatch in one of two ways.

Some aggregate violent incidents up to the level at which existing demographic or other explanatory information may be matched, be it cities (Wilkinson 2004; Spilerman 1970, 1971), counties (Olzak 1992; Tolnay and Beck 1995), or even regions (Petersen 2002). While such aggregation may be necessary to test competing explanations, it does entail a loss of information, in this case, spatial variation in violence. The higher the level of aggregation, the poorer the fit is likely to be between the values of the explanatory variables at the higher level and the values the variables would have had had they been measurable at the micro-level locations where the incidents actually took place. Consider again the effort to explain the pattern of lynching in the postbellum U.S. South. It is, of course, an important finding that there is a negative correlation across counties between the popularity of parties supporting amicable relations between whites and blacks and the incidence of lynching (Tolnay and Beck 1995, 197). However, this fact by itself tells us little about whether localities *within* counties where those parties were popular were the places that had the fewest lynchings. Inferring the local outcomes from the county results is tricky even with ideal data and exemplary methods (Achen and Shively 1995; King 1997). Even analyses of cities, where aggregation is less of an issue, still have to deal with the problem of urban bias.

Other researchers eschew large-N analysis in favor of case studies (e.g., Brass 2003; Gross 2001, 2006) or small-N comparisons (e.g., Varshney 2002). We do not gainsay that much can be learned from these exemplary studies and the research traditions they represent. Indeed, the harrowing account of the 1941 Jedwabne pogrom in Gross (2001), with its provocative claims regarding Polish anti-Semitism and collaboration with the Nazis in the extermination of the Jews, led to a passionate debate about the reason for the pogrom and a surge of research on other pogroms, of which the present study is a part. But the nuance that is gained through rich description of a small number of cases is inevitably paid for in conclusions of questionable external validity. Many aspects of Gross's characterization of Jedwabne have been challenged, but even if his account were wholly accurate, we still would not know how representative Jedwabne is of localities where pogroms occurred. In fact, as we show in chapter 4, Jedwabne is not at all like other pogrom localities in its neighborhood.

We employ a large-N, quantitative approach that minimizes information losses that are due to data aggregation while still retaining a great deal of descriptive information about the sites where violence did or did not take place. We match electoral and census data (to be discussed in chapter 3) at the lowest geographic level at which they can be matched. For our six voivodships, this yields over two thousand localities, ranging in size from small towns to large cities, leaving out only villages that had fewer than five hundred electors. These data represent the most comprehensive evidence systematically available to rule out competing hypotheses and to allow us to describe the overall distribution of pogroms across the universe of settlements.

An additional advantage is that this design permits a qualitative cross-regional comparison between two Polish-dominated voivodships in the northeast and three Ukrainian-dominated voivodships in the southeast. Comparing the quantitative results across the two regions allows us to assess the effects of different combinations of ethnic groups, the historical legacies of having dwelled in different empires before Polish independence, and differing Polish and Ukrainian notions of statehood and the role Jews might play in each.

A Roadmap

Chapter 2 begins the analysis with a historical overview of ethnic relations in the eastern Polish borderlands until the German invasion of the Soviet Union in June 1941. The roots of anti-Jewish animosity predate the founding of independent Poland after World War I. We first show how nineteenth-century debates on Jewish emancipation and the merits of ethnic versus civic forms of nationalism were recast during the interwar period into partisan struggles over state ownership, economic redistribution, and the proper limits of minority autonomy. We then discuss how these debates grew sharper and more ominous for Jews (and some non-Jews) with the rise of fascism in Germany and the 1935 death of Marshal Piłsudski, whose political party favored a reasonable accommodation with the minorities.

In chapter 3 we discuss our data and methods. Our analysis is based on an original data set consisting primarily of demographic information from the 1921 and 1931 Polish censuses, electoral results from the 1922 and 1928 national parliamentary elections, and pogrom information gleaned from both primary and secondary sources. We collected the data at the lowest level of aggregation at which the census and election could be matched, the *gmina* (commune), which yielded a database of over two thousand large and small settlements, which we refer to collectively as localities. We test our hypotheses largely through large-N statistical analysis, including differences in medians, nonparametric models, and ecological inference.

Chapters 4 and 5 test our argument in two regions of Poland, the northeastern provinces of Białystok and Polesie (chapter 4), where Poles predominated alongside substantial Jewish and Belarusian minorities, and the southeastern provinces of Volhynia, Lwów, Stanisławów, and Tarnopol (chapter 5), where Ukrainians predominated over significant Jewish and Polish minorities. In both chapters, we consider the Soviet occupation of 1939–1941, which spelled the end of Polish independence and further thwarted Ukrainian national aspirations. Because Polish and Ukrainian nationalist historiographies argue that the 1941 pogroms were a response to perceived Jewish collaboration with Soviet oppression, we discuss Jews' and others' attitudes toward Soviet rule. In both regions we find that interwar support for parties advocating Jewish national autonomy and ethnic tolerance correlate with the likelihood of a pogrom. We see some evidence for the deleterious effects of economic competition between Jews and non-Jews, more limited support for the anti-Semitism hypothesis, and no evidence that sympathy for communism led to pogroms.

Chapter 6 extends the argument beyond Poland. We first examine other areas that experienced pogroms in 1941, especially Lithuania and Romania, where in both cases the targets were Jews. Here we expect the same factors to be relevant as in Poland—Lithuanians and Romanians perceived Jews and the Jewish struggle for national recognition in broadly similar ways to Poles and Ukrainians. We then discuss the role that Jewish emancipation in Russia and Germany played in generating the logic of strength in numbers that made Jewish demographics and political sentiments a concern of ordinary non-Jews. Finally, we bring the story to contemporary India and the postbellum U.S. South, where the dynamics of ethnic riots (India) and lynchings of blacks (United States) bear resemblance to our Polish case despite the difference in the identities of the perpetrators, victims, and historical context.

In chapter 7 we conclude the book with a discussion of the broader implications of our findings. First, we revisit contemporary debates on the merits of minority assimilation for reducing intergroup violence. The traditional argument holds that assimilation ought to reduce such violence because the process of acculturation reduces the majority perception that the minority is a distinct group. According to this view, Orthodox Jews, who were by far the most resistant to acculturation and the most visibly different from non-Jews, ought to have been the principal target of pogroms. But the pogroms were not about "otherness" in this specific cultural sense. In fact, Orthodox Jews were among the least sympathetic to Jewish national aspirations, and at least in part supported "Polish" parties in hopes of securing their religious rights. Our findings suggest that cultural assimilation is no guarantee of safety, but also that something less demanding of minorities than cultural assimilation may be sufficient to secure that safety. Where minorities can find common ground with majorities in the political sphere, majorities may feel just enough solidarity with them to ensure peaceful intergroup relations.

Second, we weigh in on the still-sensitive issue of civilian collaboration. Many Poles and Ukrainians are loath to accept responsibility for persecuting Jews because it challenges their self-image as victims and resistors of Nazism. On the Polish side, this was amply demonstrated by the hue and cry over what really happened during the Jedwabne attacks (Brumberg 2002). Contrary to the claims of the nationalists, however, local civilian populations were not victims of the war in the same way as Jews were. Ordinary Poles and Ukrainians may have died at the hands of both the Germans and the Soviets, but some also willingly killed Jews, both in collaboration with and independently of the Germans. The victimizers were also victims. It is also true, however, that the vast majority of Poles and Ukrainians never participated in a pogrom. In our view, the small number of pogroms relative to the number that could have taken place requires replacing the notion of *national* responsibility with a proper recognition of the local circumstances under which ordinary people committed such ghastly crimes. Perhaps then the painful issue of guilt and culpability can be put in proper perspective.

Finally, we elaborate on the implications of our findings for the prevention of pogroms in other contexts. The summer 1941 pogroms constitute a hard case for prevention due to the lack of state actors capable of reigning in civilian violence. Still, there are options that involve changes in minority behavior, the creation of local demographic and political contexts that discourage potential perpetrators, and the manipulation of identities such that the majority feels greater solidarity with minority pogrom targets.

2
ETHNIC POLITICS IN THE BORDERLANDS

Our core contention in this study is that interwar political orientations and behavior predicted the spatial distribution of violence in summer 1941. This chapter sets the pre-1941 political scene in the borderlands of eastern Poland (referred to in Polish as the *kresy wschodnie* or simply *kresy*).[1] In what follows, we explore how the diffuse ethnic divides of the era of nationalist mobilization during the nineteenth and early twentieth centuries reemerged as specific partisan disputes in independent Poland. These political disputes—over economic redistribution, state ownership, and the proper limits of minority autonomy—colored life in virtually every community and provided the context in which the deadly violence of 1941 would ultimately occur. By translating ethnic demography into political weight, democratic politics in interwar Poland heightened ethnic tensions. Where powerful and articulate Jewish nationalist political parties and movements emerged, Poles and Ukrainians came to understand that the region's Jews would not and could not be part of their respective nation-building projects.

We first show how the Jewish question of the late imperial era shaped the party landscape in independent Poland. We then turn to the worsening of ethnic relations during the 1930s. In the final section of this chapter, we examine the dramatic ethnic upheaval that accompanied the Soviet occupation and annexation of the eastern borderlands from 1939 until the German invasion of 1941.

Jews and Their Neighbors

Although industrialization in the kresy had barely begun by World War I, Jews from this region had long been disproportionately active in commerce, the professions, and especially petty trade. The division of labor remained ethnically specific. Poles performed political and bureaucratic functions, Jews commercial functions, and the surrounding villages consisted mostly of a nationally indifferent Slavic-speaking Christian peasantry who would soon refer to themselves as Ukrainians and Belarusians. Following the general rule in Eastern Europe that the more backward a region, the more prominent the role of the Jews in commercial life, in the kresy, "the Jews were *the* commercial class" (Mendelsohn 1983, 25). Some of this changed during the 1930s, as both Poles and Ukrainians sought to displace Jews from dominance in shtetl trade, but the image of an early modern, ethnically segmented social structure remained a staple of journalism and popular literature of the day.

Demographically, the small market towns and other places where Jews dwelled in the kresy were diverse. Jews, while frequently a plurality of inhabitants, rarely constituted a clear majority. They lived in close proximity to ethnic Poles, Ukrainians, and Belarusians with whom they cooperated and competed. Jews and

FIGURE 2.1. Poland 1939, with the six kresy voivodships investigated in this study crosshatched.

their non-Jewish neighbors may have dwelled side by side but frequently possessed a different sense of space and time. Christians, while aware of Jewish festivals, remained "remarkably unaware of their religious content" (Klier 2000, 31). Churches and synagogues, days of work and days of rest and celebration, the language of prayer and that of laughter, all occupied an important place in the life of the shtetl, but each community experienced them differently. Yet, as Klier (2000, 30) notes in his study of the pre–World War I shtetl, the most important space was truly nondenominational—the marketplace: "Here, Christians, Jews, and others mingled freely. In the main relations here were friendly, but there was always the possibility of squabbles and fights between buyers and sellers. Low-level violence was not unusual, but only in the rarest and most extreme cases did it take the form of pogroms. Having said that, it should be noted that when a pogrom did break out, the marketplace was always in the middle of events."

Divided, then, by religion and frequently by language and economic station, the peoples of the shtetlach and surrounding rural communities could not easily build relations of deep trust. Violence, it is true, remained the exception, and there are many examples of sustained cooperation and interethnic harmony (Aster and Potichnyj 1983; Snyder 2005). All too often, however, Jews found themselves caught between competing imperial and national projects, with each side accusing the Jews of siding with its enemy. The most traumatic of these episodes bookend the early modern era and the founding of modern Poland—pogroms in the wake of the Ukrainian uprising against the Polish nobility in 1648 and the widespread massacres following the Russian Revolution from 1918 to 1920 (Rosman 2003; Sysyn 2003; Abramson 1999).

It is important, of course, not to project the ethnopolitical identities of the twentieth century backward in order to account for premodern conflicts. The pogroms of earlier eras do not map very well on to those of 1941. Imperial rule in the kresy, first under the Polish-Lithuanian Commonwealth (1569–1795) and then, after 1795, under the Russian and Habsburg partitions, left a complex melange of ethnic and religious communities. During the nineteenth century both the Russian and Habsburg imperial governments (the former ruled the northeastern borderlands and the latter eastern Galicia) had at various times counted and attempted to categorize the inhabitants. Historians have taken an interest in the region precisely because the shifting and ill-defined identities and the uncertain allegiances of the population illustrate the contingent and socially constructed nature of belonging (Brown 2004; Stauter-Halsted 2001). At the outset of the twentieth century, the residents of the region were frequently multilingual or spoke "impure" versions of national languages, making it difficult for would-be nation builders to match a particular person to a nation. Sometimes, if it suited their interests, people wavered or switched back and forth between national affiliations. A nontrivial number remained uncertain exactly "what" they were in national terms

By World War I, however, most inhabitants of the borderlands were being mobilized into one or another national project: Polish, Lithuanian, Jewish, and increasingly Ukrainian and Belarusian. The demise of empires, the Bolshevik revolution, and the creation of national states after World War I lent new urgency to the competing identity projects and made it far more difficult to claim more than one ethnic allegiance or to remain fuzzy on the question of ultimate loyalty. The ethnic carnage in the two years following the war in these territories all but sealed the matter. By 1920 most people knew "what they were" and "who" their neighbors were. The vast majority of Polish speakers in the borderlands knew they were Poles, Lithuanian speakers understood they belonged to a Lithuanian nation, and Ukrainian speakers, at least in eastern Galicia, were increasingly certain they were members of a Ukrainian nation.[2]

And Jews knew they were Jews. The Jewish enlightenment of the eighteenth and nineteenth centuries had begun to alter the structure and practices of shtetl life in important ways, but most Jews remained easily identifiable (and self-identified) by their distinctive religious practices, dietary laws, dress, economic functions, and modes of expression (Bauer 2009). The "Jewish question" throughout Eastern Europe revolved around what to do about this fact: What was to be the position of Jews in increasingly modern societies? Should Jews be granted full membership rights in the community? One solution corresponded, roughly speaking, to that pursued by the Habsburg rulers incrementally after 1848: emancipation in the hope of eventual assimilation or some sort of reasonable communal accommodation. The alternative model was that of imperial Russia: delay emancipation, restrict Jewish settlement in carefully prescribed areas in order to limit Jewish cultural influence, protect non-Jewish entrepreneurs, and encourage emigration (Vital 1999, 205–208).

The creation of constitutional states in east-central Europe after World War I did not resolve the Jewish question but instead displaced it onto the stage of modern politics by translating it into electoral struggles between political parties. Nowhere was this question more acute than in the kresy of interwar Poland, a multinational region that for the first time in almost 150 years belonged to one state.

Could Jews be Poles or Ukrainians?

The Polish debate on membership in the nation, conducted under conditions of partition, followed the imperial contours only imprecisely, for here the questions concerned whether the Jews and other minorities could be (or rather become)

Poles. One stream of thought, associated with Józef Piłsudski and the Habsburg lands, harkened back to the premodern Polish-Lithuanian Commonwealth and viewed Polishness more as a matter of state allegiance than ethnic belonging. Such a relatively open idea of the Polish nation accommodated ethnic diversity even with the Polish language as the first among equals. Jews (and other ethnic groups) could join or assimilate to the Polish nation without giving up their communal ties or, within reason, their mother tongue (Michlic 2006, 35).

Other Poles rejected the multiethnic idea as unworkable in the modern era and advocated Jewish assimilation. As long as Jews were willing to speak Polish, shed their customs, and convert to Christianity, they were, so the argument went, Polish. This idea presumed the existence of a malleable Jewish population (Cała 1989). Under conditions of partition, however, Jews might prefer the imperial German, Austrian, and even Russian to Polish culture.[3] They might also choose to remain Jewish linguistically and culturally or even become increasingly Jewish politically.[4]

It was in fact an ethnolinguistic-Christian ideal of Polishness that gained ascendancy in the late nineteenth century. Under the formidable intellectual leadership of Roman Dmowski, the National Democrats (referred to as the Endecja in reference to the letters *N* and *D*), viewed the world in social Darwinian terms, as a relentless struggle between unified ethnic groups for domination of territory and culture (Porter 2000). Poland's Slavic minorities in the East constituted suitable material for assimilation. Poland's Jews, on the other hand, did not. Jews could not become Poles. In Dmowski's *Thoughts of a Modern Pole*, published in 1902, he wrote of the Jews: "[They] have far too many characteristics that are alien to our moral code and that would play a destructive role in our lives. Mingling with the majority of them would lead to our destruction: the young and creative elements on which the foundation of our future existence depends would be dissolved by the Jewish elements" (Dmowski 1902, cited in Michlic 2006, 66). Their very presence weakened the Polish nation and its domination of modern sectors of the economy and society. The preferred approach to the Jewish question was legislative, but included economic boycotts, social exclusion, and, when needed, violence.[5]

The resurrection of Poland after World War I transformed these theoretical debates into questions of state policy. How would Poland's Jews and other national minorities fit into the new "nationalizing" state (Brubaker 1993, 84–86)? Would Poland's elites adopt a civic or an ethnic definition of political membership?

The early signs were not promising. The armistice in November 1918 brought an end to major hostilities in the West, but a bloody and brutal three-way war between Bolshevik Russia, Poland, and a proclaimed independent Ukraine continued to rage in the East. All three sought sovereign control over the same territory. Jews disagreed among themselves about the best course of action. From the communists came the promise of revolutionary equality; from Ukrainians, an

TABLE 2.1. Ethnic profile of six eastern voivodships, 1921

	NON-POLISH POPULATION (PERCENT)	JEWISH POPULATION (PERCENT IN TOWNS)	JEWISH POPULATION (PERCENT IN VILLAGES)
Białystok	32	44	4
Lwów	53	40	4
Stanisławów	85	37	3
Volhynia	88	58	5
Tarnopol	69	38	3
Polesie	91	48	5

Note: Percentages inferred from religion and nationality data.
Source: 1921 Polish census.

offer of communal autonomy; and from the Poles, potential entrée to the West. Repeated Jewish declarations of neutrality convinced nobody and were met by accusations from all sides of favoring the enemy. The result was widespread pogroms in the Russian partition and scattered atrocities in eastern Galicia carried out by Polish, Ukrainian, and Russian regular units and local warlords. Abramson (1999, 110), following Gergel (1951), puts the Jewish civilian death toll between 1918 and 1920 at nearly 50,000.

Diplomacy in Paris in 1919 and a spectacular reversal of military fortune under the leadership Marshal Piłsudski in 1920, which drove the Red Army back into central Belarusia and Ukraine, left Poland in possession of territories in the East with nearly five million Ukrainians; two million Belarusians, who lived mostly in rural areas; and three million Jews, who comprised almost half of urban residents in the eastern borderlands. None of these groups were happy in the new state. Most dissatisfied were the Ukrainians of eastern Galicia who had briefly tasted national independence in 1919 (Kuchabsky 2009, 314–327). Although the Belarusians and Ukrainians from the Russian partition were less politically mobilized, by 1922 they, too, could look across the frontier into the Soviet Union where national republics carried the names of both groups. How these ethnically aware minorities were to be accommodated, assimilated, integrated, or expelled became a key question of interwar Polish politics. The ethnic makeups of the eastern voivodships studied in this book are shown in table 2.1.

The National Cleavage in Interwar Polish Politics

Not everything went well for Poland's nationalist elites in Paris. As a condition for international recognition, the Entente powers presented Poland (and other successor states) with a Minorities Treaty as part of the Versailles Peace Agreement. Poland's leaders objected to the treaty as an unwarranted and hypocritical intrusion on the new state's sovereignty and approved the document only after roundly denouncing it. Vigorous Jewish appeals in Paris, both from within Poland and from abroad, for communal autonomy constituted "evidence" of Jewish ill will (Rothschild 1974, 39). In fact, the treaty did not meet Jewish demands for reserved ethnic representation in Polish parliament, for democratically elected autonomous Jewish communal institutions, or for a Jewish national council. It did, however, call for state-funded Jewish schools controlled by the Jewish community (a promise never fulfilled) and called on the new state to respect the Jewish sabbath (a promise only partially kept) (Mendelsohn 1983, 35).

Poland's elites nonetheless considered themselves part of the general European family of nation-states. The question for the Polish majority was how to reconcile reaping the rewards of state ownership, which included asserting the preeminence of the majority language and culture throughout the entire territory, with the presence of substantial and geographically concentrated minority populations that sought to preserve as much autonomy as they could. Polish elites were not completely free to do as they pleased within their new state. The constitution approved by the Constituent Sejm in 1921 conformed to the basic liberal democratic norms of the day. Citizens, regardless of ethnicity, were accorded equality before the law—a fundamental departure for the Jews of the formerly Russian partition of Eastern Poland, which amounted to nothing less than the long-awaited emancipation (Tomaszewski 1994). It also provided guarantees to religious and ethnic groups to pursue their own cultural development (Mendelsohn 1983, 36). The electoral law, passed in 1922, provided for universal suffrage for all adults over twenty-one years of age.

Democratic Poland's institutional structure efficiently translated the preexisting ethnic tensions of the imperial era into heated partisan contests over ownership of the modern democratic state. It did so by making this ownership dependent on electoral success. The constitution created a strong parliamentary government and a weak presidency (elected by a majority of members of the lower house—the Sejm). This institutional outcome represented a victory for the Endecja, which expected to outperform the Social Democratic war hero Józef Piłsudski in any nonplebiscitary national election (Rothschild 1974, 46–47).[6] Highly proportional electoral rules ensured a broad spectrum of representation in the Sejm. At the same time, in order to restrict the influence of the minorities, the principle of proportionality was watered down through a careful division of the country into sixty-four multimember constituencies with fewer seats allocated to the constituencies located in the eastern borderlands and a bonus for parties that could garner votes in at least six constituencies, a feat no minority group could manage (Bernhard 2005).

The first national election encompassing virtually all of Poland took place on November 5 and 12, 1922 (for the Sejm and the Senate, respectively). Twenty-two parties ran on the state list and dozens of others ran on regional lists. In most cases, these parties grew out of preexisting organizations from one or more of the imperial partitions. As elsewhere in Europe, this was the golden age of the ideological political party as a mass organization. Parties saw themselves as more than operations to attract votes. They published their own newspapers, supported youth leagues, reading clubs, civic associations, and generally attempted to provide a coherent set of organizations and ideas to guide followers from early adolescence to old age.

Poland's party system in the run-up to this election reflected the preindependence fissures among Poles and between Poles and the country's ethnic minorities. In the following sections, we describe the main parties of interest to this study. We restrict our discussion to the parties competing in the eastern borderlands.[7]

Polish Parties

On the right, the National Democrats teamed up with various Christian Democratic parties to run as the Christian Alliance of National Unity (Chrześcijański Związek Jedności Narodowej, or Chjena). The Endecja set the tone, however. Economic policy was viewed through the lens of nationality. The main threat came from ethnic economic competition in the urban areas, from Germans in the West, and from Jews in the rest of the country. Jews as Jews with rights equal to ethnic Poles constituted a mortal threat to Polish sovereignty (Golczewski 1981, 324). Proposed policies advantaged Polish over Jewish businesses and restricted civil service employment to ethnic Poles. In those areas of the eastern borderland thinly populated by ethnic Poles, military settlers were to be given land and tax incentives.

The Polish Peasant Party (Piast) led by Wincenty Witos (who ultimately served as prime minister three times), the bourgeois Polish Center, and the working class National Workers Party occupied the center of the political spectrum. All three of these parties took moderate stances on socioeconomic issues, but on nationality questions their positions did not deviate a great deal from that of the National Democratic–dominated Chjena.[8]

Polish parties on the left wavered between an optimistic assimilationism and some version of reasonable accommodation with the national minorities. Despite some talk of "federation," the discussions remained highly theoretical. In practice, the issues were far more mundane: funding for schools, the mandating of rest days, and various employment quotas in public administration and universities. The Polish Socialist Party (PPS) focused on working class voters and the urban intelligentsia but remained open to support from the country's minorities. In the kresy, low levels of industrialization kept support for the PPS very low in most shtetls. The left-wing peasant party Liberation (Wyzwolenie) pitched its message at land hungry peasants and advocated accommodation with nonethnic Poles.

Communist Parties

The Communist Party called for a Soviet-style republic and was declared illegal before election in 1922. Nevertheless, it managed to run under easily decipherable labels (such as "Union of Proletariat of the City and Countryside"). It remained a tiny organization, and its members worked according to the rules of revolutionary conspiracy (Dziewankowski 1959). Jewish presence in the leadership raised suspicions among Poles that Jews favored the destruction of the Polish state and among Ukrainians that they opposed national independence. A not-insignificant number of Ukrainians and Belarusians also supported the Communists and they received assistance from across the border in the Soviet Union. The party's campaign in the eastern borderlands spoke both to land hunger and to minority rights (Radziejowski 1983, 25).

Mainstream Poles considered communism to be treasonous. Even so, this revolutionary movement constituted perhaps the only forum where Jews, Poles, Ukrainians, and Belarusians could speak with a single voice and agree on the fundamentals of politics. In this sense, communism served as a nonliberal form of universalism, a drastic choice to be sure, but one that could potentially attract voters among the losers of ethnic politics. In a sign of just how deep the ethnic cleavage ran in interwar Poland, even the communist movement, symbol of universalism par excellence, featured Polish, Jewish, Ukrainian, and Belarusian versions.

Ukrainian Parties

Like Polish political parties, Ukrainian political parties in interwar Poland grew out of their pre–World War I counterparts. Given their general boycott of the 1922 elections, however, Ukrainians did not enter the political fray until after it became clear that the question of Ukrainian statehood would not be quickly resolved. The Ukrainian National Democratic Alliance (UNDO) was founded in 1925 and, until the mid-1930s, dominated Ukrainian political life (Magocsi 2010). Led by urban Ukrainian intelligentsia and Greek Catholic clergy, the party's luminaries included Dmytro Levytsky and Vasyl Mudry (who would later become speaker of the Sejm). The UNDO positioned itself as a party of the middle class (and therefore had a frequently cordial but never easy relationship with urban Jewry), but it faced challenges from the anticlerical and agrarian Ukrainian Socialist Radical Party and, on the far left, by the Communist Party of Western Ukraine. Like other Ukrainian parties, the UNDO considered Poland's rule on Ukrainian territory to be illegitimate and advocated independence. Until independence could be achieved, however, the party's leaders supported working within Polish institutions and rejected violence. Ukrainian political parties advocating violence reemerged on the political scene after 1928 under the leadership of Organization of Ukrainian Nationalists, an entity we discuss later in this chapter.

Jewish Parties

Jewish parties, as Mendelsohn notes, shared a common dilemma given the regime's initial view of the state as narrowly Polish: "How could the Jewish minority, which constituted only ten percent of the population and which lacked powerful protectors abroad, hope to reverse the policies of the Polish Government and thus protect the interests of the three million Polish Jews" (Mendelsohn 1974, 204). Zionism, religious orthodoxy, and Yiddishist autonomism constituted the three main options for the Jewish electorate.

Zionism

The founder of Zionism, Theodor Herzl, considered the downtrodden masses of Eastern Europe's Jews, especially those in the heavily mixed Galicia and Russian borderlands, as prime candidates for resettlement in a Jewish homeland. But in the absence of this homeland, other Zionists, such as Ahad Ha'am (Asher Ginzburg) argued that the movement's primary purpose must be the development of a separate Jewish national consciousness and a full-chested defense of Jewish interests and values where Jews actually lived. The prospect of a large-scale Jewish departure interested non-Jewish nationalists and emperors even before World War I, but they also worried that, failing this departure, a rising Jewish national consciousness would impede the construction of unified national states.

As far back as 1903, the czar's anti-Semitic interior minister, Vyacheslav von Plehve, noted in a meeting with Herzl that he was sympathetic to Zionism, "so long as it works toward emigration," but any non-"Palestinian" talk "about culture, organization, and Jewish nationalism," he noted, "doesn't suit us" (Avineri 2014, 224).

A similar dynamic unfolded in newly independent Poland. The Zionists of interwar Poland were Jewish nationalists, who already before the war had fractured into various streams that ran the gamut from socialist to religious. The General Zionists struck a moderate note on socioeconomic issues and religion and enjoyed the greatest popularity among the Jewish national parties. Their leader in the lands of the Russian partition, Yitzhak Grünbaum, related in his memoirs how his encounter with Polish literary classics "awakened my love for the Poles who fought for their rights" and was a factor in his decision to become a Zionist (Mendelsohn 1981 345). As all Zionists of the day, Poland's General Zionists were committed in principle to establishing a Jewish homeland. Practically, however, they were focused mainly on *Gegenwartsarbeit* (work in the Diaspora), which meant protecting Jewish interests in Poland and promoting Hebrew education. Contrary to the stereotype of implacable enmity toward languages other than Hebrew, the General Zionists repudiated a radical rejection of Yiddish and even Polish; working for Jewish interests and honor in the Diaspora was a good in its own right (Weiser 2011, 193).

What did voting Zionist mean? Jews who supported Zionist parties did not for the most part plan to leave Poland. Instead, supporting the General Zionists meant favoring a new kind of Jewish politics, one that was proud and assertive. A vote for the General Zionists was a signal of support for a vigorous and public defense of Jewish national interests. It signaled above all an unwillingness to join the nation-building project of either the Poles or the Ukrainians. The Zionists loudly proclaimed their liberation from the "ghetto" and confronted Polish politicians publicly about the shortcomings in their treatment of the country's Jews. As Mendelsohn puts it, the General Zionists "would work to improve the condition of the Jews, but never at the expense of Jewish honor" (Mendelsohn 1974, 205). Zionism, because it remained flexible on both class and religious questions, dominated Jewish politics in the kresy through the late 1930s.

Polish and Ukrainian views of the Zionists were complex. One would think that the prospect for a Jewish departure might have warmed the heart of Polish and Ukrainian nationalists, but, as Plehve's reaction to Herzl's Zionism of an earlier era, interwar Polish and Ukrainian nationalists worried about the new and assertive Jewish politics. For nationalists, Zionists epitomized Jewish unwillingness to join other nation-building projects, Polish or Ukrainian. As a practical matter, however, negotiations between Zionists and the Polish and Ukrainian leaders never ceased. Very few Jews preferred Hebrew over Polish, Yiddish, Russian, or German in conducting their daily affairs. The General Zionists of the Russian partition—under the aggressive leadership of Grünbaum—tended toward parliamentary confrontation, whereas those of eastern Galicia, led by Leon Reich, worried about provoking their Polish and Ukrainian neighbors and saw the benefits of accommodation. A tangible sign of this divide is that in both 1922 and 1928 the General Zionists in eastern Galicia refused to run on the Bloc of National Minorities list, but instead fielded their own.[9]

Yiddishist Autonomy

The main nationalist alternative to Zionism was Jewish nationalism that sought recognition for Jews as a distinctly "Yiddish" nation within Poland. The smaller of the two Yiddishist parties, the Folkists, led by Noah Pryłucki, favored Jewish cultural autonomy and pitched its message largely to the Jewish middle classes (Marcus 1983, 288). Pryłucki spoke just as ardently and loudly as the Zionists, and his behavior in the Sejm earned him a great many enemies and few friends (Weiser 2011).

Similar demands were made by the Jewish Workers Bund, a larger organization, which called for revolution as a prelude to Jewish cultural autonomy (Johnpoll 1967). On socioeconomic issues, the Bund and the Polish Socialist Party were ideological allies, but they were also rivals, as the PPS considered itself (justifiably) as the largest Polish party that attempted to attract Jewish working-class voters and even included Jewish candidates on its electoral lists. As with the PPS, economic backwardness and the absence of an industrial working class deprived the Bund of any significant voter base in the kresy. Its calls for communal rights and autonomy ultimately did not differentiate it enough from the Zionists.[10]

Religious Traditionalism

Agudas Yisrael represented a third and very different path for Jewish politics. Led by the Hasidic Gerer rebbe Avraham Mordechai Alter and the non-Hasidic Chaim Ozer Grodzinski of Wilno, this party espoused the politics of religious traditionalism (Bacon 1996). Whereas the Zionists considered the role of the *shtadlan*, the discreet negotiator with the gentile community, to be humiliating, followers of Agudas Yisrael considered him a wise hero. Zionists and Bundists, from the traditionalists' standpoint, failed to understand the precariousness of the Jewish position in Poland.

Orthodox Jews organized not so much to oppose Polish discrimination but rather in response to Zionist and Bundist mobilization of the Jewish masses and the fear that unless they responded with their own civic associations, newspapers, and a political party, the Jewish public (and ultimately the private and religious) sphere would be monopolized by secularists. A vote for Agudas Yisrael was therefore a vote for Jewish traditionalism, both in political style and substance. Aguda opposed Jewish secularists on educational issues and consistently spoke against mandatory Sunday closing laws or the refusal of the Polish army to grant Jewish soldiers leave for certain religious holidays. At the same time, a vote for Aguda was also a vote for loyalty to the Polish state. "Our policy in the Sejm," the party's main paper editorialized in 1922, "remains the same—an understanding with the Polish government and society. We want to build our lives on the basis of friendly coexistence with our Polish fellow-citizens for the good of the Polish Republic for which we will spare no sacrifice" (Bacon 1996, 255).

The Bloc of National Minorities

To circumvent the institutional impediments to their parliamentary representation, the German and a number of Jewish, Belarusian, and Ukrainian parties ran in 1922 under the umbrella Bloc of National Minorities (BNM). Conceived initially by a German politician, Edwin Hasebach, the idea was eagerly taken up by General Zionist leader Yitzhak Grünbaum. But from the outset, negotiations between the politicians of different minority groups indicated that the BNM would never become more than an electoral marriage of convenience between parties representing ethnic minorities who otherwise viewed each other with indifference or hostility. Parties, not individuals, joined the bloc. Some parties, such as Agudas Yisrael, joined only reluctantly and made clear to its voters that the bloc was a purely electoral device and would not influence its legislative votes. The absence of any unified program provided further evidence of its purely electoral rationale.

Not all minorities parties joined the BNM. Several Jewish parties (such as the General Zionists in eastern Galicia, to which we return later in this chapter) and Ukrainian parties (such as the Ukrainian Peasant Party in Volhynia and the pro-Polish Ukrainian Chliboroby) chose to run on their own. Some refused to join the bloc on ideological grounds; others worried about Polish and (in the case of the Galician Zionists) Ukrainian opinion. Although the Ukrainians of the former Russian partition participated in the election, the Ukrainians of eastern Galicia boycotted it altogether (and backed up the boycott with violence) to protest the founding of a national Polish state on Ukrainian territory.[11] The Bund, the Folkists, and the Labor Zionists, Poalei Zion, refused to join the General Zionist–

dominated Bloc of National Minorities in 1922. This amounted to a serious error, as none gained a seat in the Sejm.

Notwithstanding its tactical as opposed to principled origins, most Poles viewed the BNM as a grave danger to the Polish state. The prospect of a third of the population voting en masse for non-Polish parties, some of which cultivated links to "kin" states across new and insecure international frontiers, alarmed not only the Polish Right but also the Left who had hoped to attract voters from the minorities. Jews who supported the Bloc were, in effect, supporting irredentist Germans, Ukrainians, and Belarusians (Weiser 2011, 205).

Victory for Ethnic Politics

The campaign in the run-up to the election in 1922 was rancorous. Among Polish parties, the National Democrats forced virtually all challengers to engage in a game of ethnic outbidding. Rallies and speeches drew in large crowds and occasionally led to brawls. The Endecja warned Poles not to "split" the Christian vote and worked with local priests and Catholic associational networks to mobilize the population. The Left was accused of dangerously coddling the national minorities. Even PPS candidates felt obliged to reassure voters that their candidates were "genuine Poles" (Zloch 2010, 54–71).

The electoral rules guaranteed an ethnically Polish party majority in the Sejm but also encouraged party fragmentation. The vote yielded a parliament consisting of eighteen parties, five of which had only one or two seats (Polonsky 1972, 103). No party or ideological bloc came close to gaining a parliamentary majority. Poles split their vote among the Right, led by the National Democrats (28% of the seats); the bourgeois centrists (20% of the seats); and the parties of the Left, led by the Socialists (21% of the seats). Parties representing the national minorities won 20 percent of the seats, a number that underestimates their potential parliamentary strength because of the Ukrainian boycott in eastern Galicia. The results constituted a victory for the National Democrats. Not only did it capture a plurality of votes but it fielded the only party list to perform well in all regions of the country, winning a significant percentage of the ethnically Polish votes in the eastern borderlands. The real shocker, however, was the strong performance of the Bloc of National Minorities. Whereas in the Constituent Sejm that was elected in 1919, parties representing national minorities received a mere 3.2 percent of seats, the 20 percent figure in 1922 demonstrated the hazards of having included the eastern borderlands within independent Poland.[12] In those new areas the Bloc of National Minorities received almost half of all votes cast

(Groth 1960, 146). According to Korzec (1980), even where few Jews resided, Poles frequently held the Jews responsible for the BNM's performance.

With these results none of the Polish party blocs could form a majority government without the cooperation either of another Polish bloc or with the minorities. The assassination in 1923 of Poland's president, Gabriel Narutowicz, after being elected by the Sejm with the support of Socialist and Jewish deputies, removed any possibility of minority participation in government. In the end, the National Democrats formed a coalition with the centrist (but reliably nationalist) peasant party, Piast.

The government's policies made clear that this was to be a Poland for Poles. Polish would be the only official language; national minorities could establish their own schools, but only at their own expense; polonization of the bureaucracy, public schools, and religious institutions became official policy; ethnic Polish military colonists were moved into "insecure" eastern borderlands; and minority political representatives would be frozen out of all cabinets. The Lanckorona Pact, signed in May 1923 among the coalition members (National Democrats, Piast, and Christian Democrats), called for a limit to legal, cultural, and economic ownership by the country's national minorities and for the dominance of Poles in all areas of public life. In the kresy, these measures were aimed not only at Jews but also at Ukrainians. Ukrainian institutions of higher learning in eastern Galicia were shut down, and even the use of the word "Ukrainian" was proscribed in official communication. The Polish term for the region, "Eastern Little Poland," seemed designed to offend (Chojnowski 1979, 29–54; Snyder 2003b).

Zionists leaders disagreed over how to deal with this situation. The General Zionists in eastern Galicia pursued the path of negotiation with the government but faced harsh criticism from within their own ranks and accusations of betrayal from Ukrainians for having "sided" with the Poles. The Ugoda (agreement) of 1925 was signed by Jewish and Polish parliamentary representatives and promised an end to anti-Semitism and the recognition of Jewish communal rights. Ultimately, the Polish government did very little to honor the agreement (Mendelsohn 1983).

The Coup d'Etat, the Sanacja, and the 1928 Election

The right-wing Polish coalition confronted a basic problem: its seat total made it vulnerable to minor defections, which in turn threatened government stability (Bernhard 2005, 95). Between 1922 and 1926, several governments tried to formulate and implement viable policies on a broad range of issues having little to do with ethnic politics, but without the support of the Left and the national minorities, they could not. The result was legislative gridlock, budgetary impasses, and labor unrest. With the Endecja and Piast about to form a new government in May 1926, Marshal Józef Piłsudski, who had temporarily retreated to private life, led a coup d'etat. Although the Sejm elected Piłsudski president of the republic, he refused the office and chose instead to rule primarily from behind the scenes.

Piłsudski was a soft authoritarian, but he was not an anti-Semite. On nationality questions more generally, the Piłsudskiites were guided by the idea of "prometheanism," in which the melding of the country's minorities within an overarching Polish statehood could transform Poland into a leader in Eastern Europe, simultaneously securing domestic peace and successfully navigating the treacherous irredentism of its neighborhood (Snyder 2005). National assimilation was to be replaced with state assimilation, and discrimination would be supplanted by a serious attempt at ethnic accommodation. In return for the state's support for their cultural development and economic security, the minorities were to cultivate a sense of coresponsibility for the country's fate and a devotion to the broader Polish state project (Chojnowski 1979, 24).

The election of 1928 was held not primarily to choose a new government but rather to provide the Polish citizenry with proof that Piłsudski's statist ideal enjoyed majority support. The Piłsudskiites sought to unite a coalition of Poles (hived off from existing parties of different ideological orientations) and non-Poles (who could be attracted away from ethnic parties or whose parties would declare themselves to be pro-Piłsudski) (Chojnowski 1986). The revealingly named Non-Party Bloc for Cooperation with the Government (Bezpartyjny Blok Współpracy z Rządem, or BBWR) emerged as the primary vehicle for mobilizing voters. At the communal level, the BBWR's party organizations consisted primarily of local officials and dignitaries, but a great deal of effort was made to mobilize and integrate local ethnic minorities, especially Jews and Ukrainians.[13]

The BBWR's propaganda stressed a number of changes since 1926. First, the government appointed a committee to amend the bill on compulsory Sunday rest and ultimately passed the law On Repealing Special Regulations Related to Origin, Nationality, Race, or Religion of the Republic of Poland. In 1927, the Ministry of Religious Affairs and Public Education introduced mandatory Ukrainian and Belarusian classes to Polish high schools in the eastern borderlands. Even though Poland's government failed to meet its Versailles obligations to establish Jewish public and elementary schools, it did grant "public rights" to a handful of Ukrainian, Belarusian, and Jewish schools in 1927 and 1928 (Chojnowski 1979, 135–137).[14]

The party espoused an ideology of state and bureaucratic rectitude (from which Piłsudski's regime earned its popular moniker, Sanacja, or "moral cleansing"), but it was ultimately an antiparliamentary party designed to demobilize the population once the election results were in. Snyder (2005), in his study of Volhynia, characterizes the BBWR as a top-down attempt to reconstruct the political "center" in Poland. In this he is correct: the BBWR tried to attract support across social classes and ethnic groups, but in doing so it was required to remain far more ambiguous in its plans for ethnic accommodation than parties of the nonrevolutionary and revolutionary Left such as the PPS and the various communist parties. Even so, the BBWR in the Polish context represented a genuine attempt to politically assimilate Poland's minorities to the broader national project.

The electoral campaign of 1928 remained every bit as rancorous as that of 1922. Once again the Polish Right mobilized the Catholic Church on its behalf. Catholic bishops had issued a pastoral letter calling for overcoming party divides. The National Democrats took this as their cue. "If you do not vote for List 24 [the National Democratic list], Poland may collapse." Another election flyer proclaimed, "Whoever is a real Catholic votes for the national list without hesitation. Poland must be big, strong, and wealthy!" Piłsudski, they predicted in election rallies, would close churches or otherwise attempt to separate church and state. The most hysterical analyses likened members of the Sanacja government to a "satanic" conspiracy. "Rich Jews," it was claimed, were running on the BBWR slate and, on the whole, Jews were the main beneficiaries of the Sanacja regime (Zloch 2010, 269).

The vitriol was not restricted to the hard Right, however. *Piast*, the main newspaper of the center-right Peasant Party of the same name, although faced with periodic censorship, gave ample room to its leader Wincenty Witos to discuss the situation in eastern Galicia. On June 12, 1927, Witos published an article, "My Observations on Eastern Galicia." Witos maintained Piast had been successful in 1922 because of the Ukrainians boycott, but this success would not be repeated in 1928. Ukrainians harbored a "hatred of all things Polish." Witos criticized the Sanacja's "concessions" to the national minorities, stating how central eastern Galicia was to Poland's identity. Two weeks later, *Piast* warned of a "Jewish-Ukrainian Bloc" (June 20, 1927). In the run-up to the election, the paper carried a series of articles under the rubric "On the Campaign Trail" with the headlines: "Jews on the Government List" and "All Jews Back List Number One" (February 19, 1928); and on the eve of the election: "Don't let yourselves be fooled. Piast's former list, number one [now the number of the BBWR], is today the property of saboteurs, Jews, and aristocrats—the peasants' list is number 25!"

Notwithstanding a modicum of repression and fraud in the eastern voivodships (especially in Volhynia) and a far-from-level playing field throughout the country, the 1928 elections, which were held on March 4 (for the Sejm) and

March 12 (for the Senate), were remarkably free and fair considering the circumstances in which they were conducted.[15] The best evidence for this assertion is the failure of the BBWR to attain its parliamentary majority.[16]

The results of the 1928 election differed from that of 1922 in important ways. First, the Right's totals dropped dramatically from 29.1 percent to 8 percent of the vote. A good portion of the electorate had clearly tired of the confrontational politics of the right-wing governments. Second, the performance of both the non-revolutionary Left and the Communists improved significantly. The Communist Party had divided along ethnic lines, with sporadic attempts at coordination. The Belarusian and Ukrainian Communists (as well as the pro-Soviet Jewish Poalei Zion-Left) performed so well in the eastern borderlands that in some locations their ballots were invalidated by electoral commissions with the connivance of the government in Warsaw.[17] Although Poland's national minorities continued to vote strongly for their own ethnic parties, our own calculations from Galicia (where the vote was free and fair) show that the BBWR did succeed in garnering a significant share of the Jewish (18%) and Ukrainian (15%) vote. The pro-government bloc was not only the most popular Polish party among Ukrainians and Jews but also the front-runner among Poles (33%). Evidently, at this stage a majority of Poles in Galicia preferred the rather more "tolerant" politics of the Piłsudskiites and the Left (which received 22% of the Polish vote) to the ethnically exclusionary politics of the Right.[18]

The essence of integrating the minorities, however, would entail rendering them the distributional beneficiaries of the new order. In this respect, the Ukrainians, as the largest group, were crucial. Starting in 1929, Henryk Józewski, the governor of Volhynia, undertook an experiment to reintegrate the region's Ukrainians and stave off the tide of communism and nationalism. The main components of the program were improving public administration (through including Ukrainians in all local administrative structures), maintaining bilingual schools, making Ukrainian culture part of "Polish" culture, and strengthening Ukrainian churches against both Polish and Russian influence. Józewski also set up common Polish-Ukrainian economic and cultural organizations: Społem, a food-producing cooperative; and the Ridna-Khata, a cultural and pedagogical society (Schenke 2004, 243–254).

This experiment and a similar one in Lwów produced a modicum of change, but the resources devoted to them were too little and arrived too late. By the first years of the 1930s, most Ukrainians were already solidly mobilized into nationalist politics, and the Jewish parties had refused to support the government's budgets in the face of continued high levels of urban taxation (Chojnowski 1979, 124). The election of 1928 was to be the last relatively free and fair one of the interwar era. Thereafter, pro-government majorities were either manufactured or, after

1935, constitutionally guaranteed. Alternating highs and lows in relations between the Sanacja and the national minorities ultimately alienated all sides, but until Piłsudski's death in 1935, the government managed to maintain a measure of social peace.

Polarization after 1935

With the tolerant dictator gone, Poland's politics in the years after 1935 drifted inexorably to the right. Elections were now fully "managed," and ethnic relations deteriorated significantly. Liberalism had fallen into crisis throughout Europe following the Nazi seizure of power in Germany. In Poland the impact was a return to the politics of the Endecja. This time, however, most pretense of liberal restraint was cast aside in pursuit of ethnic advantage. The new ruling party, the Camp of National Unity, explicitly prohibited Jews from its ranks. The regime did prevent the fascist fringe from gaining state power but it sought renewed support among the nationalists' core urban and rural constituencies (Wynot 1971). The state introduced credit programs privileging ethnically Polish enterprises and engaged in a not-so-subtle program of harassing Jewish businesses through regulation and taxation. Jewish credit cooperatives attempted to fill the gap, but the high cost of credit left this source beyond the means of increasingly pauperized Jewish merchants. The American Jewish Joint Distribution Committee assisted in the creation of Free Loan Societies (Gemilad Hessed) throughout the kresy, and a large percentage of Jews made use of these small loans (approximately $12 per member), but their spread indicated more the downward mobility of the kresy's Jews than their affluence (Marcus 1983, 140–141, 349–366, 379–380).

State policy was met more than half way by Polish civil society, which was willing to go beyond what the law sanctioned, especially when no punishment was expected. In the years after 1935, ethnically Polish civic groups and religious institutions called for boycotts of Jewish businesses. These boycotts were frequently initiated and then enforced with scattered public violence and even the bombing of synagogues, retail shops, and apartments (Żyndul 1994).[19] Several professional organizations prohibited Jewish membership (Marcus 1983, 216–217). The tone was further reinforced by National Democratic members of the Sejm who called for outlawing Jewish butchers practicing kosher slaughter—an obvious attempt to capture a significant portion of the retail trade in meat. University administrators acquiesced in the creation of "ghetto benches" (segregating Jewish students in lecture halls) at some universities, and Jewish students faced the danger of attack from right-wing students. None of these excesses was investigated or punished by the authorities despite repeated requests by Jewish Sejm deputies.

Entreaties by Jewish communal organizations similarly met with no response (Tomaszewski 2002, 47–52).

Ukrainian politics also turned to the right (Motyl 1980). The Organization of Ukrainian Nationalists (OUN) was founded in 1929 with roots in eastern Galicia. In contrast to the UNDO, the OUN accepted violence as a legitimate tactic and espoused a clear ideology of Ukraine for Ukrainians. Scholars disagree on whether it is properly categorized as integral nationalist or fascist, but during the 1930s its leaders were deeply anticommunist, anti-Polish, and profoundly anti-Semitic. Jews were considered a "foreign" and "enemy body" in the "national organism" and were depicted in OUN literature both as dominating the urban capitalist economy and as the primary supporters (along with Poles) of the Communist Party on Ukrainian territory (Bruder 2007, 46–47). Polish police reported multiple instances of OUN violence against both Jews and Poles during the late 1930s (Bruder 2007, 99–100).

Jewish, especially Zionist, politics also changed. Revisionist Zionism, under the leadership of Vladimir (Zev) Jabotinsky, gained a foothold in Poland. It called for a Jewish state in Palestine on both banks of the Jordan River, a clear rejection of socialism, and a break with any General Zionist tendency to negotiate with the Polish government over Jewish rights within Poland. The goal no longer concerned improving conditions "here" but on the attainment of a powerful state "there." With declining opportunities for emigration to Palestine in the last years of the 1930s, the surge of the Bund in local elections in 1938 in central Poland (but much less so in the north- and southeastern borderlands) signaled a continued Jewish desire for national autonomy and a declining confidence in the ability of the Zionists to realize this goal (Marcus 1983, 468). When the Soviets invaded the eastern borderlands in September 1939, they entered territory where ethnic tensions had been stoked by almost two decades of partisan ethnopolitics.

The Soviet Occupation

The Molotov-Ribbentrop Pact, concluded between Nazi Germany and the Soviet Union in mid-August 1939, sealed the fate of Poland and the Baltic states. In addition to the nonaggression pact, a secret protocol carved up the territories between Germany and the Soviet Union into regions of German and Soviet control. Germany invaded Poland from the west on September 1, 1939. The Soviet Union invaded Poland from the east two weeks later to occupy its share. Moscow imposed Soviet rule, which lasted from September 1939 until Germany invaded the Soviet Union in June 1941.

The destruction of Poland and integration of these territories into the Soviet Union constituted a reversal in ethnic fortunes for all groups (Petersen 2002). Poles lost their state, the Ukrainian nationalist leadership was decimated, and Jews were now the equals, both in law and fact, of their non-Jewish counterparts. Moscow immediately set about ensuring that the old order would not revive. The new authorities expropriated property, arrested, imprisoned, and deported local elites and showed a callous disregard for local languages and religious traditions (Gross 2002).

The NKVD (Soviet Secret Police) was particularly active in seeking out opposition to Soviet rule. According to Pinchuk (1990, 34), the NKVD established a network across the whole region within a matter of weeks, and a "fine net of informers was spread throughout the territories, in every institution, factory, enterprise, and tenement."[20] The NKVD successfully recruited from all ethnic groups, though as Pinchuk (35) further notes, "Local Jewish communists played an important role in locating former political activists and compiling lists of 'undesirables' and 'class enemies.'" Mass arrests and deportations of individuals connected to the outgoing regime and other influential people followed. NKVD brutality reached a crescendo at the end of Soviet rule, just as the Soviets were about to retreat in the face of rapidly advancing German forces, when thousands of massacred Poles, Ukrainians, Lithuanians, and Jews were found in its prisons.

Those who were not deported by Soviet authorities were subject to sovietization. Although the liquidation of the old system was not immediate, in the end the state took control of industry, agriculture, schools, and cultural production. Religious life was highly constricted, and Soviet propaganda was everywhere. When the Polish currency, the złoty, was abolished in early 1940, millions were immediately impoverished (Pinchuk 1990, 44). It is safe to say that for many, Jew and non-Jew alike, Soviet rule constituted one long ordeal of degradation and humiliation (Gross 2002). When the Germans invaded in 1941, the stage was set for neighbor-on-neighbor violence. Just how we account for which communities turned deadly is the question we turn to next.

3
MEASURING THREAT AND VIOLENCE

We constructed our data set of localities in interwar Poland's eastern borderlands from three main sources: primary and secondary materials documenting which localities experienced at least one pogrom in summer 1941, published materials from the 1921 and 1931 censuses listing the national and religious makeup of localities and the economic structure of the larger counties, and published materials containing the disaggregated results of the 1922 and 1928 national parliamentary elections. This chapter first provides details on these data, their important statistical properties and limitations, and how we use them as indicators for our explanatory variables. It concludes with a discussion of the methods we use in chapters 4 and 5 to test our hypotheses.

Pogroms

Those who study ethnic violence under settled political conditions usually have the benefit of being able to rely on information from the press or other organizations that, while certainly not wholly unbiased, at least do not have a direct stake in the conflict. Uncovering the actual distribution of violent acts is difficult even under these circumstances because of selection effects: only larger episodes may get reported, and events outside towns may be poorly covered or ignored entirely. The resulting urban bias almost certainly underestimates the true extent of violence and blinds us from uncovering causes that might be particular to rural areas.[1]

Obtaining accurate information on pogroms in summer 1941 poses even more difficult challenges. There was a war going on, and the pogroms were taking place in the "bloodlands" (Snyder 2010) between Germany and the Soviet Union, where the fighting was harsh and the treatment of both Jewish and non-Jewish civilians brutal. Indeed, most Jewish communities were ultimately annihilated in the Holocaust, leaving no survivors to testify about any pogroms that might have occurred. This is particularly true for small communities, which were easier to wipe out. Nearly 25 percent of the pogroms we have identified were in communities with fewer than one hundred Jews. The fragmentary evidence we have of what happened comes from a combination of German military and police reports; Soviet military correspondence; non-Jewish reminiscences; and, above all, the testimonies of perpetrators and survivors (when available).[2] The secondary literature is even larger, and we draw on it in the following two chapters and reference it where appropriate. Frequently we revisit the sources cited in these studies in order to understand the context in which the pogroms occurred.

Needless to say, the amount and quality of information is highly variable. There is an ongoing debate among Holocaust scholars, for example, about the extent to which survivor accounts, which may be affected by faulty memory, antipathy toward members of other groups, and "contamination" by postwar discussions, should be accepted at face value in the absence of corroborating information.[3] The same can be said for non-Jewish reminiscences, which suffer from similar problems and tend toward the self-exculpatory. This is not even to speak of Nazi and Soviet sources, which have every reason to exaggerate local civilian culpability or to blame the other for the deliberate murder of Jewish populations.[4]

The often-contested accounts of what happened in particular localities necessitate a minimalist approach to classifying pogroms. Adapting Horowitz's (2001, 22) definition of a deadly ethnic riot, we define a "pogrom" (against Jews) as a collective attack on one or more Jewish civilians that is geographically limited in scope and in which the perpetrators are primarily non-Jewish civilians. Although for some places it is possible to reconstruct important information such as the number of victims or the demographic profiles of the killers, the available source material is too uneven to replicate that feat across most localities. This does limit the types of analyses we can perform. Spilerman (1976), for example, has sufficient information to statistically analyze the severity of U.S. race riots. Wilkinson (2004) is able to investigate riot proneness with data on the frequency with which violence occurred in particular localities. We are not so fortunate. Our main dependent variable is thus simply whether or not at least one pogrom occurred in a given locality. The locations of these pogroms are visible on the map in figure 3.1. We also list each locality where pogroms took place, together with the source(s) for information about that pogrom, in the appendix.[5]

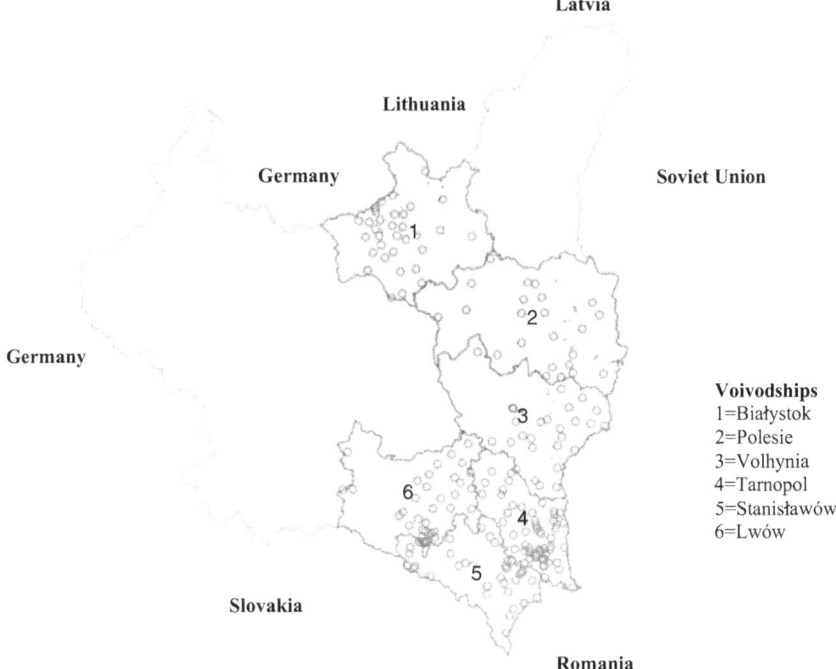

FIGURE 3.1. Six voivodships in the eastern borderlands, with small circles indicating where pogroms took place in summer 1941.

Even reconstructing such minimal information about a locality requires overcoming two big challenges. The first concerns identifying localities where pogroms did *not* occur. The evidentiary material tends to report instances of violence, but because of the war, the Holocaust, and the passage of time, it can be unclear for some places whether the absence of documentation means there was no pogrom or just that neither perpetrators nor victims are alive to tell their stories. We compensate for this problem by capitalizing on a recent surge in scholarly interest in the culpability of local civilian populations in anti-Jewish violence. Spurred in part by the passionate reaction in Poland to accounts of what happened during the Jedwabne pogrom, historians have begun the painstaking work of locating and sifting through multiple source materials to reconstruct what happened in even the smallest communities in summer 1941 (e.g., Machcewicz and Persak 2002; Rubin 2006). Our pogrom database builds on this research.

The second and related challenge is that not every instance of anti-Jewish violence counts for us as a pogrom. A key feature of pogroms is that the perpetrators be primarily civilians. Given that the pogroms were occurring in the middle of a war, it is thus important to establish for a particular place that the violence in question was not carried out by the military. In some cases sources generally agree that the German military itself directly killed Jews, such as in the city of Białystok, where police battalion 309 burned alive between eight hundred and one thousand Jews in a synagogue (Szarota 2004, 215). For us, such acts do not count as pogroms.

In the vast majority of cases, however, the evidence suggests that Germans were either not present or were present but did not take a large role in the actual violence. Nationalists in Poland and Ukraine argue that even when the Germans refrained from direct participation, civilian populations were not responsible for pogroms because the Germans compelled them to commit the crimes (see, e.g., Chodakiewicz 2003). We do not doubt that there may have been instances of such coercion, but the available evidence does not support the broader inference. The general presence of German army units, police battalions, and mobile killing units in the region is of course indisputable. It is also clear that the Germans preferred their dirty work to be done by locals in so-called self-cleansing actions. For example, on June 29, 1941, SS-Gruppenführer Reinhard Heydrich noted in a telegram that "nothing is to be put in the way of the self-cleansing actions of anti-communist and anti-Jewish circles in the newly occupied areas. On the contrary, without trace they are to be unleashed and, when necessary, to be intensified and to be steered onto the right path." The question is whether such incitement and orchestration count as compulsion. In general, they do not. Few would deny that if the Nazis had truly wanted to compel the locals to act, they could have succeeded in doing so—the Nazis felt little restraint in using force and intimidation to get their way. Yet there is evidence that the effort to incite pogroms had only uneven success (e.g., Brown 2004, 208; Dumitru and Johnson 2011) and no evidence that local populations were ever penalized for having failed to act on German instigation (see, e.g., Goldhagen 1996). In short, while Germans wanted the locals to act against the Jews, they stopped well short of forcing the issue. Therefore, the German presence does not automatically absolve civilian populations of responsibility. We give more specifics about the German presence in chapters 4 and 5.

Census Data

A different set of challenges relates to the local-level interwar Polish census data. The outbreak of World War II precluded a general census in 1940–41. The war itself destroyed the municipal results from 1931. Our main source of disaggregated data on the ethnic and religious makeup of the country thus comes from the 1921 census. We were unable to locate electronic versions of local-level 1921 census data and thus had to create an original electronic data set from the published volumes (Główny Urząd Statystyczny 1925). The census collected a broad range of religious and nationality information. Religious affiliations included Roman Catholic, Greek Catholic, Eastern Orthodox, Protestant, other Christian confession, Jewish, other confession, and "not indicated." National affiliations included Polish, Belarusian, Ruthenian (Ukrainian), German, Jewish, other nationality, and nationality nondeclared. There was a further category of "Local," referring to people who identified with or were identified by their locality. Such locals were found primarily in the voivodship of Polesie, an underdeveloped region that neither Poles nor Ukrainians had succeeded in nationalizing.

Our data span six voivodships (provinces) within the region that the Soviet Union occupied as a consequence of the Molotov-Ribbentrop Pact: Białystok, Polesie, Volhynia, and the east Galician provinces of Lwów, Stanisławów, and Tarnopol. These six divide nicely into regions where the principal national groups were Poles, Belarusians and Jews (Białystok and Polesie), and those where the principal groups were Ukrainians, Poles, and Jews (Volhynia, Lwów, Stanisławów, and Tarnopol). Because of missing census volumes, we were unable to include two voivodships: Nowogródek and Wilno. The absence of Wilno means that we are unable to include an analysis of pogroms where Lithuanians were the main perpetrators. In total, we employ religious and nationality data for 2,304 localities.[6]

The 1921 census is known to have overcounted Poles and undercounted national minorities. To compensate, we follow Tomaszewski (1985) and infer national affiliation from the more accurate data on religious adherence. Roman Catholics are equated with Poles, Jewish religion (the Mosaic faith) with Jewish nationality, the Orthodox with Belarusians, and Greek Catholics (Uniates) with Ukrainians. This solution does miscategorize nontrivial numbers of Orthodox Ukrainians (in Volhynia) and Jews (by religion) in Galicia who categorized themselves as Poles by nationality. We address these issues in two ways. First, we assess the sensitivity of our results when areas likely to contain such populations are included and excluded from the analysis. Second, for reasons we elaborate further in chapter 5, we analyze pogroms in Volhynia separately from those in Galicia, where the overwhelming majority of Ukrainians were Greek Catholic.[7] Thus, in practice, little bias is introduced by using religion to proxy for nationality.

The local-level 1921 census is the lowest level of aggregation for which we have systematic demographic data for interwar Poland. These data will be crucial for establishing the character of localities where pogroms occurred, as we shall see in chapters 4 and 5. Unfortunately, other useful information, such as economic structure and mother tongue, were collected only at one administrative level above the locality, the *powiat* (district). We collected these district-level data from both the 1921 and 1931 censuses, though for reasons of better temporal proximity to our 1941 outcome, the 1931 data are more useful. Economic variables we collected include employment in various occupations, including agriculture, industry, and services; and the distribution of farms by size. Mother tongue data include the main languages of the biggest non-Jewish national minorities in the region under analysis (Polish, Ukrainian, and Belarusian), but also Yiddish and Hebrew. We also have data on literacy, a common indicator for overall economic development (Lipset 1959). Though these data do not figure into our main results, they will prove invaluable for any future extensions to our argument.

There are two further variables that figure into our analysis. One is a dummy variable indicating a shtetl, a small market town where Jews tended to occupy higher-status occupations than their peasant neighbors and Jewish-Gentile relations could be especially fraught. We follow Bauer (2009) in defining a shtetl as a municipality with a population of at least 15,000, of which at least 30 percent was Jewish. If pogroms are about economic competition or plunder, then they should be most common in the shtetls, where competition was fierce and wealth differentials great. We also define a dummy variable indicating whether or not a given community has a free loan association, endowed in whole or part from Jews dwelling outside of Poland.[8] Very small communities did not host such associations, so we analyze these data only for places with one hundred Jews or more. Owing to the significant loss of data this entails, we do not include this variable in the multivariate analyses, though where appropriate we do discuss the propensity for pogroms of the much smaller sample of localities that had free loan associations.

Electoral Data

National parliamentary election results are the principal means by which we assess the political preferences of local populations. As discussed in chapter 2, although Poland did hold regular parliamentary elections throughout the interwar period, Piłsudski's 1926 coup d'etat meant that no election after 1928 was sufficiently free and fair to be an accurate reflection of popular views. Consequently, we use only the 1922 and 1928 results (and mainly the 1928), which we keyed in from Polish government publications (Główny Urząd Statystyczny Rzeczypospolitej Polskiej 1926, 1930). These data are less comprehensive than the census data and contain information only for localities with at least five hundred electors. This means we are unable to include small villages (with under five hundred voting-age adults) in our analysis. Fortunately, the Jewish preference for urban areas limits the amount of bias introduced. Among the localities in our analysis for which we also have census data, 104 places do not have any recorded 1928 electoral data, of which 7 experienced a pogrom. In the end, we lose only around 3 percent of the 219 pogroms in our data.

There are two other flaws with the 1922 and 1928 elections that bear on how we interpret the results. First, the Communist Party was formally outlawed. This did not prevent communists from organizing or even running for office, but they had to do so under different party names, and this surely disadvantaged them vis-a-vis competing with legal parties that could openly prepare for political competition. Actual communist support is thus higher than the published results indicate. Second, the 1928 election was marred by a modicum of administrative interference in the eastern provinces, mainly against communist parties. Fortunately for us, there is a record of these intrusions in the number of invalidated votes, which the state recorded, and the actual numbers are not significant. Beyond the restrictions on Communists and despite the fact that Piłsudski was a dictator, the 1928 elections are considered fair. Further evidence of this may be deduced from the performance of Piłsudski's party, the BBWR, which failed to secure even close to a majority of the vote. Where possible, we use the 1928 results rather than the 1922 because the former are temporally more proximate to our 1941 outcome.

In both 1922 and 1928, Poland's parliamentary electoral system was exceedingly proportional, consisting of a combination of national and regional party lists and low thresholds for parliamentary entry. The net result, as detailed in chapter 2, was that many niche parties fielded lists, and not a few of them entered parliament. Poland's highly fragmented parliaments made governance difficult (and were a big factor behind Piłsudski's 1926 coup d'etat), but the advantage for us is that it gives us very detailed information on the geographic distribution of political preferences. No fewer than twenty-five parties fielded national lists in 1928, and they offered a broad menu of choice. The most important 1928 parties for our purposes are the communist parties (lists 8, 13, 19, and 26); the National Democrats (list 24), representing Polish anti-Semitism; the Bloc of National Minorities (list 18), representing Zionism (Jewish nationalism) in areas where Jews dwelled with Poles and Belarusians and representing Ukrainian nationalism in Galicia; the east Galician Zionists (list 17), representing Zionism in Galicia; and BBWR (list 1), Piłsudski's party, representing support for a tolerant policy toward national minorities (though falling well short of endorsing minority autonomy).

We acknowledge that equating vote choice with acceptance of a party's viewpoint on national minority issues can be problematic. Clearly, voters could be motivated by economic, strategic, or candidate-centered concerns (Jacobson and Kernell 1981). However, there is good reason to believe that these other effects are minor in the Polish case. First, voters selected closed party lists rather than individual candidates, so candidate effects were minimized (Carey and Shugart 1995). Second, low electoral thresholds for entry into parliament lessened the pressure for voters to avoid small, niche parties for fear of wasting their votes (Duverger 1972). Moreover, in an era well before public opinion polls gave voters crucial information before an election on the popularity of parties, most voters would not have been aware that their votes were wasted until after the votes had been tallied.

Third, and most important, the cleavages underlying the party system support our claim. As detailed in chapter 2, each of the larger national groups had its own set of parties. Such was the importance of the national cleavage that even the communist parties divided themselves on national lines (see Kopstein and Wittenberg 2010).[9] Let us first consider the Polish parties to see why equating National Democratic support to anti-Semitism rather than economic nationalism is plausible. Parties within the Polish grouping ran the gamut on social and economic issues, but on national minority issues could still share broadly similar views. For example, the Polish Peasant Party, the National Workers Party, and the bourgeois Polish Center all favored reducing the economic influence of national minorities (primarily Jews and Germans), but only the National Democrats singled out Jews for special opprobrium. Mere nationalist voters might have supported the National Workers Party or the Polish Center, but only those Poles who also gave pride of place to anti-Semitism supported the National Democrats.

Now let us consider whether support for the General Zionists can be reasonably attributed to anything other than sympathy for protecting Jewish national rights within Poland. Like the Poles, the Jews had a panoply of their own parties, and most of them pledged to improve Jewish life in Poland. Secular Jews who did not acknowledge the need for Jewish communal rights could support the very small Jewish assimilationist party or opt for "Polish" parties such as the Socialists (PPS), which indeed enjoyed some Jewish support. Religious Jews who sought maximal freedom to practice their faith but had otherwise little desire to engage in politics could vote for the Orthodox Jewish party (or opt not to vote at all). The non-Orthodox Jewish working class was well organized and represented by the Bund and Poalei Zion, but for both these parties achieving revolutionary (socialist) transformation took priority over a Jewish nationalism that would bind Jews from different walks of life. Among major Jewish parties, only the General Zionists (and their east Galician Zionist counterparts) stood for an immediate and robust defense of Jewish interests as national equals with Poles (and Ukrainians).

We are not claiming that non-Jews were aware of the precise proportions of Jews or levels of support given to Zionist and other political parties in their communities. That is, our argument does not require that the perpetrators of pogroms or the bystanders that let pogroms happen had a precise electoral calculus in mind. Rather, what happened is that local populations experienced the strength or weakness of demographic and political groups through ordinary interactions in their everyday lives and thereby formed more inchoate but no less real perceptions of a Jewish challenge to Polish (or in some areas Ukrainian) dominance. In areas where Jews supported the Zionists, for example, non-Jews would have seen Jews advocate their national rights through vigorous participation in local social and political life. In areas where the Hasidim or other Misnagdic Jewish Orthodox (and hence support for the religious Jewish party) were more predominant, by contrast, non-Jews would have had less contact with Jews outside of economic interactions. Jews would have evinced little interest in broader community or national affairs except as they affected Jewish religious practice.

Methods

One of the peculiar features of our data is the level of skewness among key variables. Table 3.1 presents summary statistics of important demographic, economic, and political variables. To illustrate the skewness, we present the median value (50th percentile), P75 (75th percentile), and the maximum value. Focusing on the proportion of Jews, we see that across Białystok, Polesie, and the three Galician voivodships the vast majority of communities contain relatively small proportions of Jews. In Galicia, for example, 75 percent of the communities have 5 percent or fewer Jews. In Białystok and Polesie three-quarters of places (P75) have fewer than 17 percent Jews. A similar situation holds for the support for the General Zionist–dominated Minorities Bloc in Białystok and Polesie and support for the Galician Zionists in Galicia.

As a consequence, some of our results may be sensitive to the inclusion of the relatively small numbers of observations exhibiting high values for different variables; for example, localities where Jews composed a majority of the population. One strategy for dealing with this would be to treat these observations as outliers that require separate explanation, but there is no theoretical reason to do this: localities where Jews were a majority ought to pose an even greater threat to (local) non-Jewish minority dominance than those more numerous places where Jews were merely a substantial minority. To mitigate the influence of these outlying observations in descriptive statistics, we employ the median rather than the mean as our primary measure of central tendency. In chapters 4 and 5, we show that the median values of key variables differ dramatically between the subsample of localities where pogroms occurred and the subsample where they did not occur.

A second feature is that the data are ecological (aggregate) rather than individual level. The quantity we are most interested in estimating is a feature of

CHAPTER 3

TABLE 3.1. Summary statistics of explanatory variables

VARIABLE	N	MEAN (%)	MEDIAN (%)	P75 (%)	MAX (%)
BIAŁYSTOK & POLESIE					
Jews	362	14	4	17	94
Min Bloc	339	8	2	10	64
BBWR	339	30	26	39	91
Communist	283	22	7	42	91
Endecja	185	16	10	26	77
Shtetl	48				
Free loan	107				
GALICIA					
Jews	1856	6	3	5	91
Zionists	1779	4	1	3	67
BBWR	1779	25	20	35	100
Communist	1701	9	0	8	94
Min Bloc	1626	32	26	52	98
Shtetl	83				
Free loan	145				
BIAŁYSTOK & POLESIE GALICIA & VOLHYNIA					
Jews	2364	8	3	6	98
Zionists	2118	5	1	3	67
BBWR	2243	27	22	37	99
Communist	2064	11	1	12	94
Pol+Ukr Natlist	1811	31	23	50	98
Shtetl	160				
Free loan	288				

Note: The variables are percentage Jews; 1928 electoral support for Jewish nationalist parties (Min Bloc in Białystok and Polesie and Zionists in Galicia), the Government Party (BBWR), Communist parties (Communist); Polish and Ukrainian nationalist parties (Endecja for Poles in Białystok and Polesie, and Min Bloc for Ukrainians in Galicia); and the number of shtetls (Shtetl) and the number of free loan associations (Free loan). P75 represents the 75th percentile and Max the maximum values of the corresponding variable.

localities rather than individuals: the propensity of a locality to suffer a pogrom. However, we would like to know not just the observed marginal distributions of our census and electoral variables (such as the number of Jews or the votes received by the Endecja in a given locality) but their unobserved joint distributions (e.g., the proportion of Jews supporting the Zionist party or the proportions of Poles or Ukrainians supporting their respective nationalist parties). For example, in our extension to power-threat theory, Zionist Jews should pose more of a threat to non-Jewish political domination than Jews less vehement in their advocacy for Jewish national rights. If, instead, anti-Semitism is behind the pogroms, then Poles who support the National Democrats should be a greater threat to Jews than Poles who support other parties. The unobserved proportion of a national group within each locality that votes for a particular political party must be estimated from the observed census and electoral data.

To do this, we employ ecological inference methods (Rosen et al. 2001; Wittenberg et al. 2007). Extracting reliable estimates with any ecological inference procedure can be tricky when there are multiple national groups and parties to contend with, as in Poland.[10] However, we can divide our task of estimating group support for parties into two categories. In the first category are parties where it is reasonable to make the simplifying assumption that their support came entirely from one national group. These are the "ethnic" parties most central to our analysis: the General Zionists (Jews), the National Democrats (Poles), and for reasons elaborated in chapters 4 and 5, also the Bloc of National Minorities (Jews in the northeast and Ukrainians in the southeast). This assumption does not remove the need for imposing statistical assumptions, but it does simplify the problem. In the second category are parties where the assumption of single group support is unreasonable, such as the communists and Piłsudski's BBWR.

Generating estimates of group support for the ethnic parties in the first category requires three further steps. First, we assume that the proportion of adults with the right to vote from a given national group across localities reflects the proportion of that group in the (local) population as recorded in the census. For example, if 30 percent of a locality's population were Jewish, we assume that 30 percent of those eligible to vote were also Jewish. Second, we estimate overall turnout rates across Poland (rather than in each locality) for each national group using the method in Rosen et al. (2001) and compute the number of each group's actual voters by multiplying the number of eligible voters from each group by that group's turnout. Finally, we generate the desired proportion of each group supporting its ethnic party by dividing the number of votes the ethnic party gets by the number of voters from the given group. For each of our localities, then, we have at our disposal not just each party's share of the vote, but for ethnic parties such as the General Zionists and the National Democrats, each party's popularity within its target national group. It follows that in all communities not dominated by one national group, the proportion of a given group's support for a party will always be higher than the overall proportion of the votes that party received in the locality.

For "nonethnic" parties that appeal to multiple national groups, we can still employ ecological inference to estimate the distribution of group support. But these quantities represent average (group) support within a subsample of localities rather than estimates for each locality. In chapter 4, for example, we compare average Jewish and Polish support for BBWR in localities where pogroms occurred with the corresponding support where they did not occur. In the case of the BBWR, such estimates are an indicator of a group's commitment to work with the other national groups as citizens of a Polish-led common state. High support for BBWR among non-Jews is evidence against the anti-Semitism hypothesis. Unfortunately, communist support was too low and too skewed toward a very small minority of settlements to permit even such a more limited analysis.

Our general empirical strategy in chapters 4 and 5 proceeds in two parts. First, we divide the sample of localities into those that experienced a pogrom and those that did not. We then compare the median values of a panel of demographic and political characteristics for each subsample. As we shall see, this provides prima facie evidence for our claim that what distinguished pogrom places from nonpogrom places was the perceived threat of Jewish nationalism and not principally levels of violent anti-Semitism or sympathy for communism.

Second, to identify the independent effect of the perceived Jewish threat, we estimate multivariate models. The standard approach for bivariate outcomes is to employ logit models, which we have done in earlier work (Kopstein and Wittenberg 2011). The problem with parametric models such as logit is that they require specifying particular functional forms of the relationship between the outcome and the explanatory variables. In our case, however, theory does not provide much of a guide on which form to choose, and our results are sensitive to model specification. Therefore, we employ nonparametric regression methods. The advantage of such methods is that they choose whatever function of the explanatory variables fits the data, including those involving interactions among variables. The effect coefficients in such models thus represent the total effect of the corresponding explanatory variable (rather than, say, a linear or specific curvilinear effect). Nonparametric models do not solve the problem of omitted variable bias, but they do yield more robust effect estimates for those variables that are included. To minimize complexity, we do not include variables computed using ecological inference in our multivariate models. For comparison, we also estimate and present logit models using the same set of explanatory variables.

A related issue concerns how to account for error in our nonparametric model. We are analyzing a population rather than a sample of communities, so the conventional interpretation of standard errors as sampling error does not apply. One solution is to employ Bayesian analysis (see Western and Jackman 1994). In traditional (frequentist) statistical analysis, we want to know how likely it would be to obtain our sample effect coefficient (such as the effect of support for Zionist parties on the probability of a pogrom) if there were in actuality no such effect. Bayesian analysis is more straightforward. It estimates the magnitude of the effect given the data that are there, which is exactly the quantity we want to know (Schrodt 2013). We estimated Bayesian logit models with uninformative priors but do not report them because in magnitude they do not significantly differ from the corresponding standard logit model results (though the resulting "credible intervals" have a different interpretation than "confidence intervals").

We acknowledge the potential bias introduced by the disjunction between the period at which we measure our demographic explanatory variables, largely in 1921, and when the outcome occurred, in 1941. Nearly four hundred thousand Jews, over 10 percent of all Polish Jewry, emigrated from Poland between 1921 and 1937 (Hundert 2008, 1436). Very few of these were Hasidic or other ultraorthodox Jews, leaving Polish Jewry more traditionalist and almost certainly less nationalist than our 1921 demographic data would suggest. However, this poses less of a problem for our argument than meets the eye. Fewer nationalist Jews would have meant fewer pogroms overall, but in general would not have altered the relationship between local support for nationalism and the propensity of a pogrom to occur.[11]

Another source of trouble is the political upheaval Poland endured between 1928, the year we use to measure the local political context, and 1941. As we saw in chapter 2, after Piłsudski's death in 1935 Poland trended in a fascistic direction, its government increasingly brazen in the favoritism it showed to the ethnic Polish majority. The Jews, meanwhile, increasingly abandoned their full-chested assertions of national pride, whether cast in Hebraic or Yiddishist hues, and turned in some measure to the socialist Bund to protect their interests. Under the Soviet occupation of 1939–1941, there was massive social and economic upheaval that included the repression of civil society and socialist economic reorganization. According to some estimates, over 1 million Polish citizens were deported, further distorting the distribution of national groups from what it was in 1921 and probably reducing the presence of Polish and Ukrainian nationalists, who would have been targeted for deportation. But the broader question is whether by 1941 non-Jewish perceptions of Jewish political aims were updated from 1928 in ways that threaten our argument. It is undoubtedly true that by summer 1941, after two years of Soviet rule and facing an uncertain future, none of Poland's ethnic groups viewed politics in quite the same way as they had in 1928. But this does not imply that the old political identities were completely wiped away. Research on historical legacies has definitively established that such identities are resilient to far greater upheavals than what occurred in Poland between 1928 and 1941. Charnysh (2015), for example, shows how areas with anti-Jewish politics in interwar Poland also opposed European Union membership in the post-Communist era. Jasiewicz (2009) documents even longer identity persistence by drawing a connection between patterns of voting behavior in the 2005 Polish election and the empires that ruled different parts of Polish territory between the late eighteenth century partitions and Poland's reemergence in 1920 as an independent state. Throughout the intervening eighty years, Poland endured not just the Soviet occupation of 1939–1941 but also World War II, the imposition of four decades of state socialism, and the chaos of transition from dictatorship and economic central planning to democracy and free markets.[12]

No research design is perfect, and ours is no exception. However, we are not overly concerned about the limitations of our data. First, we are aware of the weak spots and, wherever possible, compensate for them. For example, to remedy known bias against counting minority ethnicities in the census, we employ the more reliable data on religious affiliation, which effectively stands in for ethnicity in interwar Poland. To account for our uncertainty about whether pogroms occurred in the smaller settlements in Ukrainian-inhabited areas (which have been less intensively researched than the Polish-inhabited areas), we rerun our analyses without those data points. We employ nonparametric methods to reduce the model dependence of our results. These robustness checks provide extra confidence that our conclusions are not the result of idiosyncratic measurement decisions or unreliable data.

Second, for better or worse, these data are the best available for establishing the economic, social, and political features of localities in interwar Poland that made them most vulnerable to pogrom occurrence. This goal requires knowledge of both the prevalence of pogroms—where they occurred and where they did not occur across all settlements where they could have occurred—and systematic and comparable economic, social, and political data for that same universe of settlements. More comprehensive data than we have collected, such as information on civil society membership or economic performance, might well be available for large cities or some other small subsample, but what is gained in the addition of potential correlates of pogroms is lost in the scope of the analysis.

4

BEYOND JEDWABNE

In this chapter we turn to an analysis of Białystok and the northeastern kresy, a region of Poland annexed to the Soviet Union as part of the western provinces of the Belarusian Republic following the Nazi-Soviet pact in 1939. We focus on the territories that had been the Polish voivodships of Białystok and Polesie before the Soviet annexation. The main ethnic groups inhabiting these areas were Poles, Jews, and Belarusians. Our analysis of 352 localities in these voivodships affirms the broad utility of power-threat theory and offers more limited support for the anti-Semitism hypothesis. The louder the Jewish call for cultural autonomy and the greater the popularity of parties such as the BBWR that advocated interethnic cooperation, the greater the perceived threat to Poles who sought a nationally homogeneous state, and the more likely a pogrom.

We begin with an overview of social, political, and military conditions in Białystok and Polesie on the eve of the pogroms. Conditions were ripe for pogroms: the hated Soviet regime had melted away and with it the violent suppression of Polish nationalism. The German army and Einsatzgruppen (Nazi death squads) came in but were not yet in full control. Our quantitative analysis starts with a comparison of Jedwabne, the locality with one of the best known of the 1941 pogroms, with other pogrom localities. We find that although Jedwabne has come to be paradigmatic of pogroms of the period, it is in no way representative of localities where pogroms occurred. We then offer prima facie evidence for the applicability of the power-threat hypothesis by descriptively comparing municipalities where pogroms did not occur with those where they did occur. Following that, we introduce a statistical model that shows that the perceived Jewish threat to Polish dominance predicts pogroms even once factors such as anti-Semitic Polish nationalism and the extent of Communist support are taken into account. Finally, we interpret these findings by turning to several narratives of pogrom violence. Poles that turned against their Jewish neighbors or failed to help prevent violence against them were motivated less by hatred, revenge, or avarice than by a perception of a threat to their political dominance.

The German Presence

It is important to recall that most of the pogroms discussed in this book occurred during a six-week period following the German invasion of the Soviet-occupied eastern borderlands on June 22, 1941. It was a period of near statelessness. The German Army Group Center moved through the northeastern borderlands exceptionally quickly. One week into the campaign, German units had encircled and destroyed Soviet forces deployed in the Białystok salient and had advanced beyond Minsk to the edge of the Pripet marshes (Stahel 2009, 192). In the face of this onslaught, public authority at the local level collapsed, as local Communist and police officials evacuated with the retreating Soviet forces.

In most towns local Poles replaced the departed Soviet officials, and, with German permission, temporarily carried out both political and police functions for the first several weeks. But the general political situation remained chaotic. Throughout the Białystok and Polesie voivodships, German army units stopped in communities to raise their flag, leave a small field troop, and then continue eastward. According to the account of Yehoshua Kales, who survived the war hidden by a Christian in the town of Siemiatycze, "Overall, the Poles had all the power in their hands for the first couple of weeks" (AŻIH 301-1463). The pattern and degrees of German involvement varied from place to place. A survivor account from Rokitno in Polesie voivodship describes how the pogrom unfolded there:

> The Soviet authorities remained in Rokitno until June 29, 1941, as well as units of the Red Army. The last to withdraw was the sapper detachment, which blew up the railway bridge and burned down several other objects. The town was then left entirely without authorities. On the night of July 3, the local Poles attacked and robbed Jewish houses. The Jews resisted, and a struggle developed during which one fell victim, whom the murderers killed with boards.... Among the local murderers, the following distinguished themselves: the Volksdeutsche Retslov and the Pole Krukowski. At the same time, a local police force of Poles was established. Retslov was appointed its commandant. No Germans had yet appeared in Rokitno. (AŻIH 301-3179)

It was not for "a couple of weeks," the narrative continues, until the "three SS men arrived in Rokitno from Tarnów and began to throw their weight around in true Hitlerite fashion." Although in some places German forces attempted to instigate pogroms, in other towns, such as Rokitno, deadly pogroms occurred before the Germans even arrived.

The Wehrmacht (the armed forces of Nazi Germany) was trailed by Schutzstaffel (SS) units known as the Einsatzgruppen. These units were tasked with killing communists and Jews. The problem they confronted was one of scale. In the areas of northeastern Poland covered in this chapter, SS-Gruppenführer Arthur Nebe's Einsatzgruppe B deployed less than 700 soldiers in a region with over 225,000 Jews. According to Dmitrów (2004, 122), "The task of the Einsatzgruppen confronted its leadership with the problem that the size of their own forces was limited compared to that of the Jewish population." Furthermore, the speed with which regular German military units moved across western Belarus forced Nebe's men to move along with them. By the first week of July, Nebe's main units had already left western Belarus and were located in Minsk. Small subunits of the Einsatzgruppen remained in the area, but they were very thin on the ground. This is one reason why the SS leadership decided to permit the local Polish and Belarusian populations to engage in "self-cleansing" actions. As previously noted, however, their efforts to encourage pogroms met with only limited success.

Legacy of Soviet Occupation

Soviet repression was experienced by the local population in a number of important ways. According to Gurianov, on the territory of western Belarus, 44,981 people were arrested during the Soviet occupation. Many were accused of having supported anticommunist resistance movements, and others were arrested for crimes ranging from membership in illegal organizations to economic "speculation" to crossing the Soviet-German border illegally. Of those arrested 48.9 percent were Poles, 24.2 percent were Jews, and 18.3 percent were Belarusians (Boćkowski 2005, 207). These numbers on their own do not suggest that Soviet repression disproportionately affected Poles over other ethnic groups. In addition to arrests, several thousand inhabitants were deported to the interior of the Soviet Union. Deportations occurred in four waves. In February 1940, landowners, civilians, military personnel who had received land for taking part in the struggle for independence, as well as foresters and their families, were the primary victims. In the second wave, in April 1940, the families of those previously jailed, of those in hiding, or those who had fled across the border were shipped eastward. Finally, in June 1940, Polish citizens who had fled the areas occupied by Germany in 1939 were deported. Whereas the earlier deportations had targeted mostly Poles, this third round focused primarily on Jews. On June 20, a final round of deportations was initiated, primarily of Poles and those who had worked in the anti-Soviet underground, as well as families of landowners, policemen, and higher officials of independent Poland. This last action, however, was never completed because of the German invasion (Wierzbiecki 2007, 32).

During the Soviet occupation, perhaps even more fateful for interethnic relations than the arrests and deportations were the dramatic changes in the ethnic composition of government, public administration, and the police. These were spheres that had been completely dominated by Poles, but in both the Białystok and Polesie regions Jews and especially Belarusians took up strong positions in all of these sectors. By October 1, 1940, for example, in the Białystok region, Boćkowski estimates that there were somewhere between 9,000 and 12,000 people working in the state administration. Of these, approximately 3,900 were Belarusians; 3,104 were Russians; 1,420 were Jewish; and 613 other nationalities. These figures represented a dramatic break with the past. Perhaps even more significant were changes outside the state administration. At the Białystok Pedagogical Institute, spaces in the class admitted in March 1940 were allotted by nationality with a clear preference for Belarusians and Jews over Poles: 25 Belarusians, 22 Poles, 18 Jews, and 4 Russians (Boćkowski 2005, 128).

It is important to note that preference for Belarusians and Jews over Poles in predominantly Polish areas began to change in fall 1940 (Boćkowski 2005, 140), when orders came down from Minsk to increase the number of local Poles in state and party positions. From the standpoint of ethnic relations, however, the damage had already been done. The state administration and civil service, which had earlier been "owned" by Poles, were now in the hands of a multiethnic political elite. On the eve of the German invasion, the Third Battalion of the Red Army stationed near the town of Ostryn sent a report up the chain of command noting, "According to the information of the local population, with regards to the moving of troops of the Red Army, Polish counterrevolutionary elements are spreading rumors about the Red Army leaving Western Belarus and they are threatening the Belarusian and Jewish population with revenge" (Wierzbiecki 2005, 34). Multiple Jewish survivor reports note that those just released from Soviet prisons were strongly represented among pogrom perpetrators (AŻIH 301-1858; Destruction of the Jews of Szczuczyn, 7). But most administrators stationed from the interior of the Soviet Union had fled with the retreating Soviet authorities, leaving the local Belarusian and Jewish population vulnerable to retribution for the ordeal of the preceding twenty-one months.

Anti-Semitic Polish Nationalism

As noted in chapter 1, both historians and survivors point to the strength of the anti-Semitic and Polish nationalist National Democrats (Endecja) as the key to understanding pogroms (Żbikowski 2007). Israel Lewin, a survivor from Wizna, was advised to flee by a Polish friend soon after the outbreak of the war because "the nationalists have already been given permission to do what they want" (AŻIH 301-4391); Szymon Datner's account of the same town testified that "Polish fascists, anti-Semites of long standing, the well-known Endeks sized up the situation and began persecuting those Jews who were in hiding" (AŻIH 301-192). Datner's account of the Kolno pogrom points to the same group: "It was not in vain that the Polish Endeks and fascists had drummed into their minds over the course of long years the notion that Jews and Communists were one and the same thing, and they were the ones responsible for their misfortune" (AŻIH 301-1996).

The Endecja was in fact particularly strong in parts of Białystok and Polesie. In 1902, of the 6,800 members of one of the main precursor civic organizations to the National Democrats in all of Poland, almost one-third (2,275) were active in the Łomża region, which makes up part of Białystok (Wolsza 1992). Most historians trace the organizational capacity of the Endecja in these regions to the size and social position of the petty nobility, the so-called *szlachta zagorodowa*, who possessed small farms and often lived no better than the peasantry among whom they resided. This group had a reputation for fanatical patriotism, religiosity, and a sense of belonging to a socially better stratum than the ordinary folk (burghers, peasants, and Jews) in their surroundings.

In independent Poland, the National Democrats emerged as the strongest party in the region, winning on average over half the votes cast in the 229 settlements of the Białystok voivodship in 1922. The party could draw on both an anti-Jewish political Catholicism and a deep resentment against Jewish economic competition in the small market towns, or shtetls. We lack systematic data for all of the towns in our two provinces, but one study of the retail sector in eleven towns in the Białystok region in 1932 found that 663 of 721 retail shops (91%) were owned by Jews. Although this proportion dropped in the face of the growth of the Polish retail sector and economic pressure applied against Jews after Piłsudski's death, by 1937 Jews still owned 563 of 873 retail shops (64%) in these same towns, providing plenty of fuel for National Democratic agitation and boycotts (Linder 1937, 17, cited in Mendelsohn 1983, 75).

In the late 1930s, these boycotts were frequently accompanied by pogroms in this region and were abetted by the growth of what social scientists today would call pogrom "networks" (Brass 2006; Scacco 2008). The existence of such networks and their connection with the National Democrats in northeastern Poland during the late 1930s is supported by a great deal of anecdotal and archival evidence. For example, in a statement to the Sejm in 1937, Prime Minister Felicjan Slawoj-Składkowski discussed his response to daily reports of anti-Jewish riots in the Wysoki Mazowiecki district of Białystok in a way strongly indicative of nationalist agitation:

> The Starosta [district prefect] told me that the man behind the disturbances was a lawyer named Jursz, leader of the National Democrats, but he never takes part in the riots personally. I sent for him. He was not at home, so I left word to tell him that Składkowski was here and said that if riots occur, he will be sent to Bereza [prison] and will be freed only if for one month after his incarceration no riots will occur. When, therefore, riots took place, we sent him to Bereza. After six weeks, we freed him, no riots having occurred.... During the time of his imprisonment they evidently endeavored not to provoke riots, and none occurred. (Segal 1938, 89)

Perceived Jewish Threat

One of the most important political vehicles of the Jewish struggle for cultural autonomy in northeast Poland was the Bloc of National Minorities, an electoral alliance that drew together all of the country's major national minorities—Germans, Jews, Ukrainians, and Belarusians. As described by Mendelsohn (1983, 53–54), the BNM was built on the idea that all the minorities shared a similar interest in gaining national autonomy. The best strategy to achieve this, given electoral districts and rules favoring the Polish majority, was to form a united front.

Popular support for the Bloc of National Minorities undoubtedly increased Polish suspicions, particularly among the landed gentry (Cang 1939), that the minorities, and the Jews in particular, were resisting a reasonable accommodation with Polish national aspirations. Indeed, given the minorities' demographic weight and the fractionalized Polish political spectrum, it could conceivably have been the largest parliamentary party. The BNM could and sometimes did hold the balance of power, as occurred when the country's minorities supported the Left's candidate for the subsequently assassinated president, Gabriel Narutowicz. The strong performance of the BNM in the 1922 elections shocked Polish public opinion and seemed to confirm the worst fears of Poles that the country's national minorities were either unassimilable or disloyal.

In northeastern Poland the key player within the BNM was the General Zionist Party, led by Yitzhak Grünbaum. The General Zionists spanned the religious/

secular divide; incorporated both workers and businessmen; and, despite all of the bluster about Hebrew (a language spoken by very few Polish Jews), its newspapers were published and party meetings were conducted in Yiddish as well as Polish. Therefore, it is probably best thought of as a Jewish "catch-all" party that took aim at the "center" of the Jewish electorate. Although Zionism's ultimate goal was a Jewish state in Palestine, for the General Zionists, day-to-day politics involved pressing demands for Jewish cultural and political rights and autonomy within Poland. Perceptions of the BNM as a vehicle for achieving such autonomy could only have increased after the Orthodox Jewish Agudas Yisrael decided to field its own list in 1928.

Poles of both the Left and the Right viewed Zionism as a danger because of the threat it posed to the establishment of a nationally homogeneous Polish state. According to Mendelsohn (1981), "The origins of the Zionists' support for the so-called minorities bloc resided in their conviction that Poland must be transformed from a nation-state into a multinational state and their search for allies in the struggle to maintain this goal." For the Polish Left, Zionists represented a failure of the project of assimilation and a return to Jewish medieval separatism. For the Polish Right, Zionism was seen as a "step toward the creation within Poland of a 'Jewish state'" (Mendelsohn 1981, 14). The General Zionists did not constitute the same irredentist threat as parties representing Germans, Ukrainians, and Belarusians, but in some ways the threat they posed was more intractable: because the Jews were urban and literate, the Zionist appeal represented a threat to precisely those modern sectors of the economy and polity that the Poles hoped to dominate.

Stachura probably best summarizes the mainstream Polish view of the Zionists in his otherwise sympathetic reading of interwar Poland's minority policy:

> If one Jewish leader personified for Poles the distrust and resentment many of them harboured toward the Jews ... it was the General Zionist leader, Yitzhak Gruenbaum (1879–1960), described by one writer as "fundamentally anti-Polish." A somewhat intemperate, doctrinaire and egocentric individual, who had returned to Warsaw in 1918 after spending many years in Russia as a Zionist activist, he made it his mission in his new life in Poland to agitate incessantly against the state, and to encourage others to follow his uncompromising example. (Stachura 1998, 75)

The Zionists' calls for government-funded Jewish schools in Hebrew and Yiddish; a transformation of Jewish communal organizations, the *kehilot*, from purely religious institutions to democratic political ones; and other forms of Jewish extraterritorial autonomy were opposed by Polish governments of all political stripes. This fear of a Jewish "state within a state" was repeated time and again, not only in the literature of the Polish Right but also, after 1935, in the platform of the otherwise centrist Peasant Party (Cang 1939, 249).

Even ethnically tolerant Poles viewed the Bloc of National Minorities as a danger.[1] The Piłsudskiite efforts to undermine it were taken with exactly this concern in mind. As noted in chapter 2, when the chief of the Interior Ministry's Political Department, Kazimierz Świtalski, was dispatched to the eastern borderlands in 1927 to meet with Jewish leaders in an effort to discourage the formation of the BNM for the upcoming national elections in 1928, both he and his interlocutors could agree that Poles considered the BNM an "anti-state organization" (Switalski 1992, 215). Although Świtalski's efforts bore some fruit in eastern Galicia (to be addressed in chapter 5), in this part of Poland his efforts failed.

The Jedwabne Pogrom in Regional Context

We now turn to our quantitative analysis. One of the advantages of our data is that they allow us to situate individual pogroms within the distribution of all pogrom localities. Recall from chapter 1 that Gross (2001) launched the recent flurry of research on the 1941 pogroms with his account of the vicious Jedwabne pogrom (Białystok voivodship), where Poles brutally murdered even young, old, and sick Jews. Although even then it was known that Jedwabne was not the only pogrom that occurred, Jedwabne has come to represent the 1941 pogroms and symbolize Polish anti-Semitism and collaboration with the Germans.

Misplaced emphasis on Jedwabne is unfortunate because it was far from being a typical Białystok pogrom settlement. Table 4.1 compares Jedwabne with other pogrom localities in the Białystok voivodship across a range of demographic and political factors. As discussed in chapter 3, we report the median percentage (excluding Jedwabne itself) rather than the mean to avoid skewness in the data, and we use religion data as a proxy for nationality. As evident in the first five rows of the table, Jedwabne was far more Jewish, less Polish, and more supportive of both the Minorities Bloc and the Polish nationalist Endecja than other localities where pogroms occurred. This polarization may be better appreciated by examining the last two rows in the table, which present estimates of the percentage of Poles supporting the Endecja and the percentage of minorities supporting the Minorities Bloc, respectively.[2] In Jedwabne strong majorities of both Poles (63%) and Jews (76%) supported their respective nationalist parties, in proportions far higher than the medians of the rest of the voivodship.

We can conclude two things from these findings. First, Jedwabne is not representative of other pogrom localities in Białystok, but is something of an extreme case of political polarization. Polish support for the Endecja (63%) and minority

TABLE 4.1. Key characteristics of Jedwabne and its pogrom neighbors

	BIAŁYSTOK MEDIAN (%)	JEDWABNE (%)
Polish	48	36
Jewish	45	62
Belarusian	.5	0
Endecja 28	16	22
Min Bloc 28	28	50
Poles for Endecja 28	38	63
Mins for Min Bloc 28	47	76
N	31	1

Note: Median values used. Variables are percentage Poles (Polish), Jews (Jewish), and Belarusians (Belarusian); 1928 electoral support for Polish nationalism (Endecja 28) and Jewish nationalism (Min Bloc 28); percentage of Poles supporting Endecja (Poles for Endecja 28); and percentage of minorities (mainly Jews) supporting the Minorities Bloc (Mins for Min Bloc 28).
Source: 1921 Polish Census, 1928 election to Polish Sejm, and authors' computation.

support for the Minorities Bloc (76%) put Jedwabne above the 90th percentile. Jedwabne was *much* more politically polarized than most other places, a fact that might account for that pogrom's exceptional cruelty. It is also worth noting that Jedwabne is the only pogrom locality that had no Belarusian inhabitants, leaving Poles and Jews in direct and unmediated ethnic competition. Second, the findings cast some doubt on the claim that it was the Soviet occupation and the suspected Jewish role in it that turned Poles against Jews in 1941. However brutal the Soviet occupation may have been, it is clear that Poles and Jews were polarized long before the outbreak of war. This is, of course, especially true for Jedwabne, but also for the other pogrom localities, where on average large minorities of both Jews and Poles supported their respective nationalist parties.

Why Pogroms?
Prima Facie Evidence

How do pogrom localities differ from places where pogroms did not occur? As a first cut at this question, we divide all 352 localities in our northeastern sample into two groups: those where pogroms occurred and those where they did not. The extent to which the two subsamples differ across important demographic and political characteristics offers prima facie evidence for what differentiates pogrom from nonpogrom localities. Table 4.2 reports median values for a range of important characteristics across the Białystok and Polesie voivodships. The top and middle sections of the table present raw census and electoral data. The bottom portion (with "for" in the label) contains estimates of group vote for particular parties, computed according to the logic presented in the previous section. Even a cursory examination shows that the two subsamples differ in important ways.

First, the results are consistent with our hypothesis on the importance of the perceived Jewish nationalist threat. Focusing on the demographic data in the top third of the table, it is clear that pogroms occurred where more Jews actually resided, both in absolute terms ("Number of Jews") and relative to the number of other nationalities ("Jewish"). The differences are in fact stark: pogrom localities had more than ten times as many Jewish inhabitants as nonpogrom localities. Moving to the middle third of the table, median support for the Minorities Bloc ("Min Bloc 28") was far greater where there were pogroms (22%) than where there were no pogroms (1%). Support for Jewish parties for which national autonomy was a secondary issue, such as the socialist Bund or the Orthodox Jewish list ("Orth Jew List 28," dominated by Agudas), did not appreciably differ across the two subsamples. The result does not qualitatively change if we consider the proportions of Jews that supported the Minorities Bloc ("Jews for Min Bloc 28" in the lower third of the table). Jews in localities where pogroms occurred were far more nationalist (51%) than in localities where no pogrom occurred (39%). Only results for BBWR ("Gov Party") do not conform to expectation.

Second, there is some support for the anti-Semitism hypothesis. The Endecja was slightly more popular where pogroms occurred (13%) than where they did not (9%). But Poles were far more nationalist in pogrom localities (39% supporting the Endecja) than in peaceful places (24%). On the other hand, if anti-Semitism were behind the violence, there is no reason why pogroms should not have broken out in localities where there were smaller numbers of Jews. These populations would have been particularly vulnerable to the Poles among whom they lived.[3] Yet as we see from the top part of the table, pogromists had a strong preference for localities with lots of Jews, both in absolute and percentage terms. In fact, no pogrom occurred in any settlement with fewer than 360 Jews.

Third, there is no support for the hypothesis that pogroms were revenge for Jewish support for communism. Although Communist support ("Comms 28") was low everywhere, it was six times as low in places that would later experience a pogrom. Our hunch is that this result reflects two significant but unappreciated facts about the sociology of Communist support in interwar Poland. The first is that, at the mass level, the Communists did not attract many votes from Jews—the strongest supporters were to be found among Belarusians in the eastern voivodships (Kopstein and Wittenberg 2003). The second is that areas where Communist sympathy was strong among non-Jews were not fertile ground for those wishing to instigate anti-Jewish violence. The Communists did not recoil from violence, but it was directed more at class enemies than at ethnic ones. Local

TABLE 4.2. Median demographic and political characteristics of pogrom and nonpogrom localities in Białystok and Polesie

	POGROM	NO POGROM
Polish	33%	43%
Jewish	41%	3%
E. Orthodox	10%	35%
Number of Jews	1574	137
Pop	5290	5000
Bund 28	0%	0%
Orth Jew List 28	4	0
Min Bloc 28	22	1
Endecja 28	13	9
Comms 28	2	12
Gov Party 28	19	27
Jews for Bund 28	0%	0%
Jews for Orth List 28	11	0
Jews for Min Bloc 28	51	39
Poles for Endecja 28	39	24
N	56	296

Note: Variables are the 1921 percentage Poles (Polish), Jews (Jewish), and Belarusians (Belarusian); 1928 electoral support for non-Zionist Jewish parties (Bund 28 and Orth Jew List 28), Jewish nationalism (Min Bloc 28), Polish nationalism (Endecja 28), and the communists (Comms 28); percentage of Jews supporting non-Zionist parties (Jews for Bund 28 and Jews for Orth List 28) and nationalist parties (Jews for Min Bloc 28); and percentage of Poles supporting Endecja (Poles for Endecja 28).
Sources: Census and electoral data and authors' computation.

non-Jewish Communists certainly opposed rightist nationalist violence and may well have also provided a haven for Jews threatened by such violence. Whatever the role Poles, Jews, or Belarusians played in abetting Soviet rule between 1939 and 1941, there was little hint of mass Communist support in the late 1920s.

Fourth, we acknowledge that the preference among pogrom perpetrators for localities with lots of Jews may have other interpretations. For example, if the objective were simply to persecute Jews, then it would make sense to focus attention where more of the Jews dwelled, in the cities. Or, if the problem was not the availability of perpetrators but finding Jews to persecute, then it makes sense that the probability of a pogrom would increase with the relative proportion of Jews in a locality. It might also be the case that pogroms were more likely to occur where Jews were more visible because in these localities the identification of Jews with the Soviet occupation was more palpable or at least believable. Where there were few Jews, by contrast, the Soviets were more likely to have relied on Poles and Belarusians, making it more difficult to blame Jews for the occupation.

Given the findings of both Jasiewicz (2001) and Brakel (2007) on the ethnic makeup of the Soviet government in the newly acquired Polish territories, however, it is not plausible to argue that a small minority of Jews occupied the majority of administrative positions.

Multivariate Analysis

Table 4.2 shows that pogroms tended to occur where there were lots of Jews, where there was greater support for the Zionist party (within the Minorities Bloc), where there was lower support for communism, and where Polish nationalism was stronger. But we would also like to know the relative significance of these factors, and for that we need a statistical model. Our central claim is that pogroms were most likely to occur where Jewish calls for cultural autonomy and the popularity of ethnically accommodationist political parties were widespread enough to threaten Polish plans for a nationally homogeneous state.

We have measured perceived threat in two different ways. Both employ the demographic weight of Jews as represented in the 1921 census and the result of the 1928 election, but differ in how they incorporate support for Zionism/Jewish nationalism. One uses the proportion of the vote received by the Minorities Bloc, while the other uses the estimated proportion of Jews supporting the Minorities Bloc. To minimize the number of statistical assumptions behind our multivariate analysis, in our models we employ only the first indicator, which relies on the raw census and electoral data.

Both the Communists and Marshal Piłsudski's BBWR advocated Polish accommodation with the ethnic minorities, and our explanation would predict a positive relationship between support for those parties and a pogrom. It should be noted that arguments attributing pogroms to Polish revenge for Jewish collaboration with the Soviet occupation also predict a positive relationship between pogroms and Communist support, so the statistical analysis alone may not disentangle the two interpretations. The BBWR was also multiethnic. Polish society was divided on nationality questions, not only between ethnic groups but—perhaps even more fatefully—within them. Ethnic Poles disagreed among themselves about the most prudent course of action regarding the country's minority population. Because Polish nationalists advocated assimilation for the Belarusians and discrimination for the country's Jews, those communities where Poles and Belarusians supported Piłsudski more strongly should have been especially threatening to the Endecja. In these settlements we expect Poles to have been especially keen to attack Jews in order to forestall any need to acknowledge Jewish rights.

Logic tells us that the relationship between the strength of BBWR and the probability of a pogrom is curvilinear: where the BBWR gained no support, clearly it did not constitute a threat to local nationalists; where it was dominant, nationalists were too weak to initiate anything. It is in the middle range, where the vast majority of localities are found, that the rising popularity of the BBWR among Poles and Belarusians should have stiffened the resolve of local nationalists to poison the atmosphere and pave the way for pogroms. As noted above, we proxy Polish anti-Semitic nationalism with the proportion of the vote for the Endecja (the National Democrats). Arguments emphasizing the importance of Polish anti-Semitism would predict a positive correlation with the probability of a pogrom.

Recall from chapter 1 that economic arguments for pogroms claim they were more about economic competition and plunder than about racism or revenge. Narratives of actual pogroms lend support to this hypothesis. Petseye Shuster-Rozenblum's 1946 testimony on what transpired in Jasionówka after the departure of the Red Army is representative:

> The darkest elements of the Polish people soon sense Jewish weakness, and don't even wait for the Germans to arrive, but soon men come from the farms, boldly enter Jewish homes, in broad daylight taking what they can, and what they can't they destroy where it is. They soon felt as if they had broad shoulders: the Germans would certainly allow their actions, and even condone them. Of course, this is only done by those Poles with base instincts; the shtetl workers resist and drive the robbers from the village.... Here village peasants harness up the wagons, there they bring the stolen bundles to close neighbors in the shtetl in order to be able to run and grab something else, it's such a good opportunity, they'll be set for life, the shtetl never had such a holiday, the Christians call it *valny targ* (supermarket) and take pains not to let the opportunity slip away. (AŻIH 301-1274)

We test economic arguments with the dummy variable "Shtetl." If pogroms are about economic competition or plunder, then they should be most common in the shtetls, where competition was fierce and wealth differentials great. We also use the dummy variable "Freeloan." As noted in chapter 3, these data are available only for larger communities, and thus cannot be used in the multivariate analyses. However, we do present some bivariate results.

Figure 4.1 presents the results of both the logit and nonparametric analyses for the Białystok and Polesie voivodships. The explanatory variables are listed on the left. The circles and triangles represent the effect coefficients of the nonparametric and logit models, respectively. The horizontal bars are 95 percent confidence intervals. If those bars cross the vertical line indicating zero (only the one for the nonparametric model is shown), then the corresponding explanatory variable is not statistically different from zero.

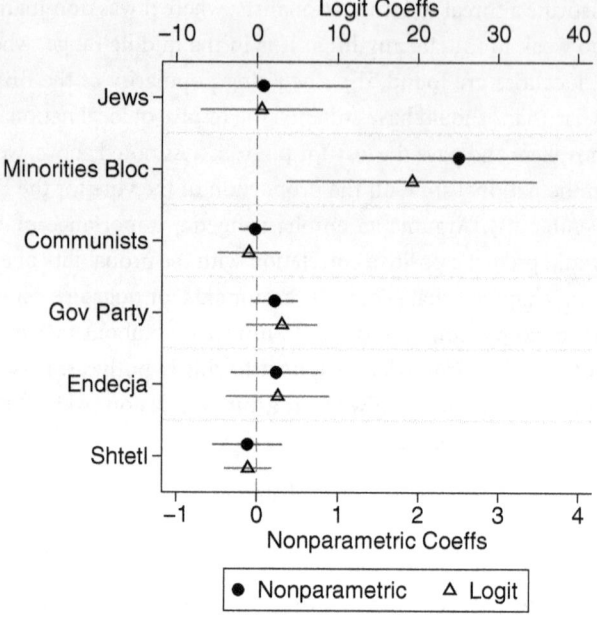

FIGURE 4.1. Results of nonparametric regression and parametric logit analyses of the determinants of pogrom occurrence in Białystok and Polesie voivodships. Point estimates are given by circles (nonparametric) and triangles (logit); 95 percent confidence intervals are given by the horizontal bars. N=129.

There are two findings highlighted in this figure. First, the results support our claim that the probability of a pogrom increases in tandem with the popularity of parties advocating Jewish national equality ("Minorities Bloc"), which is the only explanatory variable statistically different from zero. Anti-Semitism ("Endecja"), revenge for alleged Jewish support for communism ("Communists"), economic competition ("Shtetl"), and non-Jewish ethnically tolerant parties ("Gov Party") had zero effect. The result for anti-Semitism is perhaps surprising given the importance that many pogrom narratives ascribe to Polish anti-Semitic nationalism. At the same time, however, by saying that one cannot predict where a pogrom would take place based on the strength of the local Endecja organization or its political support, we can better appreciate the surprise and shock, expressed in so many Jewish narratives, that Poles with whom Jews had lived side by side and with whom they had gotten along reasonably well would, under the right conditions, turn on them.[4] The environment conducive to pogroms was less one of Polish nationalism—for this was strong everywhere—than a large Jewish population calling for Polish recognition of its cultural and political rights.

Despite these encouraging results, it would be premature to dismiss the alternatives. The reason has to do with sample size ($N=129$, owing to missing values) relative to the number of explanatory variables and some of those variables' limited variance. We shall see in chapter 5, for example, that economic factors are also important. On the other hand, the qualitative similarity between the nonparametric and logit results gives us some confidence in our use of nonparametric methods. The magnitudes of the coefficients are different, as expected, but both models identified the same significant and insignificant factors.[5] Also, although we have not included the presence of free loan associations in the multivariate analysis, the bivariate results among the subsample that was eligible for these associations, which were funded by Jewish organizations outside of Poland, are instructive; 39 percent of places that had free loan associations experienced a pogrom, whereas the frequency for those that lacked them was only 17 percent. This runs counter to the plunder argument, which is that the places that need free loan associations are poorer and thus less likely to be targeted for their wealth. It is consistent, however, with a different explanation that views pogroms as an expression of non-Jewish envy at the resources open to poor Jews that are unavailable to non-Jews.

To assess the model's prediction of the strength of the relationship between perceived Jewish threat and the probability of a pogrom, we computed predicted pogrom probabilities for values of Minorities Bloc support ranging from 0 to .5. These are illustrated in figure 4.2, where Minorities Bloc support is on the horizontal axis and probability of a pogrom is on the vertical axis. As before, circles refer to the nonparametric mode and triangles to logit. Focusing on the nonparametric results, we see dramatic jumps in pogrom probability as the popularity of Jewish nationalism increases. For example, there is roughly a 5 percent probability of a pogrom in a community with no Minorities Bloc support. That probability jumps to around 30 percent with 10 percent Bloc support, and to nearly 75 percent with 30 percent Bloc support. This is a strong effect given that pogroms occurred in roughly 10 percent of all municipalities. Note that the 95th percentile of Minorities Bloc support is just 32 percent in the estimation sample, so any estimates beyond that are relying on very few observations.[6]

Discussion

As Stola (2001, 2004) notes, the pogroms involved a great deal of participation, both "active" and "passive." Where the population felt a sense of ethnic threat, Poles from across the political and economic spectrum were more likely to give in to the temptation to commit violence, more tolerant of others committing

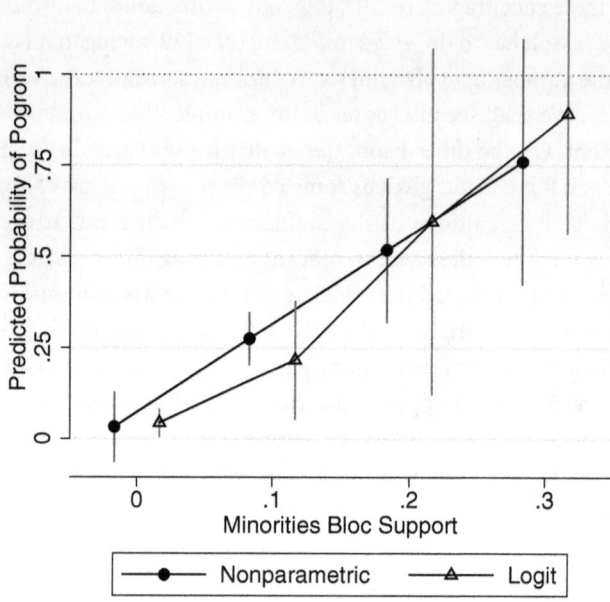

FIGURE 4.2. Marginal effects of different values of the fraction of support for the Minorities Bloc on the predicted probability of a pogrom for both the nonparametric and (parametric) logit models. Point estimates are given by circles (nonparametric) and triangles (logit); 95 percent confidence intervals are given by the vertical bars.

violence, and less likely to come to the aid of the victims. In short, the community expectation in pogrom localities either encouraged or at least failed to discourage Polish violence against Jews. Our statistical analysis is consistent with such an account. Even so, these events were complex. We are not able to account for all the spatial variation of pogrom occurrence, nor do the numbers give us a concrete understanding of how the social and political background created the facilitating conditions for pogrom occurrence, how the pogroms unfolded, and why they sometimes did not occur even though they "should" have. In what follows, we turn to two cases that provide an illustration.

Szczuczyn

An account of one less known pogrom—Szczuczyn, on June 27, 1941, in which approximately 300 Jews were killed by local Poles—may help illustrate the underlying causal relationships we seek to illuminate, the communal context in which a pogrom was likely to occur, and the mix of emotions at work. Located northwest of Białystok near the German and Lithuanian borders, Szczuczyn was a county seat in interwar Poland. Jews and Poles had long lived in the town side by side. Although nationalist tensions increased over the course of the 1930s, photographs from Szczuczyn show both communities serving together in volunteer fire departments and broad contact in both commerce and education (Levine 2002). The town even had a Jewish mayor at one point in the interwar era, which is not surprising because a majority of its inhabitants were Jewish. The 1921 census reports 2,506 Jewish inhabitants, 56 percent of the population. It is reasonable to assume that by the time of the war, this number rose to approximately 3,000, although the proportions of Jews to Poles remained constant.

Testimonies regarding Polish-Jewish relations in the interwar period report them to have been cordial but never close. Intercommunal contact occurred mostly on market days but rarely socially. Polish and Jewish communities tended to live in different worlds, both socially and spiritually. Jews especially avoided Catholic religious processions, and Christians hardly ever understood the meaning of their Jewish neighbors' customs or religious holidays. Friendships between younger Jewish and Polish schoolmates did develop, but contact also led to "playground fights and bloody noses" (Tryczyk 2015, 394). As Tryczyk notes in his collection of (mostly) Polish testimonies, Poles who survived World War II could easily name other ethnic Poles who had perished but could frequently remember only their Jewish neighbors as Jews, not by name. Jews, on the other hand, could easily identify by name not only prominent personalities in Szczuczyn but also their tormentors who came from various social strata.

Zionists dominated Jewish politics in Szczuczyn. Jews spoke Yiddish, Polish, and sometimes Russian, but political life was built around the myriad of Zionist youth organizations, cultural clubs, summer camps, sports and scouting associations, a library (with books in Hebrew, Yiddish, and Polish), and a broad range of Zionist charities and organizations, all of which espoused the full-chested new Jewish politics. A moderate number of Jews departed for Palestine in 1925, but the vast majority either could not or would not leave and remained in close contact with other Zionist groups in nearby towns. Access to the local Jewish cooperative bank, cofounded by the head of the Szczuczyn's General Zionists, Boruch Fishl Zeml, provided its 350 members with small loans that gave Jewish business a leg up, at least until the late 1930s, against their Polish competitors. Yeshiah Skubelski's recollection in the town's memorial book notes that Jews operated the majority of local businesses: "Only a few were of Christian proprietorship."[7] Taken together, the political and economic landscape of the town did little to promote solidarity between the Polish and Jewish communities.

Relations among the Polish and Jewish communities, as elsewhere in Poland, deteriorated in Szczuczyn in the 1930s. Both communities suffered during the global economic downturn, and Piłsudski's death in 1935 ushered in an anti-Semitic turn in local politics. In Szczuczyn the right-wing anti-Semitic National Party (the successor organization to the Endecja of the 1920s) situated its reading room on the main town square among Jewish-owned businesses. The movement to boycott Jewish businesses also found a toehold, but evidence is mixed as to its efficacy. Smashed windows and low-level violence, however, were not uncommon (Tryczyk 2015, 294).

The Germans briefly occupied Szczuczyn on September 7, 1939, after the outbreak of the war. Tensions immediately rose when, in the face of the inevitable collapse of the Polish state and the devaluation of its currency, Jewish shop owners closed their doors. Local Poles, unable to purchase needed goods, responded with indignation and went to the German authorities, who advised them to take matters into their own hands, a message reinforced during a meeting with the parish priest. This "prepogrom" atmosphere passed only with the intervention of the Germans, who on the following day began to round up Jews for forced labor and on September 9 arrested three hundred Jewish men, locked them in a synagogue, and ultimately took them away (the vast majority of them ultimately perished as the Germans retreated over the next two weeks back to the lines established according to the Molotov-Ribbentrop Pact).[8] Before departing, the Germans burned the synagogue and two smaller houses of study.

The Soviet occupation that followed spawned both resistance and resentment among Szczuczyn's Poles. A small contingent of citizens welcomed the Soviet military, but any warmth of reception was skewed heavily toward the Jewish community, who felt a deep sense of relief after the Germans departed.[9] The NKVD (Soviet secret police) immediately arrested a handful of town officials, a few wealthy Poles, and members of the local intelligentsia. Other Poles determined to resist took to the woods, but many known nationalists landed in NKVD prisons or were deported to Siberia. Jews enjoyed civic equality under the Soviets and served in state apparatus, but their share of positions did not exceed their proportion in the population. In fact, one document indicates it was far less. A list of the Szczuczyn's Communist Party Committee, prepared for a meeting in January 1940, indicates less than 15 percent of committee members were Jewish. Of the 46 attendees, which included the local chief of the NKVD, the prosecutor, and the newspaper chief, only seven were Jews judging by their full names (name, patronymic, and surname).[10] Any measure of Jewish participation in Soviet rule, and undoubtedly there was some, must be set off against Jewish commercial loses and political defeats. During the three rounds of deportations to the interior of the Soviet Union (February 10 and April 13, 1940, and then June 20, 1941) of the 130 people deported, 29 families were Jewish–drawn from Jewish political and economic elites–indicating that Jews as well as Poles fell into the jaws of the Soviet repressive apparatus (Tryczyk 2015, 299).[11] The perception of Jewish "collaboration" in Szczuczyn was shaped by political and social polarization that antedated the arrival of the Soviets.

Operation Barbarossa began two days after the last deportation. Chaya Soika-Golding, one of the local Jewish survivors of the war, described the events in a letter to a friend immediately after the war from safe refuge in the West. The Germans quickly swept into town on June 22:

> They hung up their swastika flag and pushed on further. The city lay in chaos. Authority passed to the hands of the Poles. This lasted about two weeks. All kinds of rowdies were let out of prison: Dombrovski, Yakubtshuk, the well known Polish arrestees under the Bolsheviks—Shviatlovski, chief of the guard and Yankayitis, the director of the school, and others. They were full of rancor for the Bolsheviks and the Jews. Friday night when the entire city slept quietly, the slaughter began. They [the Poles] had organized it very well: one gang in the new section, a second in the market-place, a third on Lomzher Street. . . . There in the new section they murdered Romorovske's family (the tailor), Esther Krieger (your neighbor with the youngest daughter), Soreh Beylkeh, Eynikl, Pishke, Yashinski, Mayzler (the head of the yeshivah)—all in their own houses . . . and many more. They had killed Rozental's children in the marketplace. They had also killed Kheytshe with her six month old child at breast and her older boy Grishen. . . . Later the squads divided up the possessions of their victims amongst themselves. On readied wagons they loaded the corpses and led them just outside of the town. The *goyim* immediately washed the bloodied floors including the stones on the street. A few hundred sacrifices had taken place and still, the murderers informed us, the massacres would continue for two more nights" (Former Residents of Szczuczyn [1954] 1987, 10–11).[12]

The elements are all there. The Soviet occupation; the collapse of authority; the riot agitators; the hatred and fear; the rage of the nationalist crowd; the thirst for revenge, blood, and booty; and, ultimately, the intimate violence perpetrated by people well known to the victims are all contained within this short narrative. To the extent that this pogrom followed the pattern of others, the primary victims in the first round were adult males. What came next, however, provides crucial clues to the permissive communal context in which the pogrom could occur and deepen:

Those remaining were stricken with fear. What do we do? How can we save ourselves? My mother ran to the priests to beg for the Jews. They offered no help. With Chana, Libe, Zeml, and Salen, I ran to the Polish intelligentsia. There too we found no salvation. My mother with other women ran after help in Grayeve [a nearby town]; they were not let into the town—curfew. What do we do? Night was falling upon us. Approximately 20 Germans entered the city—a field troupe. We were afraid to show ourselves before them. Then I had an idea: to try our luck with the soldiers, maybe they would help us. With great difficulty we chose a delegation and departed. The group of Germans consisted of soldiers and two officers. In the beginning they declined to help us, "This is not our business, we are fighting on the front, not with civilians," they explained. However, when I offered them soap and coffee, they softened up. They guarded the city at night and all remained quiet. I, with two other women, began to work for them, and later we were placed to work in the German headquarters. And so, in this manner, the pogroms in Szczuczyn were stopped for a while. (Former Residents of Szczuczyn [1954] 1987, 10–11)

The passage strongly indicates that what allowed the pogrom to get off the ground and intensify was the quite obvious indifference of key members of the local Polish community toward the fate of the town's Jews. Szczuczyn's Jewish women expected something different. Their first instinct once they understood their predicament was to turn to the priest and the intelligentsia, whom they believed could have stopped the bloodshed. But neither the priest nor the intelligentsia—a broad category in Eastern Europe that refers to the prominent and educated, especially doctors, lawyers, and school teachers—were moved by the frantic appeals of the petrified Jewish women to intervene, a point stressed in several testimonies written at different times and places. Neither lifted a finger or showed any sign of solidarity with their fellow citizens. The women did not encounter hatred in their demarches (although there was much to be found in the street); they reported no reaction, "no help," "no salvation," "nothing." They met indifference. Whether they also offered "soap" and "coffee" to these men remains unknown.[13] It is also difficult to determine whether the town's Polish spiritual and educated elite set the tone for the pogrom or merely reacted to the context in which they lived. Our statistical analysis, however, points to the importance of the political context and the preexisting social distance between Poles and Jews generated by the town's politics. Over 80 percent of Jews supported Jewish parties and the Communists attracted a mere two percent of the vote. Poles surely viewed Jews as a threat to their cultural dominance and were, therefore, at best, indifferent to the Jews' fate. The stage was set for a pogrom.

Polish testimonies taken after the war largely confirm the Jewish narratives and highlight the different individual motives at work. Avarice is a common theme, as many accounts point to the looting of Jewish property, from clothing to silverware, gold, watches, and other valuables (Tryczyk 2015, 308, 309, 311, 313). Many Polish testimonies also point to anti-Semitism in the phrases and encouragement doled out by the pogrom ringleaders to solicit popular assistance in carrying out the pogrom. Most striking, however, is the intimate quality of the brutality. Beatings and murders occurred at close quarters on the street or in the apartments of terrified Jews using knives, clubs, or gardening implements. (Tryczyk 2015, 310, 316). One Polish eyewitness reports a Jewish child being grabbed by his foot and his head being smashed on the ground (315). These events had a certain carnival-like atmosphere to them. Interestingly, the Jews' putative support for the Soviet occupation does not come up often in the testimonies, but that may be more a product of Communist era investigations of which these testimonies were part. The existing sources point to little or no German presence for any of these atrocities, but their presence provided the overall context in which the tragedy unfolded.

The narratives and our interpretation of them also shed light on what in the literature is considered the critical position of the Catholic priests and the local intelligentsia. In fact, within Holocaust historiography more generally, crimes and salvation are frequently cast in terms of individual character—victims, perpetrators, bystanders, and saviors (see, e.g., Hilberg 1961). As important as such a perspective is for establishing individual innocence and guilt, our analysis, by focusing on the local context in which pogroms did or did not occur, suggests that in many cases (though clearly not all) it was either easier or much more difficult to do the right thing. Shimon Datner, in his account of one of the most deadly and brutal pogroms of the region, which took place in Radziłów, writes that once the German military had pulled out of the shtetl,

> the scent of massacre is in the air. . . . The situation would not be so desperate, were it not for the outspoken and hostile behavior of the local Poles. . . . Finally people try one more thing: the local Catholic priest, Aleksander Dagalevski, is the greatest authority among the Radziłów Poles and Mrs. Finkelstein is a close acquaintance of his. She goes to him in order to persuade him to exert influence on his parishioners, and get them to cease perpetrating their outrages. Mrs. Finkelstein goes on her holy errand and receives the answer that all Jews, great and small, are communists, and that he has no interest in protecting them. To the question how small children could be guilty of anything, he answers that they aren't really guilty, but that he can't put in any good word for the Jews, because his own sheep would toss him in the mud. The holy man's

answer shook the shtetl's Jews, and revealed to them the hopelessness of the situation. (AŻIH 301-1994)

Delegations of Jews turned to the elite of the town with the same request, "but everyone everywhere shrugged, evaded, and avoided giving a clear response" (AŻIH 301-1994). Datner also mentions the town's only doctor who turned away the Jewish injured and other officials who refused to "swim against the tide." This account suggests that rather than casting priests and the local intelligentsia as categorically either heroes or villains, a great deal can be learned by examining more closely the political contexts in which they lived. In Radziłow, where virtually every eligible Jewish voter voted for Jewish parties in 1928 and 42 percent of the Polish electorate supported the Endecja in the same election, even those who might have had an interest in tamping down violence could not muster sufficient sympathy to prevent a pogrom. Even the bare minimum of solidarity between the two communities was absent.

Białystok

Many places that "should" have experienced a pogrom did not. Białystok is one such location that is worth reconsidering for a moment to understand one limiting feature of our account. The same factors associated with pogrom violence in our model were also present in Białystok, perhaps in even greater intensity than in Szczuczyn, and yet no pogrom occurred.

As the administrative center of a large voivodship in independent Poland bordering on the Soviet Union, Białystok possessed a large and vibrant, although mostly working-class, Jewish community. Following the suppression of the Polish rebellion of 1863, Russian authorities promoted Jewish migration to Białystok and favorable internal customs frontiers initiated a boom in growth, especially in the textile industry. In 1897, about 42,000 Jews lived in the city (64% of inhabitants), and despite a significant influx of Poles once the area became part of independent Poland after World War I, the 1921 census put the Jewish population at 76,792, still 51.6 percent of the city's population. Poles from the outset considered Jewish demographic weight a serious and persistent threat to the political and cultural dominance in Białystok, one that would not dissipate.[14] In 1939 a Polish Ministry of the Interior report on Jewish demographics in Białystok dwelled on demography and characterized the Jews as "morally corrupt, self-serving, and rapacious" and described Jewish political loyalties as "governed by expedience" (Bender 2008, 47).

As in Szczuczyn, national politics dominated Jewish life, a process that began in Białystok very early, even before the twentieth century. Rabbi Samuel Mohilever, Białystok's chief rabbi, was one of the key figures in the early proto-Zionist organization Hovevei Zion (Lovers of Zion) and a founder of the city's Mizrachi movement, which sought to bridge the divide between traditional religious Judaism and the new politics of ethnic assertiveness. As Bender observes, even after the first Zionist Congress in Basel in 1897, "Białystok continued to serve as the spiritual center of both the Odessa Committee and the Zionist Organization as a whole.... As cultural activity flourished, Russian and Hebrew were spoken as well as Yiddish, and Zionist ideology became a constant source of debate" (Bender 2008, 10). In addition to the religious Mizrachi, the catch-all General Zionists, and dozens of other Zionist cultural and youth organizations, and Labor Zionism (Poalei Zion) also found a strong following. In fact, Białystok's high level of industrialization made it rather unique in eastern Poland and created an island hospitable not only to Hebraic working-class politics but, perhaps more importantly, the Bund, whose leaders spoke in a language that inspired the migrant Jewish workers flowing into the city from the surrounding towns (Kobrin 2010, 48). Bundists and Zionists competed for Białystok's Jewish working-class votes, and both enjoyed success at different times.

Białystok's Jews were just as unlikely as Szczuczyn's to join Poland's nation-building project after World War I. The city's first Jewish-sponsored (but Russian language) newspaper after the war, *Golos Belostoka* (Voice of Białystok) openly doubted whether Poland would adhere to its promises to the country's ethnic minorities and called for a plebiscite on whether Białystok should be annexed to the Soviet Union, be merged with Lithuania, or enjoy some sort of special status. Community leaders tried a more diplomatic approach but from the outset felt constrained to oppose mandatory Polish-only street signs and attempts to draft the city's Jews into the Polish army. The local Polish press responded with anti-Semitic characterizations of Jews as "foreigners," traitors," and what became the standby epithet of the interwar era and beyond, "Jewish Communists" who wanted the city to be part of "Jewish Communist Russia" (Kobrin 2010, 138–139).

Białystok had long known anti-Semitism of various sorts, from religious to social to economic, and certainly no less than Szczuczyn. Samuel Iwry, in his memoir of interwar Białystok, highlights traditional Christian anti-Semitism, "I remember every Sunday when the services were held and processions were conducted, my mother kept all the children inside.... These processions—the same thing happened in Christmas in Białystok. The mothers would run out onto the street to remove their children.... This being a strictly Catholic country, and we, the Jews, knew that we were not a part of it, there was a kind of seriousness on these holidays." Although he did not experience violence, "the idea was that it was better to be at home" (Iwry 2004, 9). Charles Zabuski's memoir, however, recalls "anti-Semitic hooligans" attacking children during Jewish school outings in the forests. "On such occasions—and there were many—the biggest and strongest Jews in Białystok would come running ... carrying sticks and knives or whatever they could find" (Zabuski 1996, 32). In the background of these interwar skirmishes lay the memory of the deadly 1906 pogrom (in which eighty-eight Jews perished and hundreds were injured) and much smaller bouts of violence immediately after World War I.

If Szczuczyn's small cooperative bank became a source of tension between Jews and Poles, Białystok's large and highly philanthropic Jewish Diaspora unwittingly generated much more serious resentment.[15] Donations from abroad helped expand Jewish welfare agencies, hospitals, and cultural institutions. In the first years of independent Poland, Kobrin notes this assistance accentuated "the divide between the economic fate of local Poles and Jews." Perhaps more crucially, emigre assistance fostered a bold Jewish public sphere and press and a sense of independence from the Polish state. "Emboldened by the absolute support of emigre philanthropists, the Yiddish press in Białystok continued to question Polish sovereignty and cultivated a new vision of Białystok as an international city. . . . Many editors continued to publish inflammatory editorials, under such titles as 'The Lithuanian Question' or 'The Beginning of the End,' that argued unceasingly against the inclusion of Białystok in the Second Polish Republic" (Kobrin 2010, 141, 146). Perhaps unsurprisingly, in its 1939 analysis Poland's Interior Ministry drew attention to Jewish Białystok's ties to international Jewry as one the main negative features of the community (Bender 2008, 47).

What then differentiates Białystok from Szczuczyn? Perhaps most decisive was Białystok's size and regional importance. After a brief but deadly German occupation in 1939, the Soviets occupied the city and rapidly transformed it into the capital of Western Belarus. As a major administrative center, Communist Party officials frequently visited, and the city had a large secret police contingent that subjected the locals to the full force of Sovietization. Polish disappeared immediately and was replaced by Russian. Jewish life changed overnight. Jewish communal institutions shut down; parties and party elites fled, were arrested, or went underground. Jewish-owned factories were quickly nationalized and absorbed into the planned economy, and, as elsewhere in the Soviet Zone of occupation, jobs in education and the state administration opened up to all ethnic groups, even if Belarusians were now favored as the titular nationality. The Jewish population swelled as tens of thousands of refugees poured into the city from German-occupied Poland, placing a serious strain on both housing and food supplies (Bender 2008, 66–69). In short, the Soviet presence and previously existing political divides were more than enough to cause a pogrom in Białystok. There should have been one.

Why did a pogrom not occur? Białystok's importance made it a prime target for rapid conquest. Three companies belonging to German Police Battalion 309 occupied the city without a fight on June 26, 1941. Whereas in Lwów, as we shall see in chapter 5, the Germans could rely on well-organized Ukrainian nationalists to carry out a massive pogrom, in Białystok they did not. Had they not arrived or had they elicited Polish nationalist support, there most likely would have been a pogrom in the city, as all the other conditions were present. But the Germans were both willing and able to do it themselves, albeit with some assistance from local Poles who pointed out Jewish houses and provided information about how many Jews lived in each. After engaging in rituals of humiliation, such as cutting the beards of religious Jews and forcing others to dance, soldiers of Battalion 309 murdered Jewish patients in the hospital, shot hundreds more near Branicki Palace, and in a final act of the day herded hundreds into the Great Synagogue, locked the doors, drenched it with kerosene, and set it on fire (Bender 2008, 91–93). In one day, June 27, 1941, it is estimated that two thousand of the city's Jews died. In Białystok, because of its military and political importance, the Germans arrived in sufficient numbers and stayed long enough to carry out their own massacre.[16]

Political Integration and the Minimum of Solidarity

Why, then, were some communities so much more toxic than others? Our analysis shows that political integration was key. Where Jews and locals opted for nonnationalist political parties, pogroms were more often prevented. This brings us to the complex role of Marshal Józef Piłsudski and his BBWR. The BBWR was a party that, as we have seen, advocated toleration and accommodation of the country's minorities. Piłsudski's plan was for a reconstructed, technocratic, and ethnically tolerant, albeit authoritarian, party to guide the country to a "statist" as opposed to an "ethnic" order. The vehicle for this plan was the BBWR, which was founded in time for the 1928 election but was not a typical political party with grassroots organizations.[17] The leadership at the local level consisted primarily of state officials and local dignitaries. It was, however, the one Polish political party that tried to bridge both class and ethnic divides and thereby neutralize the influence of the National Democrats. Its electoral success signalled an ethnically less-polarized politics.

The question is whether Jews might have avoided pogroms if more of them had been supportive of the BBWR instead of Jewish parties. Our data do not permit us to estimate the ethnic composition of the BBWR at the settlement level—unlike in the case of the National Democrats or one of the Jewish parties, it is not plausible to assume that the BBWR's vote came from only one national group.

TABLE 4.3. Ecological estimates of support for the BBWR in Białystok and Polesie, 1928

	SUPPORT FOR BBWR (%)	
	POGROMS	NO POGROMS
Poles	36 (14,57)	30 (23,39)
Jews	9 (2,18)	18 (9,31)
Bela	40 (26,54)	33 (28,37)
N	37	159

Note: Estimates indicate percentage of the corresponding national group that supported the BBWR in localities with and without pogroms and where Poles and Jews each constituted at least 1 percent of the population. For example, in places where pogroms took place, 9 percent of Jews voted for BBWR. Variables are percentage Poles, percentage Jews, and percentage Belarusians (Bela). Associated 95 percent confidence intervals are in parentheses.
Sources: 1921 Polish Census, 1928 election to Polish Sejm, and authors' computation.

But, as noted in chapter 3, we can use ecological inference techniques to estimate BBWR support among different groups. These results, computed for both pogrom and nonpogrom subsamples, are displayed in table 4.3.

The estimates are consistent with the argument that pogrom occurrence is associated with a decreased Jewish vote for minority-friendly "Polish" parties. Jews were half as likely to support the BBWR in pogrom areas (9%) as in nonpogrom areas (18%), the only statistically significant difference in the table. Jewish support for Piłsudski was not lost on the local population—an image that carried through the 1930s and even lasted into the early years of the Soviet occupation. In his report to Stalin written one week following the Soviet occupation, after characterizing the Belarusian population as decidedly pro-Soviet, First Secretary Panteleimon Ponomarenko restricted his remarks about the Jews to the following observation: "One has also to note that Piłsudski is popular not only among the Polish population, but also even among the Jews. They say he was a real human being—that with him it was much better than later" (cited in Boćkowski 2005, 45).

Some historians maintain that Jewish support for the BBWR came from a mixture of semiskilled artisans, small merchants, and the Orthodox community (e.g., Bacon 1996). It is difficult, therefore, to maintain that this integration was cultural, much less religious. What it was, however, was a form of *political* integration that may have constituted one possible path to reducing the hostility and indifference between Poles and their Jewish neighbors at the local level. This kind of integration was not the thick solidarity of a nation, but it may nevertheless have provided just enough communal cohesion, the bare minimum, to prevent the worst sort of depredations when all other factors pointed in that direction.

This chapter has shown that the distribution of intimate anti-Jewish violence in northeastern Poland in summer 1941 cannot in general be explained by the role of the Germans, the crimes of the Soviet occupation, or even Polish anti-Semitic nationalism. Instead our analysis points more to the failure of the Polish state to integrate its Jewish citizens and the decision of many Jews to opt for the politics of nationalism, to advocate for the same rights enjoyed by their Polish conationals. This finding should not be interpreted as blaming the victim. Jewish support for the Bloc of National Minorities did not mean implacable resistance to integrating into Poland's social and political life. Representatives of the parties of minorities in Poland's Sejm would have jumped at the opportunity to be part of a governing coalition, but they were never given the chance. Although Jews appeared on the electoral lists of the Polish parties (primarily the PPS and the BBWR), in the end not one Jewish (or Ukrainian, Belarusian, or German) cabinet member from among the minority parties was chosen in the entire interwar era. Responsibility for that properly lies with the Polish parties who were forming governments, not with the Jews who were seeking the best way to address their communal concerns.

Poles nevertheless considered the Jewish vote for nationalist parties as proof of the Jews' unwillingness to integrate into Polish political life. This logic is consistent with power-threat theory, according to which Poles in localities with a large Jewish population calling for a recognition of Jewish communal autonomy and rights would view their neighbors as an ethnic threat. At the same time, this sense of threat could be mitigated by the presence of a sturdy communist organization that advocated for a nonethnic, universalist politics.

This chapter also points to the potential importance of political integration in fostering the absolute minimum of solidarity necessary for preventing intercommunal violence. Our findings are consonant with those of Varshney (2002), who extols the advantages of interethnic civic engagement. By highlighting the vote and politics, however, as opposed to the thicker ties of civil society, our threshold for preventing violence may be even lower than that considered by Varshney. Given the strength of anti-Semitic nationalism in much of northeast Poland and the highly permissive conditions provided by the Nazi invasion, our analysis paradoxically shows that it was extraordinarily difficult to start pogroms and actually required very little to prevent them.

5
UKRAINIAN GALICIA AND VOLHYNIA

In this chapter we explore the pogroms of summer 1941 in western Ukraine, in what had been the voivodships of Volhynia, Stanisławów, Lwów, and Tarnopol in pre-1939 Poland. Ukrainians constituted a majority of all inhabitants in the four voivodships. They lived predominantly in the rural townships surrounding the numerous small towns, but also constituted a nontrivial percentage of city and town dwellers. Poles lived primarily in towns, but the region also featured a number of rural Polish "military" settlements, the inhabitants of which had been given land in return for their service during the struggle for national independence before 1920. Jews lived mostly in small towns (the shtetls) and cities, where in some instances they constituted a majority or plurality, but smaller numbers were scattered throughout the Ukrainian countryside. Lwów, the largest city in the region, was considered a Polish city—in 1921 half the population was Polish and 35 percent Jewish, with the remaining 15 percent Ukrainian, proportions that remained largely unchanged until 1939 (Kubijovyč 1983). In the smaller towns, the proportion of Jews was frequently much higher and Poles much lower.

Extending the analysis to the southeastern region confers distinct advantages. First, the Ukrainian areas allow the further exploration of hypotheses that were only tentatively testable in Białystok and Polesie due to the limited number of observations. Our analysis encompasses 1,943 localities (where Jews and non-Jews dwelled together), of which 153 experienced a pogrom. This many observations provide more robust evidence not only of whether the small market towns are more apt to experience pogroms, as the economic competition hypothesis would predict, but also whether areas of greater Jewish wealth are vulnerable, as the looting hypothesis claims.

In what follows, we proceed in a similar fashion to chapter four, highlighting both similarities and differences with the Northeast. We first discuss the German presence and role establishing the context in which pogroms could take place. We then survey, for the Ukrainian context, each of the main hypotheses we will subsequently test: the Soviet occupation, Ukrainian nationalism, and Jewish support for national equality. Our quantitative analysis is split into two parts. For the Galician voivodships of Stanisławów, Lwów, and Tarnopol, we estimate multivariate models of pogrom occurrence, with results broadly similar to what we found in the primarily Polish and Belarusian areas of the Northeast. Though Ukrainian nationalism and economic tensions play some role, our most robust finding is consistent with power-threat theory: localities where Jews sought national equality with Poles and Ukrainians were the most vulnerable to pogroms. For Volhynia, where our data are of much poorer quality, we limit ourselves to basic comparisons. Here we find further evidence that popular support for communism immunized against pogroms.

The German Presence

On June 22, 1941, German forces under General Gerd von Rundstedt, swept into western Ukraine with forty-two divisions, of which five were armored and three were motorized Panzer divisions (Bauer 2009, 58). Although encountering stiffer Soviet resistance than in western Belarus, by June 28 Równe in Volhynia had been taken; on June 30 the largest city in western Ukraine, Lwów, fell into German hands; and by mid-July the German army stood at the prewar Polish-Soviet border, poised to move on central and eastern Ukraine. Units of the Einsatzgruppen and Ukrainian nationalist operatives moved into western Ukraine on the heels of the Wehrmacht (Pohl 1996, 68–69). Meanwhile, prewar Soviet (and Polish) political authority rapidly melted away amid the chaos and confusion of the German advance. There is evidence that Jews most active in the preceding Soviet administration attempted to flee with the retreating Red Army; for example, four hundred of the seven thousand Jews in the town of Kostopol, in Volhynia. But the vast majority of Jews either would not or could not flee.[1]

The German high command was eager for local Ukrainians (and Poles) to attack their Jewish neighbors. Heydrich's telegram on the importance of initiating and directing local "self-cleansing" actions, discussed in chapter 1, applied as much to Volhynia and eastern Galicia as it did to other occupied areas. The

Germans persecuted and killed Jews, sometimes by themselves and sometimes with the assistance of locals. Magocsi (2010, 631) notes, for example, that "the Germans helped to circulate rumors that 'Jewish Bolsheviks' had been involved in the murders of thousands of Ukrainian political prisoners killed by the Soviet authorities before their hasty retreat," and that between June 30 and July 7, 1941, German Einsatzgruppen units killed around four thousand Jews with the assistance of Ukrainians.[2]

But in these crucial weeks after the German invasion, between the collapse of Soviet authority and the establishment of full German control, German-initiated violence does not tell the whole story. In other localities the Germans stood back and let the Ukrainians "have a fling," as Basia Levkovitch characterized the violence in Borysław (AŻIH 301-5881), or gave them a "day off" to kill Jews, as in Drohobycz (AŻIH 301-344). Consider Regina Wildner's testimony on the pogrom in Drohobycz:

> On the second day, the jail was opened on Piłsudski street, with the intention of demonstrating something. Bodies of murdered Poles and Ukrainians were found there. They were in terrible shape—burned and cut into pieces and so on. That was the first call to kill Jews because Ukrainians as well as Poles thought that the Jews were the perpetrators. . . . In addition people arrived from neighboring villages, men with horse drawn carriages and sacks for looting. There was not a single home that did not suffer from this wildness. From the floors or buildings, women and children were thrown, their hands were cut off so they could take their rings. The Jewish neighborhood of "Lan" suffered the most. The Germans did not take part in, nor did they intervene in these personal attacks. (AŻIH 301-1277)[3]

The Germans were certainly present, either as actual perpetrators or as sympathetic bystanders, for many acts of anti-Jewish violence in the weeks immediately after the invasion. It is difficult to believe, however, that their presence can account for the distribution of pogroms we observe. Consider our three Galician voivodships: Stanisławów, Lwów, and Tarnopol, where 125 pogroms occurred across 1,820 municipalities where Jews dwelled with non-Jews. Killers from Einsatzgruppe C roamed the west Ukrainian countryside but, as in the Polish Northeast, the rapid advance of German forces rendered their presence thin. Given the paucity of German boots on the ground, it would have been logical for whatever German forces that were devoted to persecuting Jews to concentrate on places with the most Jews. Although the median number of Jews in places where pogroms occurred (565) is far higher than in places where pogroms did not occur (34), fully one-quarter (around 31) of all Galician pogroms took place in municipalities with 52 Jews or less. By contrast, there were 545 municipalities with greater than 52 Jews and 80 places with greater than the median number of Jews that did *not* experience a pogrom. If the German presence had been the key factor, there is no reason the Germans would devote scarce resources to so many places with relatively few Jews while ignoring a large number of places with greater numbers of Jews.

One might argue that German incitement could cause violence even in the absence of any actual Germans present at the time of the violence. "After the movement of the front to the east," testified Abraham Scholl about his hometown Niemerów, "the Ukrainian nationalists began their activities by arresting 38 Jews from a list and executing them outside the city. The Ukrainians took over the administration" (AŻIH 301-4950). Scholl's testimony does not speculate on Ukrainian motivation, but it might well have been German encouragement. Certainly, this would be the view of those who seek to absolve local Ukrainians and Poles of responsibility. Yet, as Golczewski (2008, 132) notes, incitement only works when heard by a receptive population. Where Ukrainians were less apt to view Jews in such adversarial ways, the German message might have fallen on deaf ears, regardless of whether German personnel were present during the violence or not. According to Dumitru and Johnson (2011), such was the case of the Ukrainians in Transnistria, which was a part of Soviet Moldova during the interwar period. They argue that the overall unwillingness of Transnistrian Ukrainians to accede to German requests for "self-cleansing" actions can be traced to prewar Soviet policies promoting interethnic amity. Relative to their Galician Ukrainian cousins, who had spent the 1920s and 1930s in a Poland that discriminated against both Ukrainians and Jews, Transnistrian Ukrainians were less likely to commit pogroms and more likely to help Jews avoid persecution. The paucity of anti-Jewish violence in regions that had been incorporated into the Soviet Union twenty years earlier is ironic given the rather different effect that the Soviet occupation of eastern Galicia between 1939 and 1941 is purported to have had among both Ukrainians and Poles.

Soviet Occupation

Much ink has been spilled on the welcome given to Soviet soldiers as they entered communities of western Ukraine. Although generalization is hazardous, most scholars agree that the Soviets were met by the Jews with relief (in the words of Levin [1995], as "the lesser of two evils"), by the Ukrainians with a measure of hope (for genuine autonomy and ethnic advantage), and by the Poles with a good deal of fear (as the conquered *Staatsnation*) (Gross 2002). Of course not all Jews,

Ukrainians, and Poles fit these categories, but they are probably appropriate characterizations of the average reaction. A minority of Jews and Ukrainians (and a smaller number of Poles) greeted the Soviets enthusiastically (Bauer 2007).

Soviet rule in western Ukraine replicated the experience in western Belarus. Ethnic Poles immediately lost their "ownership" of the state. They were replaced by local Ukrainians and Jews, as well as officials arriving from the East. Polish schools became Ukrainian. Nationalization of Polish and Jewish businesses quickly followed, artisans were compelled to join cooperatives, and virtually the entire spectrum of political parties and civic organizations disappeared overnight. Religious institutions faced new and draconian restrictions. In his account of Brzezany, Shimon Redlich (2002) reports,

> Various kinds of restrictions and harassment now affected local churches and synagogues. Of all the synagogues only two, the Large Synagogue and Rabbi Yidel's synagogue, continued to function under the Soviets. The others became residential quarters for Jewish refugees. The main entrances to Polish churches and to the Ukrainian church in the center of Brzezany were closed. People had to enter through back doors. Services were severely limited and electricity was cut off to some churches during midnight Christmas prayers. (85)

Many Ukrainians initially looked on the new order as a chance for genuine autonomy, but were quickly disabused of this by the reality of Soviet rule. The new rulers removed national symbols, replaced Ukrainian narratives with internationalist ones, and doled out police and other bureaucratic functions along political rather than ethnic lines. None of this corresponded to the desires of Ukrainian patriots for national independence and was fiercely resented by the underground network of the Organization of Ukrainian Nationalists (OUN).

We argued in chapter 1 that the evidence we have of collaboration with the Soviet occupation shows that Jews were not disproportionately supportive of it. Other evidence from eastern Galicia suggests that the Jews were not spared from Soviet violence, and in one area were disproportionately victims of it. For example, the 66,563 arrests in western Ukraine between September 1939 and May 1941 were divided among ethnic groups as follows: 22,045 were Poles; 23,221 were Ukrainians; and 13,164 were Jews. Almost 20 percent of arrests were Jews, a percentage roughly double their proportion of the population. This included Jewish politicians and Zionist leaders, who on the night of April 14, 1940, were arrested and sent eastward, deep into the Soviet Union (Mick 2007, 250).

Still, perception mattered more than reality, and those Jews who were willing to work for the Soviet regime did achieve a measure of "equality" with Poles and

Ukrainians that they never enjoyed under Polish rule. Rightly or wrongly, Jews came to be associated with the Soviet regime and, in particular, with its crimes. Of the 20,094 prisoners in custody in western Ukraine on June 10, 1941 (the majority Ukrainian but a nontrivial number of Poles and Jews), approximately 4,500 were deported to the east; 7,000 suspected petty or serious criminals remained in prisons temporarily; and more than 8,700 in the hands of the NKVD were murdered just before the Germans arrived (Hryciuk 2007, 193). Henryk Szyper's unpublished memoir, written just after the war, succinctly expresses the unfortunate consequences for Jews:

> All Ukrainian and Polish grievances against the Bolsheviks found their expression in antipathy toward the Jews, who were seen as accomplices. After all, Jews were 'close' and the Bolsheviks 'far away.' It was easier to express anger on the former for the sins of the latter.... The average person, a Pole or a Ukrainian, could not forgive the Jews their equality. This had to be avenged. (AŻIH 301-4654)

Alas, vengeance was near. During the pogroms, ritualized humiliation, akin to what occurred in the Northeast, also occurred in western Ukraine. In Turka, Schulem Nagler testified that after the arrival of the Germans, "Jews were beaten by the Ukrainians" and that the Jews were forced to "bury Stalin." "In the morning, they collected all the portraits of the Russian leaders and all the Russian books from the bookstores. Jewish children were forced to carry this material. A big grave was dug in the cemetery. The children were ordered to sing Hatikva and also Ukrainian songs. Five were shot, the rest were saved because the commander of the customs office chased everyone away" (AŻIH 301-4975). In Kolomyja, according to Szaje Feder,

> The pogrom was initiated by Ukrainians, the militia, and the civilian population. All the Jews from the city were forced to come to the market square, where a statue of Lenin stood, which the Jews were forced to take down with ropes. They were beaten while doing this. Then they were herded to the city garden where a monument of Stalin and Lenin stood, and they repeated the same thing. To make this more entertaining for themselves the bystanders put a Jew in place of the statues and told the Jews to yell "you stupid Stalin."(AŻIH 301-1398)

Although Kolomyja's Ukrainian mayor brought the spectacle to an end just before a mass execution, Feder concludes her account of the episode as follows: "As they [the Jews] left, Ukrainians stood at the entrance gates and beat and tortured them."

Ukrainian Nationalism

Habsburg Galicia had long been culturally and politically dominated by a Polish nobility. As a counterweight to the Poles' desire for independence, Vienna had also cultivated Ukrainian nationalism on the same territory. Following World War I and the failure of the Western Ukrainian Republic, Ukrainian lands were divided between the Soviet Union in the East and Poland in the West. In the Ukrainian areas of the kresy, the state apparatus, educational institutions, and even policies toward religion all fell under the heavy influence of polonization. Land reform benefited Poles, and Ukrainian higher education was mostly shut down. Investment and tax policy favored other regions (Magocsi 2010, 631). All too frequently, Poles in this region treated Ukrainians with contempt. Ukrainian political elites responded with a combination of passive resistance, a boycott of Polish institutions, and sometimes violence. Polish policy throughout the 1920s and 1930s alternated between attempted political inclusion and repression, with the latter strategy clearly dominating during the 1930s as the politics of both sides hardened (Snyder 2005, 147–167).

Ukrainian political parties—dominated by the moderately nationalist Ukrainian National Democratic Organization (UNDO)—ultimately entered Polish politics, but they enjoyed little success in reversing Polish educational, linguistic, or religious policy. Violence constituted the main nonparliamentary alternative. The Ukrainian Military Organization under the leadership of Ievhen Konovalets had tried during the 1920s to dislodge the Poles from eastern Galicia, but its campaign of burning Polish estates, destroying buildings, sabotaging railroads and telegraph lines, and even assassinating political leaders ultimately failed. In 1929, again under Konovalets's leadership, the Organization of Ukrainian Nationalists (OUN) was founded in Vienna with underground cells in Poland and abroad.

Geopolitics created a community of interest between German revisionists and Ukrainian nationalists of all stripes (Golczewski 2010). Ideology, however, cemented relations between the OUN and the Nazis. From the outset, the OUN was anticommunist, anti-Semitic, anti-Polish, and deeply influenced by European fascism (Bruder 2007; Carynnyk 2011). The Polish government responded with a pacification campaign in the 1930s, which entailed mass arrests, the closing or banning of Ukrainian cultural institutions, and the imprisonment of the OUN's leading cadres. Undeterred and perhaps even spurred on by Polish repression, throughout the early 1930s the OUN continued its activities in eastern Poland, culminating in the assassination of the Polish Minister of Interior Bronisław Pieracki in 1934. Notwithstanding periodic attempts at reconciliation (including naming the Ukrainian Vasyl Mudry as vice-marshal of the Sejm in 1935), Polish-Ukrainian relations never recovered. The OUN fiercely resisted any attempt at reconciliation and intimidated UNDO moderates with threats and violence (Bruder 2007, 101, 104).

Scholars continue to debate whether the OUN is rightly categorized as fascist or not. OUN politicians frequently deviated from German positions. Some were ardent anti-Semites, declaring in April 1941 that Jews were "the most secure support of the ruling Moscow regime and the vanguard of Moscow imperialism," though also explicitly abjuring violence against Jews (cited in Bartov 2007, 39). Others viewed Jewish questions as a distraction from the more important struggle with Poles. The destruction of Poland in 1939 brought the OUN (and its internal divisions) out into the open, at least in Nazi-occupied western Galicia. The organization had already split into competing factions—one led by the older and more conservative Andrei Melnyk (OUN-M) and the other by the younger Stepan Bandera (OUN-B). Bandera's faction had formed two units under German supervision, one of which (Nachtigall) entered eastern Galicia with the German army on June 22, 1941. Additional Banderite operatives under the leadership of Iaroslav Stetsko also returned to western Ukraine with the Germans on June 30, 1941, and proclaimed (without German support) the existence of a Ukrainian state.

The case for Ukrainian nationalist and especially OUN involvement in the pogroms is strong. Immediately after the invasion and until the end of July 1941, OUN leaflets openly called for the elimination of "the Jews, the Soviets, and other enemies" (Bruder 2007, 125). Pohl (1996, 49) refers to an OUN-B meeting in Lwów on July 19, 1941, where Stepan Levkanskyj, the propaganda chief of the OUN-B said, "Concerning the Jews, all methods should be accepted that lead to their extermination." During the same time period, the temporary head of the new Ukrainian state, Iaroslav Stetsko—by this time in German custody—expressed in writing his "support for the destruction of the Jews and the expedience of bringing German methods of exterminating Jewry to Ukraine" (Berkhoff and Carynnyk 1999, 171).[4]

Jewish survivor testimony frequently refers to Ukrainian nationalists and militia officials wearing blue and yellow armbands [of the Ukrainian nationalists] among those assisting the Germans or carrying out atrocities without any German prompting or even presence (Melamed 2007, 229). According to Janislaw Korczynski's testimony about the Lwów pogrom, "On the second day after the Germans came in, I saw a group of Ukrainians, with yellow-blue armbands, and they were taking a group of Jewish men and women, around 70 people, to the prison by Zmarstynowskiej street" (AŻIH 301-1809). Other accounts, such as those of Richard Ryndner also from Lwów, Erna Klinger from Borysław, Sewerwyn Dobroszklanaka from Równo, Dr. Grossbard's from Kulików, Szaje Feder from Kolomyja, name the "Ukrainian militia" (AŻIH 301-18, 301-583, 301-1091, 301-1222, 301-1398) as the main perpetrators of pogroms in early July. OUN advance groups had organized these militias. The results of NKVD interrogations, suspect as they might be due to coercion, are nonetheless consistent with survivor testimony.[5]

Perhaps most damning, a document generated by the OUN-B itself after the fact suggests preparation for a cover-up of its own activities in June and July 1941 (Carynnyk 2011). On October 17, 1943, as the Ukrainian Insurgent Army (organized by the OUN-B in 1942) was preparing its retreat and dispersion in the face of advancing Soviet forces, a decree was issued to regional, district, and county commands. The most important part of the decree for our purposes concerns documents that local forces were ordered to collect over the subsequent thirty days. After calling for evidence from Polish, Soviet, and German sources indicating "anti-Ukrainian acts" carried out by Poles, the document asks officers to assemble "records that indicate that anti-Jewish pogroms and liquidations were carried out by the Germans themselves, without the assistance of the Ukrainian militia and, instead, before the shootings they [the Germans] made the Jews or the perpetrators give written testimonies of Ukrainians being present and engaged in the pogroms." This constitutes an important piece of evidence for the historians' equivalent of mens rea—evidence of a guilty mind in criminal law. As with other archival documents from this region, this one should be treated with care, but in the context of public statements by the OUN's leadership, Jewish testimonies, and NKVD interrogations, all of which point in the same direction, this document provides one more piece of evidence that Ukrainian nationalists stoked the summer 1941 pogroms.

Perceived Jewish Threat

At the end of World War I, Jews found themselves caught between two competing state projects, Polish and Ukrainian. To the extent that they learned a language other than their own, eastern Galician Jews as a practical matter learned Polish or German (or even Russian). Jewish acculturation to Polish was especially strong in this region. In the 1921 census, a significant number of Galician residents who declared themselves to be Jewish by religion also declared themselves Polish by nationality, and by 1931 approximately 30 percent of Jews in eastern Galicia considered Polish to be their mother tongue. Jewish political elites, including the powerful General Zionists, might communicate with each other in Yiddish, Hebrew, or Polish, but rarely Ukrainian.

The short-lived West Ukrainian Republic had promised the region's Jews cultural and political autonomy, something the new Polish state had refused (Kuchabsky 2009, 57). The Ukrainians' offer, however, was matched by Polish military strength. In this dispute between Ukrainians and Poles, which culminated in a short but bloody conflict as World War I came to an end, Jewish communal leaders decided to take the middle course and declared their neutrality (Mendelsohn 1981, 100).[6] This proved to be an extraordinarily difficult game to play, as both sides considered Jewish diffidence to be treasonous. In 1918, as Polish military units conquered Lwów, unit commanders accused the Jewish community of siding with the Ukrainians and instigated a pogrom in which approximately 72 Jews were killed and hundreds of others were injured.

Jewish leaders, especially the east Galician General Zionists, sympathized with the Ukrainian dilemma (some had even sided with the Ukrainians before 1918) but ultimately pursued the traditional Jewish strategy of seeking compromise with the ruling nationality. First, Leon Reich, the leader of the east Galicia's General Zionists, refused to join the 1922 Ukrainian electoral boycott, which yielded the Zionists a large seat share in the resulting Sejm. Second, it refused to join the Bloc of National Minorities in 1928 and therefore seemed to back the Piłsudskiites' plan to diminish the influence of the national minorities as a collective, oppositional political force. Third, and perhaps most divisive, was the 1925 signing of the Ugoda (agreement) between the Zionists and the National Democratic Polish government. The Ugoda was, above all, a project of the east Galician General Zionists that attempted to reconcile Polish nationalism with some measure of Jewish autonomy. Although it never lived up to its original promise, it did represent one which, in exchange for recognition of Polish dominance within Poland, Jews could live peacefully as Jews.

Ukrainian politicians, even moderate ones, considered the Ugoda a betrayal of solidarity with Ukrainian national aspirations, which in their more moderate variant were prepared to offer Jews a much larger measure of national autonomy in a future Ukrainian state. The Ugoda seemed to most Ukrainians as nothing other than a Jewish plot to strike a "separate peace" with the Polish state. Immediately following its adoption, the Ukrainian nationalist press let loose a series of articles insulting Jewish political leaders. The otherwise moderately nationalist newspaper *Dilo* was especially harsh in its criticism of the moderate Zionist organization El-Livnot and the leader of the east Galician Zionists, Leon Reich. The polemics quickly escalated, inflaming Ukrainian public opinion, alienating the Zionists, and further dividing the two communities. The conflict simmered. Troubled by the growing split, Dmitryo Levytskyj called in *Dilo* for a healing of the rift between the two communities and for "a better future in relations between the two peoples who live next to each other on Ukrainian soil." But his well-intentioned words merely reflected the depth of the divide.[7]

Despite these serious political disputes, Jewish and Ukrainian parties also cooperated. The left-wing Ukrainian Party of Labor and the Ukrainian Social

Democratic Party, for example, worked closely with the Jewish Bund and Poalei Zion, and the press of all these parties discussed the normalization of Jewish-Ukrainian relations (Honigsman 2001, 95). But these were all working-class organizations that attracted few votes in this predominantly rural and less developed part of Poland. Most Ukrainians wanted their own state, and there was only so much that most Jews would do to help them. The east Galician General Zionist program, even one that purported to be neutral on the Polish-Ukrainian dispute, still called for an independent Jewish school system, equality for Hebrew and Yiddish with other languages in the region, and a distinct Jewish ethnic constituency (*Wahlkurie*) that would give Jews guaranteed proportional representation (Mendelsohn 1981, 100). Therefore, in its essentials their program differed little from that of the General Zionists of the Russian partition.

Why Pogroms?
Prima Facie Evidence

As in our analysis of northeastern Poland in chapter 4, we divide our sample of east Galician settlements into those that experienced at least one pogrom and those that did not experience any. Although our explanation for Galician pogroms is largely similar to that for the Polish and Belarusian areas, some of the explanatory variables differ. Most noticeably, the demographics and politics of Galicia were different from those of the Northeast. Pogrom perpetrators were largely Ukrainian, and pre-war politics involved the Zionists and Ukrainian parties in addition to Polish parties. For example, the perceived Jewish threat is measured in terms of support for the Zionists rather than for the Minorities Bloc, as discussed in chapter 4.

Table 5.1 illustrates the differences between pogrom and nonpogrom localities across various demographic and political factors. It is divided into three sections (separated by empty rows in the table). The first two sections present median raw demographic and electoral data, respectively. The third section contains ecological estimates of Jewish and Ukrainian support for political parties and blocs (assuming, as in chapter 4, that the vote for those parties comes only from one national group).

Our indicators of economic competition and Jewish prosperity are the proportion of small market towns ("Shtetls") and municipalities with Jewish free loan associations. Recall from earlier chapters that if pogroms were about looting wealthier Jews, then we would expect them to be more frequent in small market towns, which to a greater extent than elsewhere featured wealthy Jewish merchants and comparatively poor non-Jewish customers. The presence of a free loan association, by contrast, indicates a less prosperous Jewish community. For clarity

TABLE 5.1. Median demographic and political characteristics of pogrom and nonpogrom localities in Galicia.

	POGROM	NO POGROM
Polish	24%	18%
Jewish	24%	2%
Ukrainian	43%	77%
Number of Jews	545	35
Pop	2621	1401
Bund 28	0%	0%
Zionists 28	7	0
Orth Jew List 28	0	0
Min Bloc 28	16	27
Comms 28	0	0
BBWR 28	25	19
Turnout 22	49	27
Jews for Bund 28	0%	0%
Jews for Zionists 28	81	43
Jews for Orth List 28	0	0
Uks for Min Bloc 28	48	43
N	126	1694

Note: Sample excludes settlements with no recorded Jewish population in 1921. Variables are the 1921 percentage Poles (Polish), Jews (Jewish), and Ukrainians (Ukrainian); number of Jews (Number of Jews) and overall population (Pop); 1928 electoral support for non-Zionist Jewish parties (Bund 28 and Orth Jew List 28), Jewish nationalism (Zionists 28), Ukrainians nationalism (Min Bloc 28), Government Party (BBWR 28), and Communists (Comms 28); turnout in the 1922 election (Turnoutr 22); percentage of Jews supporting non-Zionist parties (Jews for Bund 28 and Jews for Orth List 28) and nationalist parties (Jews for Zionists 28); and percentage of Ukrainians supporting Ukrainians nationalist parties (Uks for Min Bloc 28).
Sources: 1921 Polish Census, 1928 election to Polish Sejm, and authors' computation.

we leave these variables out of the table and discuss them after introducing the demographic and political results.

The results are consistent with our hypothesis on the importance of the perceived Jewish political threat, but also indicate some support for economic factors. In table 5.1, our basic measures of political threat are the popularity of political parties advocating ethnic tolerance, such as the BBWR, the party of Marshal Piłsudski; the demographic weight of Jews; and the degree to which Jews advocated national equality with Poles and Ukrainians, which we proxy with support for the General Zionists.

Median support for the BBWR ("BBWR 28") was roughly 20 percent higher where pogroms occurred. Moreover, pogrom localities averaged over ten times as many Jews, both in percentage ("Jewish") and absolute ("Number of Jews") terms, than localities that did not have pogroms. Support for Zionism was far higher among pogrom settlements than elsewhere, regardless of whether we consider the overall Zionist vote share ("Zionists 28") or our estimate of the proportion of Jews who supported them ("Jews for Zionists 28"). Significantly, pogrom and nonpogrom localities do not differ in the popularity of parties for which Jewish national autonomy was of secondary concern, such as the socialist Bund ("Bund 28") or the Orthodox list ("Orth Jew List 28"), dominated by Agudas, which advocated loyalty to virtually any regime. The threat non-Jews perceived did not emanate from Jews in general, or even from the outwardly more "foreign" Hasidic Jews, but from Zionist Jews, who were the most ardent opponents of Jews joining any other nation-building project.

We employ two indicators of Ukrainian nationalism. One is support for the Bloc of National Minorities (BNM). Unlike in northeast Poland, where the dominant force in the BNM was Jewish, in Galicia the Ukrainian UNDO predominated, and support came almost exclusively from Ukrainians. The other is voter turnout from the 1922 election. Ukrainian nationalists boycotted these elections in protest against incorporation into the Polish state. The problem with these indicators is that they do not differentiate between the moderate and extreme (anti-Semitic) wings of Ukrainian nationalism. The Polish state prevented any Ukrainian party akin to the Polish nationalist Endecja from competing, so support for the BNM would have included both moderate and extreme elements. Sympathy for the 1922 electoral boycott likewise was not limited to the extreme nationalists. What this means for our analysis is that even if the magnitudes of these indicators do not appreciably differ across pogrom and nonpogrom localities, we still cannot exclude the possibility that pogrom localities had disproportionate numbers of extreme Ukrainian nationalists.

Evidence for the anti-Semitic nationalism hypothesis in table 5.1 is difficult to discern. There are stark differences across the two samples in median support for the Minorities Bloc ("Min Bloc 28") and the 1922 electoral turnout ("Turnout 22"), but these differences appear largely contrary to what the (anti-Semitic) nationalism hypothesis would predict. The 1922 turnout was higher and the popularity of the Minorities Bloc in 1928 was lower in pogrom than in nonpogrom localities. Only our estimates of Ukrainian support for the Minorities Bloc ("Uks for Min Bloc 28") are consistent with the nationalism hypothesis, with slightly higher support in places with pogroms.

These apparently contradictory results illustrate the limitations of ecological data. The reason the Ukrainian nationalists performed more poorly in places with pogroms is that there were many fewer Ukrainians there than in places that did not have pogroms (see "Ukrainian"). In the median pogrom locality, Ukrainians were a plurality (of 43%) rather than a majority. Places where pogroms did not occur, by contrast, featured safe Ukrainian majorities. Ukrainian nationalists in pogrom localities may well have boycotted the 1922 election, but that effect could have been drowned out by higher turnout among Jews and Poles, who together often outnumbered Ukrainians. Our estimates of Ukrainian support for the Minorities Bloc ("Uks for Min Bloc 28"), which get around this ecological problem, do in fact show that Ukrainians in mixed areas, where pogroms were most likely to occur, were slightly more nationalist. These estimates also make sense in the context of Ukrainian nationalist strategy, which viewed the more Polish and Jewish urban centers as key battlegrounds in the quest for modern statehood.

Still, the relatively small difference in nationalist sentiment between pogroms and nonpogrom localities is surprising given the strength of the narrative evidence for Ukrainian nationalism. We attribute the finding to two factors. The first is the size of the OUN. The OUN undoubtedly wanted to kill Jews. It viewed them as born foes and hostile to the Ukrainian national project (Carynnyk 2011).[8] But the OUN was never a large organization, and its numbers had been severely depleted by Soviet repression. At the height of its popularity, in the first weeks of the war, the OUN's membership was spread thinly throughout western Ukraine (Grelka 2005, 255, 270).[9] Even these numbers may overestimate the number of ideologically committed foot soldiers. Like Henryk Szyper's friends in Lwów, some Ukrainians wore the yellow and blue armbands after having "only days before praised the Soviet fatherland." Just as the Einsatzgruppen were incapable of carrying out anti-Jewish massacres on their own, so too was the OUN outmatched by the scale of the task it confronted. In short, the OUN needed help from fellow Ukrainians (or Germans or Poles).

The second factor is our inability to empirically disentangle support for the OUN's more radical anti-Semitic nationalism from the moderate (and undoubtedly more popular) variant represented by UNDO. UNDO moderates may have been suspicious of Jewish motives, but usually did not view Ukrainian-Jewish relations in the same Manichean terms as the OUN. An OUN report from one of the "advance groups" (*pokhidnye hrupy*) in the Tarnopol region on July 13, 1941, complained that the people "feel hatred toward the Jews but there is no reaction there."[10] Much as Polish would-be pogromists in the Northeast had difficulty instigating violence in areas where communism was popular, so too did OUN activists encounter resistance where the population favored moderate nationalism.

Our findings for economic competition and Jewish prosperity (which do not appear in table 5.1) are mixed, but in a way that lends support to a slightly different economic argument for pogroms. Let us first consider the small market towns, the shtetls. Small market towns had an extraordinarily high (55%) probability of experiencing a pogrom, over ten times the corresponding probability for non-shtetl settlements. This is very strong evidence for the competition hypothesis, but perhaps not the most illuminating comparison in that the non-shtetl group comprises very heterogeneous localities, ranging from the smallest village to towns with few Jews. If we instead compare shtetls to towns with similar numbers of Jews but whose proportions are not high enough to be a shtetl, then the difference is less stark: 33 percent of those non-shtetl settlements experienced a pogrom. When we examine the effect of having a free loan association, the results are initially counterintuitive for arguments that pogroms are about looting wealthy Jews. While 42 percent of localities with a free loan association experienced a pogrom, pogroms occurred in only 9 percent of localities that lacked such an institution (but that had comparable numbers of Jews). In other words, pogroms were more likely to occur where Jews were *less* prosperous. It could be that free loan associations were located in places where Jews were themselves polarized into rich and poor, but it is unlikely that the Joint Distribution Committee (the primary financial backer of the free loan associations) would have devoted scarce resources if these could have been supplied by wealthy local Jews. A more straightforward and interesting interpretation is that non-Jews in settlements with these associations envied or resented Jews because they had access to capital that was not available to non-Jews in similar need. We note the irony that a program meant to help struggling Jews may have inadvertently led to more violence against them.

Finally, the popularity of communism ("Comms 28") does not differentiate pogrom and nonpogrom localities—in both samples the median level of support is zero. This result is doubly interesting. First, it constitutes yet more evidence that Jewish sympathy for communism was not a driver of pogroms. If we consider this together with evidence that the Jews were not disproportionately represented in the Soviet occupation, we can conclude that whatever preconceptions Ukrainians possessed linking Jews and communism were not rooted in any systematically measurable behaviors. Second, it differs from what we found in the primarily Polish and Belarusian areas of the Northeast, where largely non-Jewish support for communism had an immunizing effect against pogroms. We shall see later in this chapter that the same immunizing process is at work in Volhynia, but it is less visible in the Galician data because of the large numbers of settlements where the communists had no presence.

Multivariate Analysis

From the previous section we learned that in Galicia pogroms tended to occur where there were lots of Jews living among nontrivial numbers of Ukrainians and Poles with whom they experienced economic tensions and where parties advocating ethnic tolerance or Jewish national equality were popular. What we do not yet know is the relative significance of these factors. We now proceed as we did in chapter 4, with multivariate analysis. The difference between the model we use here and that in chapter 4 lies in our indicators of nationalism. As we discussed earlier, in east Galicia the General Zionists competed in the 1928 separately from the Minorities Bloc. Consequently, support for the General Zionists proxies for the strength of Jewish nationalism. That leaves the support for the Minorities Bloc as an indicator of Ukrainian nationalism.[11]

Figure 5.1 presents the results of both the logit and nonparametric analyses for our three Galician voivodships. The explanatory variables are listed on the left. The circles and triangles represent the effect coefficients of the nonparametric and logit models, respectively. The horizontal bars are 95 percent confidence intervals. If those bars cross the vertical line indicating zero (only the one for the nonparametric model is shown), then the corresponding explanatory variable is not statistically different from zero. Our analysis focuses primarily on the nonparametric results, though the logit results differ little in qualitative terms.

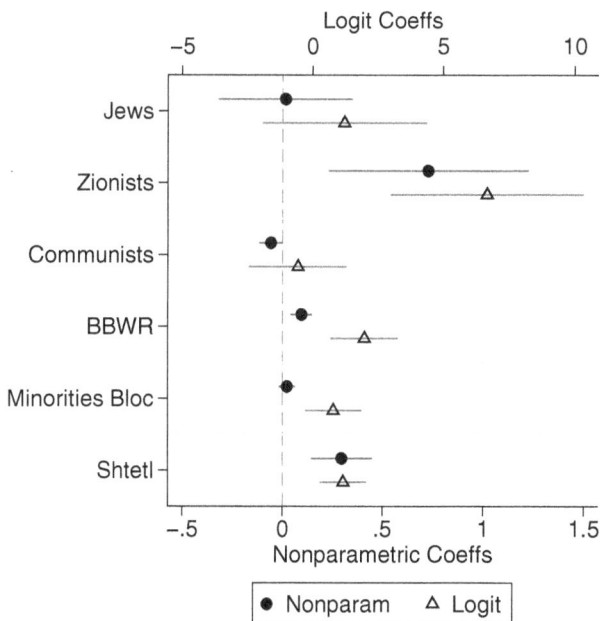

FIGURE 5.1. Results of nonparametric regression and parametric logit analyses of the determinants of pogrom occurrence in the eastern Galician voivodships. Point estimates are given by circles (nonparametric) and triangles (logit); 95 percent confidence intervals are given by the horizontal bars. Note that the Minorities Bloc proxies for Ukrainian rather than Jewish nationalism. N=1606.

The results support our argument about how the popularity of parties advocating national equality between Jews and non-Jews (Zionists and, to a lesser extent, BBWR) increased the perceived Jewish threat. However, unlike in the ethnically Polish areas of Białystok and Polesie, which we examined in chapter 4, in Ukrainian Galicia such parties include not just the nationalist (General) Zionists but also Piłsudski's government party, the BBWR. Neither Piłsudski nor the BBWR endorsed full equality between Poles and non-Poles but, as we have discussed, were much more tolerant of minorities than their nationalist rivals in the Endecja. It could be that the Poles, who were a minority in Galicia, were also more apt to view the Jews as allies against Ukrainians rather than competitors. We can also see a positive effect for economic competition between Jews and non-Jews ("Shtetl").

More intriguing is the small, but nonetheless statistically significant, negative effect for communist support (for the more reliable nonparametric results). We saw this effect in the previous chapter when we compared pogrom and nonpogrom localities for ethnically Polish regions (table 4.1), but it disappeared in the multivariate analysis. Here we have an effect despite the fact that descriptive statistics (table 5.1) do not indicate any difference in communist support across pogrom and nonpogrom localities. This finding runs counter to our main explanation because communist parties sought the abolition of national discrimination and thus in theory should have provoked a non-Jewish backlash. It also runs counter to the revenge for supporting communism explanation. Among Polish nationalist historians such as Wierzbiecki (2007), it is an article of faith that pogroms were a matter of anti-Soviet rather than anti-Jewish actions. Yet places with strong communist support during the interwar period are likely to have been the most welcoming of the Soviet occupation and therefore ought to have been the first targets of pogroms. Our results show that quite the opposite is true.

What, then, accounts for this puzzling finding? In previous work (Kopstein and Wittenberg 2003, 2011), we have shown that Jews did not vote communist in large numbers in any area of Poland. In the provinces of Białystok and Polesie communist support came primarily from Belarusians, whereas in Galicia Ukrainians supported it in greater proportions than Jews. The reason communist areas had a lower likelihood of pogroms is that communist universalism among non-Jews created the basis for intercommunal solidarity with Jews. Communist non-Jews were thus less likely to perpetrate pogroms and more likely to prevent them from happening.

The effect for Ukrainian nationalism ("Minorities Bloc") is the only one for which our interpretation would substantially differ if we had relied only on logit analysis. In investigating this discrepancy, we discovered that this effect is itself conditioned by the size of the locality. We do not show the results here, but if we add a control either for population size or Jewish population size to the nonparametric model, the effect of Ukrainian nationalism increases. This suggests that there may actually be two explanations for pogroms in Galicia: one where Jews are few in number, Ukrainians are a dominant majority, and Ukrainian nationalism is decisive (along with Zionism and Jewish demography); and another where Jews are more numerous, Ukrainians are merely a plurality or perhaps even a minority, and pogroms fail to occur despite the popularity of Ukrainian nationalism.

Figure 5.2 illustrates the relationship between perceived Jewish threat and the probability of a pogrom according to our model and values of Zionist support ranging from 0 to .5. Support for Zionists is on the horizontal axis and probability of a pogrom is on the vertical axis. As before, circles refer to the nonparametric mode and triangles to logit. Focusing on the nonparametric results, we see jumps in pogrom probability as the popularity of Jewish nationalism increases, though they are less steep than those identified for majority-Polish areas in the previous chapters. For example, the pogrom probability rises from only 5 percent where there is no support for the Zionist party to a little over 20 percent where support is 30 percent. This is substantial and also roughly the same probability that comes with being a shtetl, a small market town where economic divides between Jews and non-Jews were especially fraught. (The shtetl effect is not visible in the figure.) We were not able to incorporate the data on free loan associations into the statistical model, but an analysis of the cross-tab with pogrom occurrence is strongly suggestive of an effect similar to what we saw in ethnically Polish areas: 47 percent of the places with such associations experienced a pogrom versus 8 percent of places without an association. In Galicia both political and economic threats appear to be at work.

Discussion

The advantage of the foregoing quantitative analysis lies in its ability to pit different explanations against one another across a large number of settlements. We found that our explanation is the most robust predictor of pogrom occurrence: pogroms were most likely to occur where there were lots of Jews, where those Jews advocated national equality with Poles and Ukrainians, and where non-Jewish parties advocating ethnic tolerance (if not outright Jewish equality) were popular. This explanation holds not to the exclusion of competing explanations, but in some measure alongside them. Whatever the role Ukrainian nationalism, resentment of the Soviet occupation, or economic tensions might have played in some pogroms or types of settlements, our results show that those factors are not sufficient when we consider all localities in which Jews dwelled with non-Jews.

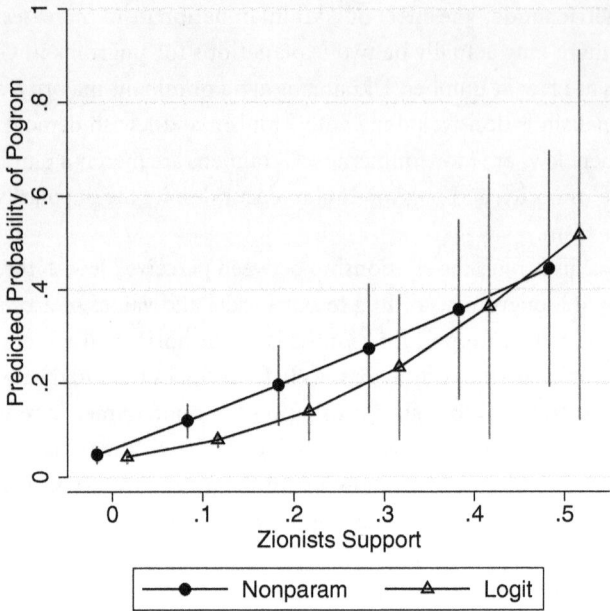

FIGURE 5.2. Marginal effects of different values of the fraction of support for the east Galician General Zionists on the predicted probability of a pogrom for both the nonparametric and (parametric) logit models. Point estimates are given by circles (nonparametric) and triangles (logit); 95 percent confidence intervals are given by the vertical bars.

Put differently, Ukrainian nationalists, anti-Soviet sentiment, and economic tensions between Jews and non-Jews may well have been present in every place where a pogrom occurred, but they were *also* present in many places where pogroms did *not* occur.

But the statistical analysis takes us only so far. It does not shed light on who the perpetrators were and what they thought, the degree of mass participation, the role of bystanders and rescuers, or the complex emotions that must have been at play among both Jews and non-Jews. Consider the pogrom in Zloczów, where an NKVD prison had also been uncovered. Bolesław Kopelman, who worked as a medic in a hospital, describes what took place:

> They brought in Ukrainians from the villages and gave them weapons. Some of the peasants didn't even know how to shoot and then the thing began. I worked as a medic at the hospital, from where they took the entire personnel, around 60 people outside. They lined us up against the wall and started shooting. Because they shot badly some managed to run

away, I was among those. As I was walking through the city, I saw Ukrainians in each entrance gate with a shovel or hoe, beating the Jews that were being chased to the citadel [the location of the NKVD prison], sometimes even killing them on the spot. (AŻIH 301-801)

In this account the NKVD prisons, a wild mob of Ukrainian villagers, and nationalist elites (who, after all, was the "they" who gave weapons to the villagers?) all enter the picture, but there is no single motive or "mechanism."

In chapter 1 we discussed the degree to which pogroms followed a certain script involving ritual humiliation, involving either Jewish religious customs or supposed Jewish support of the Soviet occupation. Another common feature of the pogroms was the intimacy of the encounter between perpetrator and victim. Whether in Drohobycz, Borysław, Lwów, Zloczów, or elsewhere, this was not the industrial, sanitized violence that the Germans would later employ in the death camps. The tools were primitive—shovels and hoes in Zloczów, clubs in Lwów, defenestration in Drohobycz, and the deed was done at close range in full view.

Sometimes the victims knew the perpetrators.[12] Some neighbors provided refuge and then became perpetrators.[13] Landlords denounced their tenants as NKVD spies without any evidence.[14] In Tuczyn, one survivor personally knew the barber, the director of the Ukrainian middle school, and a prominent local Ukrainian politician who took part in the massacre (AŻIH 301-3178).

Pogroms had a mass character, with participation—either as perpetrator, bystander, or rescuer—of heterogeneous segments of the Ukrainian public, including mayors, priests, veterinarians, lawyers, and policemen. But all of these people lived in broader communities that conditioned (if not determined) their ability to do the "right" or "wrong" thing. Consider priests, who as authoritative figures probably had the power either to prevent violence or instigate it. Testimonies frequently point to the Ukrainian Greek Catholic Church and the local priest, but priests appear both as proponents and opponents of pogroms. Thus, for example, it is well known that Father Andrey Sheptytsky, the metropolitan of the Ukrainian Greek Catholic Church, while welcoming Ukrainian independence, condemned local violence and pogroms and sheltered Jews during the war.

Survivor accounts indicate that other priests followed Sheptytsky's lead. In some locations, however, the local priest, in cooperation with the new nationalist authorities, gave his blessing to anti-Jewish violence. In Bolechów, notes Matylda Glerntner, just as the pogrom was about to start, "A few thousand people gather, most from the villages. There were Ukrainian speakers, among them Dr. Harasimow, a Ukrainian priest, and others. The priest said the Jews were a damned nation, had a damned heritage, and constituted a harmful element, that they have to be destroyed" (AŻIH 301-2145). In Sambor, a Ukrainian mob led by a priest slaughtered thirty-two Jews at a cemetery (Rosen 2005, 111). In Niezwisk, a village near the Romanian border, "Ukrainian peasants, under the leadership of the Ukrainian priest Golduniak and Dr. Jurewicz, took the Jews from the neighboring villages to Niezwisk, a village on the Dniestra, and together with Jews from Niezwisk itself, a few hundred people, locked them in the basement of a school and adjacent buildings and during the night they drowned them, throwing them from the ferry into the water. Father Golduniak took active part in this, chasing the Jews with a stick onto the ferry. Around 200 people lost their lives" (AŻIH 301-1434). In Żółkiew at "5pm the bells began ringing in the church and the pogrom ended" (AŻIH 301-1892). Priests—like lawyers, police officers, mayors, or teachers—operated in communal contexts, and it should perhaps not be surprising that the attitudes of most reflected or even followed community sentiment.

Lwów, Borysław, and Draganówka

Our statistical analysis has identified general trends across the whole population of pogroms, but it is worth examining some individual pogroms in greater detail. This illustrates how our explanation works on the ground and highlights factors that may otherwise go unnoticed. We focus on three in particular: Lwów, an "easy" case where the factors we have identified as supportive of pogroms were all present and a pogrom occurred; Borysław, a town with seemingly harmonious relations between Jews and non-Jews during the interwar period but nonetheless with high support for Jewish nationalism and a politically divided majority population; and Draganówka, a small settlement where the non-Jewish population opposed anti-Jewish violence.

Lwów

The Lwów pogrom has received sustained scholarly attention as exemplifying the anti-Semitic sources of the pogrom violence, especially the role of the OUN organized militias (Himka 2011; Struve 2015). Yet in some ways, the city was unique in the region. For one thing, it was large; on the eve of the war, it had approximately three hundred thousand inhabitants. For another, it was demographically and culturally a *Polish* city. Not only did Poles make up over 50 percent of the population, but even the city's Jewish population—at one hundred thousand, the third largest in interwar Poland—had, according to the 1921 census, heavily polonized. In the 1921 census 76,854 inhabitants of the city declared themselves to be Jewish by religion, but only 60,431 claimed to be Jewish by nationality, the rest overwhelmingly claiming Polish nationality. According to Amar (2015, 82), "Galician Jewry was the most Polonized part of the Jewish population before the Second World War." The degree of polonization varied significantly even within eastern Galicia. Despite these numbers, the Ukrainians, who made up the remaining 15 percent of Lwów's population, considered the city their own and deeply resented their political and cultural marginalization. Hopes ran high in the nineteenth century for some sort of cultural amalgam, but the intercommunal violence during and after World War I in Lwów sealed the city's reputation as one of deep political rivalry. Local Poles gravitated toward right-wing politics after independence. Ukrainians, after mostly boycotting the 1922 elections, wavered between the moderate UNDO and the hotheads inspired by Dmytro Dontsov's calls for violent struggle. Jews, many of whom had originally been assimilationist (first to German and then to Polish), now reemerged in Polish politics as General Zionists, even if they did so as native Polish speakers.[15] These undercurrents would inevitably find their way into local politics. In the 1928 elections, over 80 percent of Jewish votes were cast for the General Zionists. Whatever their status in independent Poland, Lwów's Jews would not be Poles or Ukrainians.

The size of the Jewish population, preexisting ethnic polarization along ethnic lines, and internal divisions among both Polish and Ukrainian elites between moderates and hard-liners all paved the way for a pogrom. The Soviet occupation and the war provided the spark. The presence of ethnic elites—Polish, Jewish, and Ukrainian—kept the Soviets busy after September 1939 arresting, deporting, and ultimately massacring thousands in three local NKVD prisons. As the largest Soviet administrative center in western Ukraine, similar to Białystok in the Northeast, Lwów was quickly attacked and occupied by the Germans. In contrast to the Polish areas, however, the Germans brought with them a trained and highly motivated Ukrainian force who were ready to declare the city the launching pad for their own national project and would do just about anything in pursuit of their goal.

The narration of the Lwów pogrom can therefore easily be read as one of Ukrainian nationalist–led anti-Semitic violence: the Germans and Ukrainian militias descended on the city; discovered piles of Ukrainian corpses in the three NKVD prisons, two of which were in close proximity to heavily Jewish neighborhoods; exploited popular anger at Soviet rule and stoked the latent anti-Semitism among the city's Ukrainian population, who then under Ukrainian nationalist leadership humiliated, beat, and tortured their Jewish neighbors and dragged them to the prisons to disinter the bodies. These prison courtyards became the scenes of the most infamous anti-Jewish violence of July 1941.[16]

But how much of the Lwów pogrom can be attributed to anti-Semitism? Himka acknowledges the anti-Semitism of the OUN leadership but maintains that Poles and Russians were much more the object of its hatred than Jews. When opportunity presented itself in 1939, the OUN had killed thousands of Poles, an act to be repeated on a larger scale (discussed below) in Volhynia in 1943. "The OUN's anti-Semitism made assistance in anti-Jewish violence palatable, but it is unlikely that it was an independent factor in the decision to stage a pogrom." The OUN, Himka argues, sought to impress the Germans and gain their acceptance for the *political* goals of independent statehood (Himka 2011, 234). That the pogrom itself took place as the OUN proclaimed statehood several blocks away from one of the most horrific scenes of anti-Jewish violence solidifies the connection here between "national statehood" and "national purification" (Amar 2015, 94).

What shaped the pogrom's course was the urban crowd, many members of which were unconnected to the nationalist militias (Himka 2011, 243). Much of the violence took place on streets and apartments nowhere close to the NKVD prisons and involved humiliation, sexual assault, and robbery. An account Struve (2015, 308; AŻIH 301-1737) cites is typical: "Among the perpetrators were many young women, young Ukrainian peasant women, who were no less enthusiastic than the men. . . . A Ukrainian pushed a Jew in the back and forced him to run. He hit him with a club on the head until he fell unconscious. Others did the same or tried to exceed the creativity of others. The consequence was a terrible cry of pain from the victims and a triumphal cry from the perpetrators." Both Himka and Struve describe the mocking crowd, eager to subject Jewish professionals to the humiliations of cleaning latrines and scrubbing the streets with toothbrushes, a script implemented in other places the Germans had invaded. Nobody forced the urban crowd to participate in the pogrom, but the onlookers who undoubtedly outnumbered the perpetrators did nothing to stop it.[17]

The multiple photographs and videos from the Lwów pogrom show this clearly enough. The bystanders did nothing and frequently expressed approval. Undoubtedly, much of the violence perpetrated by the urban crowd reflected popular anti-Semitism, anger over the Soviet occupation, a desire to put Jews back in their place, and the opportunity for theft and sexual license. But the ground for this violence had been well tilled in interwar Lwów itself where Jews had come to be seen as impediments to the competing projects of national dominance of both Poles and Ukrainians.[18] Anti-Semitism constituted a part of the complex mix of motivations of the pogrom crowd, but the fact that the Jews were considered outside of the community (though they had lived in the city since the fourteenth century), were present in large numbers, and were mobilized into their own nation-building project is what permitted this hatred to be acted on.

Borysław

If Lwów is an "easy" case for showing the contribution of the Soviet occupation and anti-Semitic Ukrainian nationalism in facilitating a pogrom, Borysław presents a different sort of analytical challenge. Rather than being a center of Ukrainian nationalism, politicized ethnicity did not feature prominently in this industrial town. According to Wróbel, "Neither the Polish nor the Ukrainian population of Boryslav was particularly nationalistic" (Wróbel 2012, 219).[19] The pogrom, which claimed approximately three hundred lives, came as a shock to many of the city's Jewish inhabitants.[20] According to Aleksiun, "The pogrom put into question the seemingly peaceful interethnic relations Borysław had enjoyed before the war" (Aleksiun 2016, 251).

Behind the peaceful facade, however, were several of the factors characteristic of the power-threat account of ethnic conflict. First, Poles, who constituted a plurality of the city's population, were essentially matched by large Ukrainian and Jewish minorities. By 1939, the city's population reached 44,500, with an ethnic composition of 48 percent Poles, 22 percent Ukrainian, and 29 percent Jews. Second, Borysław's population was divided politically, even though the divisions may have appeared moderate. Along with Drohobycz (located several kilometers away), Borysław was the capital of eastern Galicia's oil industry and supplied most oil produced in Poland.[21] It was one of the few places in the region where class divides could conceivably have trumped those of ethnicity. Indeed, the Polish Socialist Party (PPS) won approximately 50 percent of the vote in 1922 and retained much of this vote share in 1928.

Despite the depth of the class divide, the nationalizing Polish state induced the politicization of ethnicity among both Ukrainians and Jews. PPS voters were almost exclusively Polish industrial workers (Kopstein and Wittenberg 2011). Ukrainians mostly boycotted the vote in 1922, and their turnout remained weak in 1928. Jews, however, were heavily mobilized into Zionist politics. More than 85 percent of local Jews cast their vote for the General Zionists in both 1922 and 1928.[22] The Poles themselves were divided, with a small but active Endecja organization squaring off against the PPS. The Ukrainians remained politically sullen, mostly failing to participate in public life at all. Ethnic relations in Borysław may have been less openly charged intellectually and more moderate on the surface than in Lwów, but the communities were no less neatly sorted along ethnic lines before World War II. Borysław possessed the conditions that fit with a power-threat approach: a large Jewish population, a strong Zionist presence, and ethnic rivals divided between hard-liners and accommodationists.

After a brief occupation in September 1939, the Germans handed Borysław over to the Soviets, who quickly went about staffing the oil industry and local administration with Ukrainians, Jews, a handful of Poles, but mostly reserving the top spots for transplants from the East. Soviet rule was brutal and unfair to all groups, but unlike Lwów, Borysław was not the site of a major NKVD prison. When the Germans and their Ukrainian OUN collaborators entered the city on July 1, 1941, they nevertheless found a small lock-up with forty-four corpses. Two days later, with their Ukrainian collaborators, they instigated a pogrom that lasted for forty-eight hours (Struve 2015, 465). In contrast with Lwów, the pogrom was less focused on the prison (although Jews were also forced to clean and bury bodies there, too) and more driven by the urban crowd of Ukrainians and, to a lesser extent, Poles. Robbery on the street, looting from apartments, and murder everywhere were common. The carnival-like atmosphere comes through clearly in the testimonies. "The persecutors were pushed on by the hysterical laughing of the crowd. A general joviality ruled the street. It was a big celebration for them—a festival of killing Jews" (Struve 2015, 471). Irene Horowitz in her account notes, "When a few religious Jews were led to the NKVD yard, they were told to dance in the street and perform all kinds of tricks" (Horowitz 1992, 90). Blima Hamerman recalls that "a sixteen year old Jewish boy ran away from his Ukrainian school mate, who chased after him throughout the backyard. . . . He murdered him with an iron plug of the window shutter."[23]

Sometimes political motives cannot easily be separated from highly personal and instrumental ones. The Borysław pogrom provided an opportunity for old vendettas to be acted on. A Ukrainian barber, Michał Wyszatycki, a well-known nationalist, is reported to have had a local Jewish colleague and his entire family put to death in their apartment in order to take over his business after having threatened to do so several days before (Aleksiun 2016, 248). The case of Mikolaj Terletski is equally instructive. A member of the city's old Ukrainian elite, Terletski had been a physician before the war and counted Jews among his patients. With the OUN's recommendation, the Germans appointed him mayor after their arrival. According to most testimony, he either refused to help or was actually responsible for inciting the pogrom. "He was approached by a Jewish delegation imploring him to stop the pogrom. According to Rosenberg and other Jews testifying in connection with Terletski's trial after the war, he refused to receive it" (Aleksiun 2016, 248). Basia Levkovitsch in her testimony tells an even more gruesome tale. A representative of the Jewish community, "Dr. Taykher approached his colleague, the new Ukrainian mayor, Dr. Terletski. Terletski ordered his Jewish colleague be put to death" (AŻIH 301-5881). Although several testimonies demonstrate Ukrainian assistance to Jews during the pogrom (something to be expected, given that most evidence comes from survivors), not enough solidarity remained in the community to prevent the crowd from acting on its worst instincts.²⁴ The motives of the perpetrators were mixed; it was the local context that determined whether they could be acted on.

Draganówka

It is worth pausing for a moment on one case in eastern Galicia for which we have evidence of an entire town defending its Jewish population against a potential pogrom. Of course, there are many cases of pogroms being headed off by determined Ukrainian politicians, priests, and lawyers, but we have found only one case in eastern Galicia where Jewish testimony noted the general population as a whole opposed a pogrom. According to Jakub Zajd, forty-three years old in 1941, in the village of Draganówka, five kilometers from Tarnopol, "The inhabitants saved 16 Jews selflessly" as a pogrom raged close by (AŻIH 301-2166).²⁵ It is interesting to note that this was a predominantly Polish village (83%) and only partially Ukrainian (15%), with a respectable communist vote (15%, for the Ukrainian version of the party). Although only one locality, its strong minority community—Polish peasants in Galicia—and solid communist presence are highly suggestive of the kinds of places where Jews might (temporarily) be safe. Other scholars have pointed to the importance of "local minorities," whether they be Czechs and Poles in western Ukraine, Belarusians in Polish areas, or Ukrainian Baptists and Seventh Day Adventists, in protecting or rescuing Jews from death in the Holocaust (Spector 1990, 243; Friedman 1980, 182; Braun 2016).²⁶ When combined with a communist presence this minority effect may explain why the non-Jewish inhabitants of Draganówka saved its Jews from the larger pogrom unfolding a mere five kilometers away.

Pogroms in Volhynia

Galicia was not the only area of Poland with substantial numbers of Ukrainians. The other is the voivodship of Volhynia. There are two main reasons we analyze Volhynia separately. First, before the creation of modern Poland, Volhynia was in the Russian partition. In Galicia the Austrians tolerated Ukrainian nationalism and with it the Ukrainian Greek Catholic Church, as a counterweight to Polish desires for independence. Ukrainians in the Russian partition did not enjoy the same dispensation. Almost all of them were Eastern Orthodox and were not animated by the kind of nationalism promoted by their Galician cousins. During the interwar period, the OUN was notably weaker in Volhynia than in Galicia, and its targets were Poles as much as Jews (Snyder 2008, 83–84). Second, and more importantly, the Zionist party, on which we based our estimate of Jewish support for Jewish national equality within Poland, did not field a separate party in Volhynia, but joined the Bloc of National Minorities in this voivodship as it did elsewhere in the lands of the Russian partition. Even so, the Zionists in Volhynia enjoyed a reputation for being more assertive and less interested in compromise than in eastern Galicia. According to Bauer, Volhynia was the "center" of Zionist influence in the kresy (Bauer 2009, 24).[27] In the 1928 election the lion's share of support went to the BBWR, which was particularly popular among Jews; the Bloc of National Minorities; and the Communists, whose support came from Jews in the cities and Ukrainians in the countryside (Snyder 2008, 82). Finally, nearly 22 percent of Volhynian localities experienced a pogrom, a far higher percentage than either the Polish-Belarusian areas of the Northeast or the Ukrainian-Polish southeast.

We are not able to replicate our Galician analysis for Volhynia, but we can examine the basic demographic and political differences between pogrom and nonpogrom localities. The one important caveat concerns missing data. Although we have pogrom and census data for 114 settlements, there is a great deal of missing electoral data. This is no doubt due to political interference. As Snyder (2008, 80) notes, the Polish state was keen to minimize Soviet influence and secure this sensitive border province. This required "managing" the results, especially regarding the Communists, to a greater extent than elsewhere in Poland. The 1928 election results for both the Communists and the Bloc of National Minorities are missing for roughly half (and largely the same half) of the settlements in the voivodship. With that said, we present the descriptive statistics in table 5.2.

There are five noteworthy features of pogrom localities. First and unsurprisingly, given our prior findings, pogroms occur where Jews are the most visible, both in percentage ("Jewish") and absolute ("Number of Jews") terms. Second, pogroms occur more frequently where Ukrainians ("E. Orthodox") are more evenly matched demographically with Jews. This suggests that underlying Ukrainian aggression might have been a sense of competition with and perceived threat from Jews, who were economically dominant in the larger towns. Indeed, over two-thirds of the shtetls in Volhynia suffered a pogrom. Third, the Minorities Bloc ("Min Bloc 28") was far more popular where pogroms occurred. We are unsure how to interpret this result. It could indicate either greater Ukrainian nationalism (as in Galicia) or Jewish support for national rights (as in the Northeast).

Fourth, unlike in Galicia, where BBWR popularity was positively correlated with the probability of a pogrom (providing clear evidence for the power-threat hypothesis), the opposite is true in Volhynia. This might be evidence of a different kind of politics, but more likely it is an artifact of the data. Of Volhynia's 125

TABLE 5.2. Median demographic and political characteristics of pogrom and nonpogrom localities in Volhynia

	POGROM	NO POGROM
Polish	10%	9%
Jewish	41	3
E. Orthodox	44	85
Number of Jews	2686	320
Pop	14564	12064
Min Bloc 28	29%	8%
Comms 28	4	24
BBWR 28	43	68
N	25	89

Note: Sample excludes settlements with no recorded Jewish population in 1921. Variables are the 1921 percentage Poles (Polish), Jews (Jewish), and mostly Ukrainian Eastern Orthodox (E. Orthodox); number of Jews (Number of Jews) and overall population (Pop); and 1928 electoral support for Minorities Bloc (Min Bloc 28), Communists (Comms 28), and Government Party (BBWR 28).
Sources: 1921 Polish Census, 1928 election to Polish Sejm, and authors' computation.

settlements (that had Jews according to the 1921 census), 21 are recorded to have given at least 99 percent of their vote to the BBWR in 1928, a clear sign of electoral malfeasance. (This happened in only one place in all of Galicia.)

Finally, the immunizing effects of communism are strongly present. The median nonpogrom locality had six times the level of support as the median pogrom locality (24% vs. 4%). Of course, we can compute these figures only for localities where we know communist support. What about the 61 places where that number in missing? Presumably the Polish state would not need to manipulate the results if it knew the population supported the BBWR. The results most likely to be suppressed would be those where the communists were popular. Of the 50 settlements where we lack the data for communists but have information on whether a pogrom occurred, only 3 settlements, or 6 percent of the total, endured a pogrom.

Considering Volhynia in particular also allows us to address a potential objection to our analysis. In making the case for power-threat dynamics as the source of pogrom violence, have we not downplayed the importance of anti-Semitism? The pogroms of 1941 targeted Jews even though in other dyads (e.g., Poles and Belarusians or Ukrainians and Poles) the political threat was arguably just as strong. It would certainly help our argument if we could show that the violence was less about Jews than the *politics* of Jews. One way of doing so is to address violence against other groups, and Volhynia provides one important opportunity. Snyder's research on the ethnic cleansing of Poles by Ukrainians and Polish violence against Ukrainians in 1943 gets us part of the way there. During this episode, tens of thousands perished. Snyder writes of the violence, "The 1943 decision of Ukrainian nationalists to cleanse was, among other things, a strategic calculation based on news of the Soviet victory at Stalingrad in February 1943, and the judgement that the German occupation was both unbearable and temporary." In his depiction, ethnic cleansing in 1943 was much more about political threat and eliminating future political rivals than ethnic hatred: "It meant to preempt the return of Polish statehood by expelling Poles from west Ukraine before the war was over" (Snyder 2003a, 199, 213).[28]

And yet, this argument does not get us out of the woods completely. What about 1941? What accounts for the absence of Ukrainian pogroms against Poles or Polish pogroms against Ukrainians or Belarusians (or vice versa) in 1941? In some respects the Belarusian case is an easy one. There was a modicum of violence by Belarusians against Poles in 1939 during the Soviet takeover, but Belarusian nationalism was historically weak and therefore the account of competing national projects at the core of our argument is supported by the relative absence of intercommunal violence between Poles and Belarusians (just as it accounts for the relative weakness of Belarusian resistance to sovietization).

The lack of pogroms between Ukrainians and Poles in 1941 does pose a problem for our argument because each did pose a significant threat to the other. Here the prodding of the Germans who attempted to have locals target Jews in the weeks after June 22, 1941, probably influenced the timing of why Jews came first (and it is worth recalling that the Germans prevented Ukrainians from turning against their Polish neighbors in 1939, such as in Borysław). It is also probably the case that Jews, because of their status as urban, middle-class rivals, constituted a bigger threat to both Poles and Ukrainians than either presented to each other, and in 1941 the Germans provided a compelling reminder of this (in addition to facilitating the conditions). But the reason the Jews were perceived as a bigger threat probably *did* have something to do with anti-Semitism. Our argument does not deny that anti-Semitism played some role; what the evidence indicates, however, is that the pogroms were not *only* about anti-Semitism, which is probably best thought of as perhaps a necessary but certainly insufficient condition for the pogroms of summer 1941.

Our overall findings confirm our argument that Jewish efforts to achieve national rights in Poland were met by violent reprisals when the opportunity presented itself. Whether in underdeveloped areas of the former Russian partition, where a Polish majority contended with Belarusian and Jewish minorities, or in the historically more tolerant areas of the former Habsburg partition, where the majority Ukrainians faced nontrivial numbers of Poles and Jews, the most robust predictor of pogroms is the strength of Zionist parties. Economic tensions, anti-Semitic nationalism, and the legacy of the Soviet occupation are not absent, but even when they do play a role, it is in addition to rather than to the exclusion of the effect of Jewish nationalism.

What distinguishes the primarily Ukrainian Southeast from the primarily Polish Northeast is the absence of mitigating factors, in particular robust communist support (at least in Galicia). Whereas in the dozens of Polish and especially Belarusian towns and villages, we found that non-Jewish support for communist internationalism immunized these settlements against pogroms, in Galicia the communists were too weak to make much of a difference. Only in Volhynia do we see this immunizing effect.

Our results also return us to the question of political integration. Zionist and other Jewish parties performed better where the Jewish population was large, even accounting for other factors. On the one hand, this result is unremarkable because Jewish parties, like all parties, tended to invest their resources and attention where large numbers of their potential voters lived. But it is also worth considering whether or not a smaller Jewish population might have made it easier for non-Jewish parties to attract Jewish voters. We argue that they did. In Galicia as a whole, Jews were much more likely to vote for Polish or Ukrainian parties where they lived in much smaller numbers or as a smaller portion of a given community (Kopstein and Wittenberg 2011). In an era of party politics in multiethnic but economically backward states, where political communication was expensive, demography may have dictated party strategy and these strategies, in turn, exercised profound effects on the mobilization of ethnic groups into politics. Where Jews were mobilized into Jewish national politics, their Ukrainian neighbors turned against them. The tragedy for Jews in the Ukrainian areas is that, unlike in the Northeast, where support for Polish parties or the popularity of communists offered at least some limited protection against pogroms, in Galicia and Volhynia the conflict between Poles and Ukrainians left few options for Jews. Siding with one group ultimately meant siding against the other.

6
POGROMS OUTSIDE THE EASTERN BORDERLANDS

Can the explanation for pogrom violence against Jews in eastern Poland during the summer of 1941 account for other instances of popular anti-Jewish violence and intercommunal violence not involving Jews in other times and places? We have argued that the likelihood of a pogrom in a locality increases with the demographic weight of the target ethnic group; the degree to which the target ethnic group advocates national equality with the demographically dominant group; and, to an extent, the threat from political forces advocating ethnic tolerance. In Poland pogroms were most likely to occur where there were many Jews, where those Jews were nationalist (Zionist) in political orientation, and where some (though not necessarily most) non-Jews were ethnically tolerant.

As we argued in chapter 1, eastern Poland after the outbreak of war between Nazi Germany and the Soviet Union provides an ideal venue to study the spatial distribution of pogroms for two reasons. First, the pogroms occurred during a period of state collapse. Under settled political conditions where the state can and does punish unauthorized violence, the number of observed pogroms is always less than the number of intended pogroms because some potential perpetrators fear official retribution for their violence. Where there is state collapse, by contrast, those motivated to commit violence need not fear legal ramifications. In these situations the distribution of pogroms thus more accurately reflects underlying violent intentions in society than would be the case under a functioning state (unless that state itself sanctioned pogroms). Second, we have a lot of information for this region not just on where pogroms occurred, but where they did *not* occur. We could not easily have ruled out alternative hypotheses without recourse to a large database of multiethnic settlements with variance not just on our outcome but also on a battery of demographic, social, and political characteristics.

These two features made our analysis possible, but do not in themselves constitute scope conditions for our argument. Nationally conscious ethnic minorities can pose a political threat to majority groups even where there is a functioning state and no granular data on the distribution of pogroms. Where there is a functioning state that threatens to punish popular violence, for example, it would be necessary to consider additional factors such as the timing of violence and the role elites played in orchestrating it (see, e.g., Wilkinson 2004). In these instances, our claim would be that pogroms would occur even without elite planning. Where there are no large-N data, the role of political threat might be isolated through smaller matched comparisons, similar to how Petersen (2002) makes the case for resentment in the Polish and Lithuanian pogroms or Varshney (2002) argues for the beneficial effects of cross-ethnic civic ties.

There are two other characteristics of the Polish context, however, that do place some limits on how far our explanation extends. First, the argument as formulated relies on modern notions of ethnic politics. Before the reestablishment of an independent Poland after World War I, imperial authorities regulated the terms of interaction among the various national groups. Although there were both Polish and Ukrainian movements dedicated to protecting their respective national languages and cultures, there was no expectation of asserting their preeminence. Poland's independence changed the terms of interethnic relations. Although the treaty that brought Poland into existence provided for a range of minority rights, for Poles independence meant gaining authority to establish Polish language and culture across all of Poland. This ambition put Poles at odds with Jews and Ukrainians who sought to assert their own national rights. Pogroms were most likely to occur where such competing modern national visions clashed.

Second, embedded in the hypothesized importance of demographics and political preference is a presumption of democratic, or at least representative, politics. The power of numbers should matter most where numbers can be translated into political influence, as in democracies. If Poles and Ukrainians who sought the dominance of their language and culture across their national territories had envisioned a dictatorial future, then there would have been no need to respond to the threat of Jewish nationalism with pogrom violence. Poles and Ukrainians might have responded by simply not recognizing that Jews had any national rights. It was the democratic promise of majority rule that pitted Poles, Jews, and Ukrainians against each other as political adversaries (see Mann 2005).

We do not argue that political threat constitutes the only explanation for popular violence against minorities, but we do think its importance has not been sufficiently recognized. In what follows, we assess the strengths and limitations of our argument by considering the experiences of other countries. Our data-intensive research design gives us confidence in our results from Poland's eastern borderlands, but is difficult to replicate elsewhere, so the fragmentary evidence we present here should be viewed as suggestive for further research rather than definitive.

Wartime Lithuania, Romania, Greece
Lithuania

Lithuania is the country whose political trajectory and conditions in 1941 most closely resembled Poland's. Like Poland, Lithuania gained independence after World War I and enjoyed a short period of parliamentary democracy before sliding into authoritarianism. As in Poland, the Jews, though far fewer in number, were actively mobilized into nationalist (Zionist) politics (Mendelsohn 1983, 38–43; Eidintas 2003, 73) and played a disproportionately important role in the economy. Like their Polish and Ukrainian counterparts, Lithuania was absorbed along with eastern Poland into the Soviet sphere as a consequence of the Molotov-Ribbentrop Pact, and the Jews would be similarly blamed for the crimes of the Soviet occupation (Petersen 2002). When the Germans launched Operation Barbarossa in June 1941, they invaded Lithuania too, though they received a rather more friendly reception from Lithuanians than they did from Poles.

In the six weeks after the German arrival, more than forty cities and villages—approximately one-quarter of all Jewish communities in the country—experienced at least one pogrom, a rate higher than anywhere in eastern Poland (Arad 1976, 234–272; Levin 1990, 895–899). Between five and ten thousand Jews died during the massacres, an ominous prelude in a country where 95 percent of its 150,000 Jews would die within the first few months of the war. In one of the most gruesome incidents of the war, in the Lithuanian city of Kovno (Kaunas) on June 27, 1941, a German army photographer witnessed a pogrom in which a Lithuanian man beat to death forty-five to fifty people with a crowbar, one-by-one, over the course of around forty-five minutes. Onlookers, women and children included, clapped. When he finished, they sang along as he played the national anthem on an accordion (Klee, Dressen, and Riess 1988). In the smaller towns, Dieckmann (2011, 362) notes the combination of Lithuanian nationalists, the German presence, and bands of local thieves and hooligans who carried out pogroms such as the one in Butrimonys on June 24, 1941.[1]

Many of the same conditions that applied to Polish and Ukrainian areas of the Polish eastern borderlands also applied to Lithuania. As in northeastern Poland, Jews were a demographically weighty factor in strategic areas in the independent Lithuanian state, so much so that they were initially promised significant autonomy until it became clear in 1924 that Wilno (Vilnius) would fall under Polish sovereignty, after which Jews were increasingly seen as foreign to the body politic. As in Ukraine, a German-fueled fascist organization, the Lithuanian Activist Front, had been trained by the Germans before facilitating the collaboration of the local population with the Nazi invaders. In addition to their demographic weight, Lithuania's Jews were strongly mobilized into Zionist and other forms of Jewish nationalist politics, perhaps more strongly than anywhere else in eastern Europe. Partly because of the weakness of Hasidism and partly because of the modernizing tendencies encouraged by the previous Czarist regime, the Haskalah (Jewish enlightenment movement) dominated the Jewish population. According to Mendelsohn, the Jews of Lithuania's towns "possessed a strong nationalist, Hebraic cast" and were therefore highly receptive to "modern Jewish national and cultural movements. The combination of little acculturation and a deeply rooted Orthodox Jewish community undergoing a process of secularization encouraged by both government and the Haskalah produced an environment in which modern Jewish nationalism flourished and competed with Orthodoxy for the allegiance of the youth. Thus Lithuania became a center of Bundism, Folkism, and Zionism" (Mendelsohn 1983, 215).

Lithuania poses an easy test for our argument, but we currently lack the requisite comparative demographic and political data to compare pogrom and nonpogrom locations. Recent research on the Shoah in Lithuania (e.g., Dieckmann and Suziedelis 2006; Levinson 2006; Keys and Vasil 2011) does not systematically distinguish between the violence perpetrated by German and Lithuanian military and paramilitary organizations on the one hand and Lithuanian civilians on the other, but does point to the documentary basis on which this crucial distinction might be made. We leave this for future research.

Romania and Greece

A wave of pogroms took place in the Romanian provinces of Bukovina and Bessarabia at roughly the same time as in eastern Poland and Lithuania. These territories had been occupied by the Soviet Union since 1940 and were returned to Romanian control as a reward for Romanian assistance in the German attack on the Soviet Union. Similar to the Polish and Lithuanian cases, the chaotic and lawless period between the withdrawal of the Red Army and the restoration of political authority provided ample opportunity for anti-Jewish violence on the part of both the civilian population and the Romanian military. Most well-known is the Iași pogrom that broke out on June 28, 1941, that killed hundreds and injured thousands. In the Bukovinan town of Sadagura (Sadgora), a pogrom on

July 6 led by a local schoolmaster resulted in the murder of more than one hundred Jews. He and his band of peasants raped, beat, and looted the property of the Jews of three small towns before killing nearly all of them in a forest. "One witness testified that a baby's sobs could be heard coming from the mass grave for quite some time" (Radu 2000, 98).[2] As Hollander notes, "roving bands of militants and profiteers raped, pillaged, and murdered their way through the countryside; these actions alone must have cost the lives of tens of thousands" (2008, 232–233). There is no consensus on how many localities were affected, though it was almost certainly in the hundreds.

On this wave of pogroms, Solonari concludes that popular participation was "massive and ubiquitous," but that the violence was most murderous and locally driven where Ukrainian nationalists (in Bukovina) and Romanian nationalists (in Bessarabia) sought to exploit wartime turmoil to rid themselves of Jews (2007, 786–787). At the same time, Solonari's evidence also indicates that the extreme nationalists themselves were not the sole perpetrators and that ideological anti-Semitism was often not present.[3] "What ultimately made such massive violence against Jews possible," he writes, "was the Christians' willingness to condone it."[4] This interpretation points to the communal context. Though Solonari never specifies the conditions under which Christians may have opposed such violence, we can venture two hypotheses. One concerns local sympathy for communism, which proved important as a mitigating factor in Poland. Based on a clever comparison of adjacent Soviet and Romanian-ruled Moldovan territories, Dumitru and Johnson (2011) argue that the communist ideology to which local populations were exposed during the interwar period in the Soviet territory accounts for the complete absence of pogroms once war broke out. As in Poland, nontrivial exposure to communism immunized the population against the worst sorts of ethnic hatreds and provided the bare minimum of solidarity between communities.

Another hypothesis is more suggestive of power-threat theory. We might infer from the higher survival rate of Jews in the Old Kingdom, the territory Romania controlled before the acquisition of Transylvania and neighboring regions after World War I, that Christian sympathy for the Jewish plight was related to higher levels of Jewish assimilation. In Transylvania assimilated Jews were far more likely to identify as Hungarian or German than Romanian, which could not have much endeared them to the local Christian Romanian population. As for Lithuania, we currently lack the evidence on rates of assimilation to systematically test this claim.

Some evidence from Greece during the same period, however, supports this argument. Mavrogordatos notes that the heavily Sephardic Jewish population of Salonica tended neither to assimilate to Greek culture nor to support the local Greek irredentists. "Sephardic Jews qualify [as national minorities] not only by virtue of their Zionist majority, but also because of their persistent reluctance to accept Greek sovereignty and assimilate into Greek society" (1983, 228)[5] As in Poland, the main concern of the Zionists was to "preserve and defend the integrity and autonomy of the Jewish community against encroachments by the Greek state." When combined with other ethnic minorities who also supported the more ethnically tolerant, nonirredentist Greeks in Athens, the Jewish vote could ensure massive electoral defeats for Greek nationalists (256). Not only did Jewish demographic weight (between 20 and 40 percent of Salonica's population) and Jews' refusal to assimilate either culturally or politically sour ethnic relations with the Greek majority during the 1930s—beginning with an anti-Jewish pogrom in 1931—but all of this would have grave consequences during World War II. According to Mavrogordatos (2008), the greater cultural and political assimilation of Athenian Jews accounts for their survival under the Nazi occupation in much greater numbers than their less assimilated counterparts in Salonica. As in Poland, the majority population exploited the opportunity to condone violence to rid themselves of a political threat.

Emancipation and Anti-Jewish Violence
Germany

Jewish emancipation after the French Revolution and the advance of Napoleon changed everything, as it brought the prospect of Jewish citizenship and ultimately political mobilization and electoral participation. Could Jews also be citizens? This is the core of what was referred to as the "Jewish question." Although Russia is the locus classicus of the modern pogrom, historians have begun to unravel the relationship between emancipation and anti-Jewish riots in western Europe. Several waves of anti-Jewish disturbances swept over parts of Germany in the nineteenth century. The first widespread violence occurred in 1819, the so-called Hep-Hep riots (referring to the utterances of the rioters). Riots occurred in major populations with larger and visible Jewish populations, such as Frankfurt, Hamburg, and Würzburg, and spread to at least forty other cities (Rogger 1992, 318). Historians have settled on no single cause of this exclusionary violence (Hoffmann, Bergmann, and Smith 2002), but in two important studies Rohrbacher (1999, 2002) identifies the central role of Jewish emancipation. It was "the resistance to the process of Jewish emancipation and its local repercussions that can be identified as the immediate cause and primary reason for the eruption of anti-Jewish violence in 1819, and that ultimately accounts for the specific élan, the emotional force, and the destructive energy of the riots" (Rohrbacher 2002, 41). In 1848, during Germany's turbulent liberal revolution, further riots erupted and, according to Rohrbacher, this time "there can be little doubt that the question of Jewish emancipation stands out as the most important single factor in the anti-Jewish rioting of 1848. . . . It was conflicts over the emancipation of the Jews, particularly over their status in local society, that resulted in indiscriminate persecutions of the Jewish minority" (Rohrbacher 2002, 41–42). Similar emancipation-related outbreaks occurred in other locations in western Europe.[6] Further research is needed to determine any relationship between the localities where violence broke out and what the emancipated local Jews were advocating in the political realm.

Russia

Three waves of pogroms swept over prerevolutionary and revolutionary Russia: in 1881–1882, 1903–1906, and 1917–1920, and this violence gave rise to the term "pogrom" itself. These pogroms occurred during periods of state weakness or breakdown and generally moved over time from larger cities to smaller ones and also became more deadly. Whereas the initial pogroms that broke out spontaneously in larger cities of the Ukrainian areas of the Pale of Settlement in 1881–1882 claimed only fifty-two lives, the Kishinev pogrom of 1903 alone claimed that many, and more than three thousand would die before 1906. During the civil war after 1917, approximately fifty thousand Jews perished in pogrom violence. Most historians identify economic competition as the main cause of earlier outbreaks: market days and Jewish-owned taverns and shops constitute the core of most narratives.

The absence of genuinely democratic politics places obvious limits on the applicability of the power-threat model to these earlier pogroms. Politics, however, was not completely absent, especially during the earlier two waves, for this violence also resulted from deep anxieties about the anticipated effects of Jewish emancipation on the power hierarchy within the Pale of Settlement. Lambroza (1992, 232–233) and Asher (2008, 27) explicitly tie the distribution of pogroms in 1903–1906 to Jewish attempts to gain political rights, the first free and fair elections after 1905, and the threat that Jewish political representation posed to Russian political dominance.[7] At the same time, it should also be noted that in both 1881–1882 and 1903–1906, although state authority was weakened by events, it had not altogether collapsed. Thus, unlike in Poland in 1941, the state played an active role in encouraging or discouraging pogroms in particular places.

Before the Holocaust, the best-documented pogroms, and certainly the most deadly ones, were those that occurred between 1917 and 1920 in central Ukraine and eastern Poland. This prolonged wave, consisting of over eight hundred pogroms of often frightful violence, occurred under similar conditions to those in

1941. First, there was political anarchy in the context of World War I; the Russian Revolution; and the collapse of the German, Austro-Hungarian, and especially Russian empires. Germans, Poles, Bolsheviks, Ukrainian nationalists (primarily followers of Szymon Petlura), White armies, and countless local warlords of various (and sometimes changing) political stripes, all competed for the same territory. Second, these various competing groups were all anti-Semitic to one degree or another, and although there was no Soviet occupation for which the Jews could be held responsible, the Jews were often still accused of supporting Bolshevism.

Interestingly, however, although the non-Jewish local populations did sometimes participate, the record is clear that most of the attacks were planned and instigated by roving armies, warlords, and gangs. The violence began in late 1917 with military deserters and was continued by anti-Bolshevik Ukrainian warlords at a steady pace of approximately fifty attacks per month through late spring, 1919.[8] They reached their zenith in the summer of 1919, when, according to Kenez (1992), the White (Volunteer) armies succeeded in murdering "as many Jews as all other armies put together, because its pogroms were the most modern: they were the best organized, carried out like military operations, and the most ideologically motivated.... The White army's pogroms were largely Cossack affairs, with non-Cossack officers and local inhabitants occasionally joining them" (302). Whereas the total number of deaths resulting from neighbor-on-neighbor violence in summer 1941 is approximately twenty-five thousand to fifty thousand, the best estimate for the number of Jews killed during this earlier wave is between fifty thousand and sixty thousand (Gergel 1951).

Our argument does not consider instances of anti-Jewish violence in which the perpetrators are organized quasi-military groups. Although these attacks are usually referred to as pogroms, they do not fall under our more restrictive definition, which encompasses only attacks by civilians. We excluded (quasi-)military groups, however, primarily for pragmatic reasons. Including them for the 1941 pogrom wave would certainly have increased the number of anti-Jewish attacks that get counted as pogroms, but it would also have introduced measurement error into our dependent variable. We are confident that with our restrictive definition we can distinguish between pogroms and the German-inspired effort to exterminate European Jewry. We would be less confident in that distinction if we had expanded the potential perpetrators to include organized quasi-military groups (such as the Einsatzgruppen).

Kenez (2004) attributes the 1917–1920 pogroms to a combination of anti-Semitism, anti-Bolshevism, and looting, but bases his conclusions on beliefs he imputes to groups such as peasants and Russian White Army detachments that perpetrated the violence. As in Poland in summer 1941, however, the vast majority of Jews in this earlier pogrom wave did not experience violence. We still do not know why some settlements were spared and others were not. Whether or not the answer lies in power-threat theory or some other explanation awaits further research.

Still, our argument does point to two possible reasons why there was so little popular instigation of pogroms even when the chaos of imperial collapse presented an opportunity. First, many of these pogroms occurred in regions ruled by the Russian Empire, where restrictions on Polish and Ukrainian nationalist mobilization before the war meant that local populations would not have viewed Jews as the same kind of political threat that they did in areas ruled by Austria-Hungary. Second and relatedly, in many cases it is not at all clear that local non-Jewish populations during that period envisaged themselves as masters of their own democratic fate. During the early phase of the pogroms, these populations could not have envisaged the collapse of Austria-Hungary or the emergence of democracy in post-Imperial Russia.

Non-Jewish Targets

Although we have discussed primarily anti-Jewish violence, our approach can in principle be adapted to explain similar violence against other minority groups. We discuss two important cases. In both contemporary India and the postbellum American South, demographics and mass politics combine in ways that have led to intercommunal violence, which take the form of Hindu-Muslim riots in India and, into the early twentieth century, the lynching of blacks by whites in the American South.

India

India has been plagued by Hindu-Muslim violence for decades.[9] Scholars have repeatedly drawn the connection between Hindu-Muslim violence and political and economic competition in Indian society (e.g., Brass 2003; Varshney 2002; Wilkinson 2004; Dhattiwala and Biggs 2012) and have even highlighted specific factors that are central to our explanation: demographically significant ethnic groups mobilized into democratic politics, a desire by a titular ethnic majority to assert its dominance, and political forces seeking to defend minority rights. But they disagree on how these factors lead to violence (see esp. Varshney and Gubler 2012; Wilkinson 2013).

One major axis of debate concerns the role of the state in fomenting or tolerating mass violence. The state was not an issue in our analysis of the summer 1941 pogroms because it collapsed in the face of the German invasion of the Soviet

Union. This relieved us of the burden of having to conceptualize and measure state involvement and, we have argued, permitted us to observe in an unmediated way which settlement-level characteristics translated into violence. Scholars of India are not as fortunate. Wilkinson (2004) and Dhattiwala and Biggs (2012) develop explanations for the pattern of Hindu-Muslim violence that focus on electoral politics in ethnically divided regions. Each attributes Hindu-Muslim riots to the electoral machinations of the ruling party, which is said to foment or permit riots in places where it is politically vulnerable. This party strategy, designed to highlight the threat Muslims pose to Hindus, is used to mobilize Hindu support to win an upcoming election. Both explanations stress the importance of the perceived threat of local Muslim demographic weight to Hindu political control.[10]

Varshney (2002) and Varshney and Gubler (2013) are also interested in the pattern of Hindu-Muslim violence and acknowledge the contribution of Hindu-Muslim polarization. But they argue that in general the state in India is insufficiently powerful to be the ultimate arbiter of when and where such violence occurs. They distinguish in particular between the sparks that political elites might (or might not) set off to inflame intercommunal tensions and the resultant fires (violence) that may erupt as a result. Even if the state can control the sparks, they argue, it is in general incapable of preventing the outbreak of the fire. Instead, what prevents the violence is, following Putnam (2000), "bridging capital" (23)—the strength of local intercommunal ties between Hindus and Muslims. Towns where civil society is organized across communal lines are mostly peaceful because conflict can be regulated and resolved; violence occurs where civil society is largely intracommunal and there are no such crosscutting Hindu-Muslim social ties.

We are not in a position to intervene in this highly specialized debate, but our research does suggest a different approach to the question. We argue that the places most prone to violence are those that pit an ethnic majority seeking to maintain its political dominance against a minority challenger under circumstances in which majorities get to rule. Disentangling the effect of state actions from the effect of settlement-level characteristics in India is difficult because of the varying roles the state plays in the production of violence (see esp. Brass 2003). But one could examine Indian localities where the authorities are suspected to have attempted to foment violence but were unsuccessful. Varshney (2002) would argue that these places failed to "catch fire" because of multireligious civil society organizations. We would predict that there were too few Muslims or that the Muslims were politically organized in a way that did not challenge Hindu dominance. One could also examine the distribution of riots that did not occur around elections. This would, as a matter of design, exclude periods in which the authorities had the greatest incentive to incite or tolerate violence for electoral gain, thus allowing easier identification of other factors that make some settlements more prone to violence.

Postbellum American South

In the decades following the Civil War, whites lynched thousands of blacks throughout the former Confederacy. A lynching is, of course, not the same as a pogrom. Unlike pogroms, lynchings require the identification of a particular target, typically male, who is almost always falsely accused of a crime. Whereas pogroms might or might not involve murder, lynchings were invariably deadly. Pogroms targeted minority groups, but white mobs also lynched other whites, though blacks made up the overwhelming proportion of victims overall.[11]

Still, there are many important similarities in the circumstances surrounding lynchings and pogroms. Although law enforcement and the justice system were operational in the United States, unlike in Poland, in practice the white population did not support prosecution of perpetrators, and there were very few convictions. Thus, as with pogromists, lynch mobs could operate largely without fear of the law (McGovern 1982, 12–13). Moreover, as with pogroms, lynching was a "local affair"—according to Bailey and Tolnay, the victims were usually killed close to home, presumably by whites who were also local (2015, 87). There was also a ritual aspect to lynchings. They did not usually include humiliation, as with pogroms, but they did involve curious onlookers and other bystanders among the townspeople (8). Perhaps most important, like pogroms, lynching was meant to send a message. According to Brundage, "virtually all observers and scholars of lynching suggest that whites resorted to mob violence to shore up caste lines in the face of some perceived threat, or, more simply, to 'keep blacks in their place'" (1993, 103).

Did whites lynch blacks for reasons that were similar to why Poles and Ukrainians committed pogroms against Jews? Local context certainly mattered, as it did in Poland. McGovern conveys the conventional wisdom: "The key to the phenomenon is community approval, either explicit, in the form of general participation by the local citizenry, or implicit, in the form of acquittal of the killers without a trial" (1982, x). What researchers have yet to uncover, however, are the economic, social, and political factors that lay behind the spatial and temporal variance in such community approval.[12] Among the many explanations offered, one is power-threat theory. Blalock (1967) used the example of lynchings in formulating this theory, which argues that the likelihood of a lynching should have increased with the proportion of the population that is black and with the popularity of political parties that were perceived as relatively sympathetic to black civil rights, such as the Republicans and the Progressives.

In the ensuing decades, there has been a robust debate about the merits of the "black-threat" hypothesis. Reed (1972), Corzine et al. (1983), Creech et al. (1989), and Brundage (1993) find support for the claim that the prevalence of lynchings is positively correlated with the proportion of the black population. Tolnay, Beck, and Massey (1989a, 1989b) and Tolnay and Beck (1992) dispute these findings and also find no evidence that lynchings were more prevalent where the relatively racially sympathetic Republicans or Progressives threatened the white Democratic power structure. Indeed, they find just the opposite: increased support for Republicans and Progressives is associated with fewer lynchings. Bailey and Tolnay (2015) declare this debate inconclusive.

The biggest limitation of this body of research from our perspective is its overly aggregated county-level data. We sympathize with the lament that counties are the smallest geographic unit with which to study lynchings on a broad scale (Tolnay and Beck 1992, 39), but like pogroms, lynchings occurred in communities, and the factors underlying them should in principle also be measured at the community level.[13] There is no gainsaying that using county-level data under these circumstances introduces possible aggregation bias and likely decreases the variance (and hence potential explanatory power) of important variables such as the proportion of blacks in the population and support for the Republican or Progressive parties.

Even if the data were community level, lynching research suffers from another limitation related to the conceptualization and measurement of perceived black political threat. Although Bailey and Tolnay (2015) present pathbreaking evidence on the demographic and sociological characteristics of individual lynch victims, they lack evidence on black political affiliations and thus "were unable to specify . . . whether black and mixed-race men who were politically active, who attempted to vote, or who publicly voiced opposition to the Democratic Party experienced an increased vulnerability to mob violence" (213). It is precisely this kind of information about the magnitude of perceived Jewish threat that we have for Poland, inferred from the support given by Jews to Jewish political parties. Bounds on the degree of black support for the Republicans could be computed at the county level for the period in which blacks were still able to use their voting rights. This would, if combined with an estimate of voter turnout, provide at least an aggregate measure of the perceived black threat.

As the foregoing examples demonstrate, when countries make the transition to mass politics before their populations constitute one people, the implications can be volatile. Mass politics sows division by making ownership of the state dependent on ethnic demographics and, in the case of democracies, winning competitive elections. Where a majority group's ownership of the state is threatened by the numerical strength and communal demands of a minority group, intergroup tensions inevitably follow. Sometimes the consequence is ethnic cleansing (Mann 2005), but far more often it leads to more selective but no less deadly violence. Modern anti-Jewish pogroms, Hindu-Muslim riots in India, and the lynching of blacks in the United States serve as illustrations of what can happen when political competition turns into a source of animosity rather than legitimacy.

We have attempted to identify the conditions under which multiethnic societies with modern politics turn toxic and to extend this analysis to other cases in order to highlight the utility and limits of our account. What exactly the implications of our approach are for understanding questions of collective guilt and the politics of ethnic accommodation and preventing the worst sorts of intercommunal violence are the questions to which we turn in the conclusion to this study.

7
INTIMATE VIOLENCE AND ETHNIC DIVERSITY

Political science has only weakly incorporated the Holocaust into the corpus of its theoretical work. This is ironic because, for students of ethnic conflict, nothing would seem to be more obvious than to include what is arguably the "index case" of modern violence into the mainstream of comparative politics. But for a handful of important exceptions in comparative genocide studies (Melson 1996; Straus 2010; Valentino 2004), this has not occurred. Bauman's characterization of the relationship of Holocaust history to sociology ("Their impressively productive and crucially important work seldom finds its way back to the mainstream of scholarly discipline and cultural life in general" [1989, 15]) prefaces King's summary of the same historiography's contribution to political science a decade later ("It is an odd fact that the twentieth century's most famous instance of state-led political and social violence—the Holocaust—has remained largely peripheral to political science" [2012, 323]).

What has stood in the way? One obstacle to integrating the findings of Holocaust research back into the mainstream of political science has surely been its sheer enormity. The Holocaust unfolded over several years across multiple countries in Europe and beyond. Early research focused, on the one hand, on the impersonal and bureaucratic nature of the tragedy, organized and implemented by German *Schreibtischtäter* (desk murderers) such as Adolf Eichmann (Arendt 1963), and, on the other hand, the concentration camps, operating with the technical rationality characteristic of an advanced industrial society, as the paradigmatic site of the Jews' destruction. As Bauman memorably put it, "Modern civilization was not the Holocaust's *sufficient* condition; it was, however, most certainly its *necessary* condition" (Bauman 1989, 16).

Later research has proved this view inaccurate, or rather incomplete. We now know that by the time the gas chambers became operational, approximately half of Jews who would perish in the Holocaust were already dead (King 2012; Snyder 2015). This killing was carried out at close quarters: in apartments, in streets, in the woods, and especially over shooting pits. In all of these locations, Jews and their tormentors sometimes engaged in conversation; in the pogroms they recognized each other by social function or knew one another from work or even socially. Yet although pogrom violence transpired in modern societies, the face-to-face brutality cannot accurately be characterized as impersonal or bureaucratic or "modern" in the normal sociological sense of that term. It was intimate and cold-blooded.

This revised view of the Holocaust, one that concentrates on the local and the personal, expanded the focus of research from the death camps to killing fields across Europe, and from almost exclusive focus on Germans to the role of non-German civilians in the planning and killing. This has added not just new empirical layers but also extra normative dimensions, as the civilian populations of eastern Europe, keen to maintain their status as innocent victims of German aggression, have now been implicated in what were once thought to be exclusively German crimes. As Holocaust research has progressed, the event has become larger and more complicated and thus in principle even less amenable to being incorporated into political science.

Our strategy to overcome this obstacle corresponds to one also proposed by King: that of breaking down the Holocaust into multiple, discrete episodes. "Rather than one big thing, the Holocaust might now be described as an array of event categories" (King 2012, 326). That is, instead of seeing the Holocaust merely as one "case" of genocide, it is also productive to view it as many different events that taken together we label as one. The benefit of this "splitting" approach is that it invites theoretical innovation on important individual aspects of the Holocaust, such as within-country variation in rates of rescue and deportation (Braun 2016) and patterns of Jewish resistance (Finkel 2015), while relieving researchers of assuming the entire empirical and normative burden the Holocaust entails.

Why do pogroms occur in some localities and not others? We have addressed this long-puzzling question through an investigation of a wave of pogroms that occurred in the eastern Polish borderlands in summer 1941. Drawing on an original database of census and electoral results across Polish localities, we have found that some of the most commonly believed explanations for pogroms explain less than commonly thought. The 1941 pogroms were not orchestrated by the state and in general did not occur only where economic competition between Jews and non-Jews was fiercest, where sympathy for communism was the strongest, or where anti-Semitism was most prevalent.

Instead we find that the patterns of pogroms are better explained by power-threat theory, an approach first adumbrated by Blalock (1967) to explain race relations in the United States. It argues that where demographically weighty minorities politically mobilize in ways that challenge majority power, the majority will take actions to suppress the minority. In occupied Poland pogroms were most likely to occur where there were lots of Jews, where those Jews sought national equality with Poles and Ukrainians, and where there was some non-Jewish support for parties advocating tolerance of minorities. In those areas local Poles and Ukrainians seized the opportunity provided by the German invasion to rid themselves once and for all of future political rivals.

Our findings have implications for debates about the politics of memory and collective guilt, the breadth and depth of anti-Semitism in Poland, and the ever-difficult issue of multiculturalism and its relationship to intergroup violence. In the remainder of this conclusion, we address each of these topics and discuss the implications of our argument for the prevention of pogroms.

Collective Guilt

Assignations of collective guilt for crimes committed by non-Jewish civilians continue to burden relations between Poles, Ukrainians, and Jews. Experts disagree on the extent and type of collaboration and the attitudes of the local non-Jewish population toward its Jewish neighbors. In Poland much of the debate has centered on Jan Gross's *Neighbors* (2001), the intensive study of a summer 1941 pogrom in a single Polish town that in many ways inspired our own work. It received a mixed reception in Poland, both in the popular press, where doubt was expressed that Poles would attack Jews when they themselves were under German occupation, and among professional historians, some of whom welcomed it as shedding light on a dark period of Polish history (for various views, see Polonsky and Michlic, 2004). Others (e.g., Musiał 2004) challenged Gross's version of events and dismissed the pogrom as justified given the Jews' "anti-Polish" activities. Regarding Ukrainian civilian attitudes toward Jews, Yehuda Bauer characterizes them as "very hostile," while Shimon Redlich maintains that Ukrainians were "either indifferent or anti-Jewish" during World War II (Bauer 2009, 168; Redlich 2002, 104). Some consider any suggestion of popular complicity in the pogroms, whether spontaneous or under the leadership of nationalist militias, as a defamation of the nation and its heroes.[1]

Our findings shed light on these competing claims by subjecting different viewpoints to empirical scrutiny. One of our most important empirical discoveries is that across more than two thousand localities in Poland's eastern borderlands, pogroms occurred in just over 10 percent of localities where Jews and non-Jews dwelled together. Most Poles and Ukrainians were not perpetrators of, or even bystanders to, pogroms, and most Jews were not victims of them. Regarding the notion of national guilt, these findings reinforce the argument in Mann (2005, 20) that whole nations do not act collectively and therefore should not be held collectively responsible for the crimes committed by a minority.

Anti-Semitism in Poland

The relative rarity of pogroms is inconsistent with widely held beliefs about the extent and depth of anti-Semitism in interwar Poland. As we discussed in chapter 1, given the long history of often violent conflict between Jews and non-Jews in Polish lands, it is easy to believe that most Poles and Ukrainians were anti-Semites just waiting for a good opportunity to attack Jews. Yet if this were true, we ought to have observed many more pogroms than we do. After all, summer 1941 was a historically unprecedented opportunity to attack. The two-year Soviet occupation that had just ended had set national groups against one another and coarsened society. When the Soviet occupation collapsed, so did state authority, and with it state power to punish the perpetrators of violence. Non-Jews were free to settle scores with the Jews, with the passive encouragement if not active incitement of German forces. Yet mostly pogroms did not happen. We do not doubt that some form of informal anti-Semitism was widespread, but it was not intense enough in most places to have produced a pogrom.

A second implication of the relative rarity of pogroms relates, ironically, to the status of the 1941 pogrom wave within the Holocaust itself. Goldhagen (1996, 23–24) introduced the term "eliminationist anti-Semitism" to distinguish the German plan to exterminate world Jewry from less lethal quotidian antipathy toward Jews ("casual" anti-Semitism). Eliminationist anti-Semitism is catholic in aspiration, sparing neither the very old nor the very young. It does not distinguish between the assimilated and the unassimilated, or between the religious and the secular. The 1941 pogroms, by contrast, did not affect the vast majority of Jews in eastern Poland, and in fact were not even the most widespread or deadly pogrom wave to have struck the Polish lands. That "honor" belongs to the 1918–1920 wave, which featured eight hundred pogroms and at least fifty thousand deaths (Abramson 1999; Gergel 1951). This is not to deny the extreme and even eliminationist intent of some of the 1941 pogroms, such as Jedwabne. But it is to recognize that although the 1941 pogroms were a prelude to the Holocaust, they do not necessarily belong to it.

Cultural Difference and Ethnic Conflict

A third implication of pogrom rarity speaks to contemporary debates about the relationship between cultural difference and the outbreak of intergroup violence (Williams 1994; Brubaker and Laitin 1998). Contrary to what scholarly understanding of nation building and the integration of outsiders would lead us to expect, cultural assimilation is no guarantee of safety.[2] In fact, it may not even be necessary. The pogroms of 1941 cannot be reduced simply to Polish and Ukrainian reactions to Jewish cultural difference. Even Jews who shed the outward signs of their religious distinctiveness (and thus appeared more "Polish" or "Ukrainian") were on the whole still influenced by and respected Jewish cultural practices such as eschewing pork, avoiding work on the Sabbath, and participating in Jewish life-cycle events. Even tolerant Poles and Ukrainians would have acknowledged these practices as different from their own. For those Poles and Ukrainians who did seek to eradicate any culture other than their own, virtually all Jews should have been targets.

The pattern of where pogroms took place, however, belies the expectation that they ought to occur where Jewish cultural difference from Poles or Ukrainians was greatest. Cultural distance between Jews and non-Jews was greatest in the case of the religiously traditional Hasidim or Mitnagdim, who differed from non-Jews (and many nonorthodox Jews) not just in their dress but in their religious practices and use of Yiddish as an everyday language. Yet we find that pogroms were more likely to occur not where Jewish religious Orthodoxy was prevalent (in areas where the traditionalist Agudas was strong), but in Zionist strongholds, where Jews were far more likely to speak Polish (or Ukrainian) and to share similar tastes with their Polish and Ukrainian neighbors. This is not to claim that during pogroms traditionalist religious Jews were spared; where pogroms did occur they certainly were not and may even have made easier targets precisely because of their visibility. But traditionalist Jews were in less danger of violence in their own communities than in those dominated by Zionists.

The political character of the pogroms buttresses the argument of Mann (2005) that nationalism becomes dangerous when politicized and can be toxic when mass politics pits majority and minority nationalisms against one another. At the same time, there is an important difference between the kinds of violence that Mann theorizes and the 1941 pogroms: Mann's are top-down, orchestrated by the state; ours are bottom-up, not quite spontaneous but certainly not centrally coordinated.

This difference had important consequences for those who were targeted. As we discussed in chapter 1, Polish and Ukrainian nationalist elites sought homogeneous nation-states and shared an ideology that viewed Jews, regardless of the political and religious distinctions among them, as essentially unassimilable. If these nationalist elites had led the 1941 pogroms, the violence would have been far less discriminating and far more deadly.

Pogrom Prevention

If nationalist political competition lay behind the pogroms, might a different sort of intergroup politics have prevented them? To the extent there is a hopeful lesson from our otherwise grim analysis, it rides on the answer to this question. There has been no shortage of proposed solutions to the problem of ethnic conflict in divided societies, but most are unlikely to have prevented the pogroms. Some, such as subnational partition or federalism, assume that the minority in question is territorially concentrated or can be made so through internal displacement or forced emigration. Territorial-based solutions could not have prevented the violence in Poland because Jews were dispersed across thousands of communities.

Even if the Great Powers had countenanced the creation of a Jewish "homeland" within Poland as a condition of recreating the Polish state after World War I, such a homeland would have increased de facto Jewish "ownership" of a bounded piece of Polish territory, much as it did for the Galician Ukrainians, who were a commanding majority in eastern Galicia and resented Polish presence on their territory. A Jewish homeland would have posed an even greater challenge to Polish dominance than dealing merely with Jewish nationalist parties. Although a geographical concentration of Jews might actually have reduced the frequency of pogroms (given the resultant dearth of non-Jews able to commit them), it would also undoubtedly have increased other forms of anti-Jewish violence. Here the Volhynian Ukrainian parallel is instructive. Poles and Ukrainians did not in general commit pogroms against one another, but they did fight deadly battles during the war for control over Volhynian territory.

Other proposed solutions, such as power sharing, are in principle compatible with dispersed minority settlement and also weaken the link between the relative sizes of demographic groups and the political advantages that thereby accrue. But they are likewise highly unlikely to have prevented violence. One purpose of power-sharing agreements is to give minorities enough stake in the system to encourage them to work within rather than against the established political order. In exchange for minority moderation, the majority accedes to some of the minority's political demands. Such a setup worked in interwar Czechoslovakia, where a de facto "ethnic corporatism" involving Czechs and Germans stabilized politics for a decade. In interwar Poland, however, most Jewish parties were working within the system even without a guaranteed presence at the negotiating table implied in a corporatist arrangement. If such a power-sharing agreement had been imposed from abroad it would have granted symbolic equality to Polish and Jewish interests, which is precisely what the perpetrators of pogroms were challenging.

But these and other institutional solutions to ethnic violence suffer from an even more fundamental limitation: they all presume a functioning state and something like settled politics, both of which were conspicuously lacking across Poland's eastern borderlands in summer 1941. How can antiminority violence that emerges from mass political competition be prevented when the normal institutional tools are not available, when perpetrators may act according to their impulses, without fear of legal consequences? Our analysis suggests three possibilities.

One is for the minority to reduce its nationalist demands. Absent the perception that Jews supported a competing national project, there would presumably have been fewer non-Jewish perpetrators and greater overall solidarity between Jews and non-Jews. This is not to say that nationalist Jews bore ultimate responsibility for the pogroms. Quite the contrary is true. The Minorities Treaty that brought Poland and other East European states into existence after World War I enshrined minority-group rights, including the right to preserve minority languages and cultures. Jews and other minorities who mobilized in defense of these rights were merely acting in accord with the political order in which they found themselves. The irony of the Great Powers' emphasis on minority rights in the new East European states is that what was intended by the Great Powers to help minorities preserve their distinct identities encouraged a form of minority political mobilization that ultimately triggered pogrom violence.

A second possibility is to counteract the polarizing effects of minority nationalism. This might take the form of the "bridging capital" that results from cross-ethnic civil society organizations that reduce the social support for violence (e.g., Varshney 2002, discussed in chapter 6). Or it might be achieved by fostering the kind of political heterogeneity conducive to interethnic peace. Horowitz (1985, 646–647) argues that political fragmentation of the majority group and multi-ethnic parties can reduce ethnic conflict by reducing overall polarization. While that may be true under conditions of normal politics, our findings are equivocal on whether such heterogeneity matters after state collapse. Limitations of data and method prevent us from identifying what kinds of local cross-ethnic political alliances might have deterred any potential pogromists. For the northeastern borderlands as a whole, however, we found that in pogrom-free areas Jews were twice as likely to support Piłsudski's BBWR, the Polish party advocating ethnic tolerance, than in areas where pogroms occurred. But even then, the higher level of support was only 18 percent, promising but hardly an overwhelming or even firm basis for Polish-Jewish political solidarity.

At the same time, the popularity of parties seeking interethnic accommodation was in general positively correlated with the probability of a pogrom, a finding consistent with power-threat theory. This was not true for communist parties, however, where local support strongly reduced the likelihood of violence. We attribute communism's "immunizing effect" to its professed universalism, which at least in theory rejected the legitimacy of ethnic divisions. On the ground, local non-Jewish communists undoubtedly opposed nationalist violence and may well also have sheltered threatened Jews. Having local communists is of course not the only way to ward off pogroms. Any group that felt solidarity with Jews could have performed the same function.

This brings us to the issue of local popular sanction against pogrom violence. According to Horowitz, "The most significant facilitator of [ethnic] rioting is authoritative social support for group violence" (2001, 350). For understandable reasons, researchers have devoted more energy to documenting where and how violence occurred than to chronicling humdrum life in peaceful localities, so it is difficult to know whether or not local communities discouraged pogroms in places where they did not occur. What we do know is that where pogroms *did* occur, the social context could be neutral or supportive.

Bystanders have been relatively neglected in Holocaust research, but as our narratives in chapters 4 and 5 illustrate, they witnessed the violence. The ubiquitous presence of the urban crowd in the photographs and film clips of pogroms reminds us of something that should be obvious: the pogroms were public, social events, with an often carnival-like atmosphere. On the one hand are images and sounds of naked Jewish women cringing and running; Jewish men being shoved, dragged, or frog-marched to locations unknown; and the elderly and children standing with their hands in the air. On the other hand are the non-Jewish onlookers. Some are aghast, but more are just milling about, smiling, or even laughing as the music and church bells celebrate the violence. Under these circumstances, perpetrators surely felt encouragement rather than disapproval. We leave for future research the question of whether the expected absence of such approval prevented would-be perpetrators from actually committing violence.

The third option is to redefine the boundaries of "the people" in a way that dissolves or at least mitigates political competition between majority and minority. Since Rousseau, democratic theorists have understood that the most formidable challenge to democracy is pluralism. A people that governs itself must still define itself as a people. In parts of the West, the question of peoplehood, of nationhood, was resolved before the advent of electoral competition. In much of the world and in Eastern Europe in particular, it was not. Just who belonged, who was a member of the community, remained and remains an open and contested question.

Research on nation building suggests two modalities of identity change. One involves assimilating the minority into the majority group. Byman (2000, 159–164), for example, describes how over a period of many decades the Persians managed, through a combination of repression and co-optation, to destroy the Bakhtiyaris' distinct identity and absorb them into the Persian people. If it had been possible in interwar Poland to turn Jews into Poles or Ukrainians, then certainly there would have been no pogroms in 1941. But for Jews, as for any literate minority with an educated intelligentsia that is conscious of its own history, the chances of such assimilation were slim, at least in the short term. (It is also the case that the anti-Semitic wings of both Polish and Ukrainian nationalism, beholden at the time to biological understandings of Jewishness, did not wish to assimilate Jews.)

The second modality involves the creation and propagation of a new identity expansive enough to accommodate all ethnic groups in society. This was the strategy followed by many postcolonial leaderships who needed a way to create solidarity among otherwise disparate and feuding ethnic and tribal groups (Darden, forthcoming). It was also pursued in Czechoslovakia, Yugoslavia, and the Soviet Union, each of which had an informal ruling nationality (Czech, Serb, and Russian, respectively) that sought to create multi-ethnic "federal" identities (Czechoslovak, Yugoslav, and Soviet). As we discuss in chapter 4, this was the strategy of Marshal Piłsudski, who attempted to create a "statist" rather than an "ethnic" order that would recognize some minority group rights in exchange for loyalty to the interwar Polish state. We noted earlier that there is some evidence that pogroms were less likely where Jews supported Piłsudski's party, but it was not just a matter of convincing some Jews; nationalist Poles (and Jews and Ukrainians) would also have had to adjust their ideas of "the people," and thus who warranted solidarity and who did not. There is broad scholarly consensus that this process takes decades rather than years, too much time to have spared the 1941 pogrom victims, but at least it offers the hope of averting similar violence at other times and places.

Whatever the means by which pogroms are prevented, one thing is clear: where minorities are better integrated, they are less despised, looked on with less indifference, and more likely to be thought of as part of the community and deserving of protection. What was true in summer 1941 across communities in Poland is undoubtedly true in other national contexts: some members of the majority feel solidarity with their minority neighbors while others stand ready to commit violence or stand by and do nothing. Surviving and preventing pogroms may depend more on the presence of friends from other groups than on "enemies," and it was harder to find those friends where the bare minimum of social solidarity was missing.

Appendix

Pogroms in the Eastern Borderlands, Summer 1941

LOCALITY	SOURCE	VOIVODSHIP
Bereżne	Snyder (2008, 93); Spector, 65	Volhynia
Bereżnica	Encyclopedia of Jewish Life before and during the Holocaust, 116	Polesie
Białobożnica	Kruglov (2010, 338)	Tarnopol
Bielsk	AŻIH 301-4769; AŻIH 301-988; Żbikowski (2006, 226)	Białystok
Bóbrka	Kruglov (2010, 336)	Lwów
Bogdanówka	Kruglov (2000, 157); GARF, f.7021, op.75, d.9, l.94	Tarnopol
Bolechów	AŻIH 301-2145, 301-2146;	Stanisławów
Bołszowce	Kruglov (2010, 339)	Stanisławów
Boremel	Spector, 65	Volhynia
Borszczów	AŻIH 301-3770; Struve (2015, 555)	Tarnopol Borynia
	Kruglov (2010, 336)	Stanisławów
Borysław	AŻIH 301-1205, 301-1096, 301-1091, 301-4512, 301-800, 301-2138, 301-2198, 301-2465, 301-2575, 301-3119, 301-3120, 301-3359, 301-5434, 302-323, 301-1091; van der Linden-Wolanski, 35–38	Lwów
Bransk	Żbikowski (2006, 224)	Białystok
Brody	Żbikowski (1992, 7); Kruglov (2012, 757); Kruglov (2010, 335)	Lwów
Brześć nad Bugem	Żbikowski (2006, 224)	Polesie
Brzeżany	AŻIH 301-672, 301-3236, 301-5917	Tarnopol
Buczacz	AŻIH 301-2605; Żbikowski (1992, 12–13)	Tarnopol
Bursztyn	Kruglov (2010, 339)	Stanisławów
Busk	AŻIH 301-477	Tarnopol
Chmieliska	Kruglov (2010, 338)	Tarnopol
Chomiakowka ad Jagielnica	Kruglov (2000, 157) GARF, f.7021, op.75, d.9, l.94	Tarnopol
Chorostków	Weiss (1990, 111); Kruglov (2010, 338)	Tarnopol
Choroszcz	Żbikowski (2006, 224)	Białystok
Czortków	AŻIH 301-3754, 301-3337, 301-5710; Żbikowski (1992, 12–13)	Tarnopol
Dábrowica	Snyder (2008, 93); https://pl.wikipedia.org/wiki/D\%C4\%85browica_(miasto)	Polesie
Dawidgródek	Idan et al., 385	Polesie

(continued)

APPENDIX

(continued)

LOCALITY	SOURCE	VOIVODSHIP
Delatyn	Gilbert, 174	Stanisławów
Dereżyce	Jüdisches Komitee Drohobycz	Lwów
Dobromil	Kruglov (2004, 11); Struve (2015, 217)	Lwów
Dokszyce	Żbikowski (2006, 223)	Wilno
Dolina	Kruglov (2000, 157)	Tarnopol
Drohiczyn	AŻIH 301-1257, 301-973	Białystok
Drohobycz	AŻIH 301-1277, 301-1129, 301-344, 301-847, 301-1177	Lwów
Dubie	AŻIH 302-227; Żbikowski (1992, 12–13)	Tarnopol
Dubno	Friedman, 199; Snyder (2008, 93)	Volhynia Dzurów
	Kruglov (2010, 340)	Stanisławów
Dzuryn	Kruglov (2010, 338)	Tarnopol
Dzwingorod	Kruglov (2000, 157)	Tarnopol
Dzwiniacz	Kruglov (2010, 338)	Tarnopol
Głebokie	Żbikowski (2006, 223)	Wilno
Gliniany	Gilbert, 175	Tarnopol
Goniádz	Żbikowski (2006, 224)	Białystok
Grabowka	Kruglov (2010, 339)	Stanisławów
Grajewo	Żbikowski (2006, 223)	Białystok
Grodno	Żbikowski (1992, 12–13)	Białystok
Grzymalow	Struve (2015, 626–628); Kruglov (2004, 10); Kruglov (2010, 337)	Tarnopol
Gródek Jagiellońsi	Kruglov (2010, 335)	Lwów
Horodenka	Kruglov (2010, 339)	Stanisławów
Horochów	Kruglov (2000, 29); Snyder (2008, 93)	Volhynia
Horodyszcze	Jüdisches Komitee Drohobycz	Lwów
Horodziec	Spector, 86	Polesie
Husiatyn	Kruglov (2010, 337)	Tarnopol
Jabłonica	AŻIH 301-1398, 301-2153; Kruglov (2010, 340)	Stanisławów
Jagielnica	Struve (2015, 553); Kruglov (2010, 338)	Tarnopol
Janów	AŻIH 301-1251	Polesie
Jaryczow nowy	Lower, 63	Lwów Jaworów
	AŻIH 301-1912; Kruglov (2010, 336)	Lwów Jaworów
	Kruglov (2010, 339)	Stanisławów
Jazłowiec	Kruglov (2010, 337)	Tarnopol
Jedwabne	AŻIH 301-613, 301-1846, 301-2405; Gross (2001)	Białystok
Jezierna	Kruglov (2010, 337); Struve (2015, 589)	Tarnopol
Kamień Koszyrski	Snyder (2008, 93); Żbikowski (2006, 223)	Polesie
Kamionka Strumiłowa	AŻIH 301-613, 301-1846, 301-2405	Tarnopol
Kleszczele	Żbikowski (2006, 223–224)	Białystok
Klewań	Kruglov (2004, 11); Snyder (2008, 93)	Volhynia

LOCALITY	SOURCE	VOIVODSHIP
Knihynicze	Kruglov (2010, 340)	Stanisławów
Knyszyn	Żbikowski (2006, 223)	Białystok
Kobryń	AŻIH 201-1072	Polesie
Kolińce	Kruglov (2010, 339)	Stanisławów
Kolno	Żbikowski (2006, 224)	Białystok
Kołomyja	AŻIH 301-1398, 301-2153, 301-2579; Żbikowski (1993, 178)	Stanisławów
Koniuchy	Struve (2015, 113) Kruglov (2010, 338)	
Kopyczyńce	http://www.jewishgen.org/yizkor/pinkas_poland/pol2_00486.html	Tarnopol
Korycin	AŻIH 301-1251	Białystok
Korzec	Spector, 65; Snyder (2008, 93)	Volhynia
Kosów	Kruglov (2010, 339); Weiss (1990, 110); Struve (2015, 544)	Stanisławów
Kostopol	Spector, 65; Snyder (2008, 93)	Volhynia
Kropiwnik nowy	Struve (2015, 487)	Lwów
Kropiwnik stary	Struve (2015, 487)	Lwów
Krynki	Żbikowski (2006, 330)	Białystok
Krywka	Kruglov (2000, 48)	Stanisławów
Krzemieniec	Arad et al., 11, 31, 39; Snyder (2008, 93)	Volhynia
Kulików	AŻIH 301-1403, 301-583, 301-1801; Struve (2015, 671	Lwów
Łachwa	AŻIH 2442	Polesie
Łanowce	Snyder (2008, 93); Kruglov (2010, 337)	Tarnopol
Łastowki	Jüdisches Komitee Drohobycz	Lwów
Libuchora	Kruglov (2010, 337)	Stanisławów
Łohiszyn	Żbikowski (2006, 346)	Polesie
Łomża	AŻIH 301-4391	Białystok
Lubieszow	AŻIH 301-1174; Snyder (2008, 93)	Polesie
Łuck	AŻIH 301-1805, 301-5657; Snyder (2008, 93)	Volhynia
Ludwipol	Bauer (2009, 181); Snyder (2008, 93)	Volhynia
Łuka	AŻIH 301-1398, 302-105	Stanisławów
Łuka Wielka	AŻIH 301-1398, 302-105	Tarnopol
Luvipol	Snyder (2008, 93); Spector, 65	Volhynia
Majdan	Struve (2015, 488); Jüdisches Komitee Drohobycz	Lwów
Matków	Kruglov (2010, 336)	Stanisławów
Miedwedowce	Kruglov (2010, 337)	Tarnopol
Miasto Lwów	Pohl (1996, 2); AŻIH 301-18, 301-1403, 301-1737, 301-1170, 301-4654, 301-98, 301-339, 301-442, 301-770, 301-785, 301-1809, 301-1864, 301-2242, 301-2522, 302-24, 302-26, 302-61, 302-182, 301-4355; Himka (2011, 209–243)	Lwów

(continued)

APPENDIX

(continued)

LOCALITY	SOURCE	VOIVODSHIP
Miedzyrzecz	Spector, 74	Volhynia
Mikuńince	Struve (2015, 670)	Tarnopol
Mizocz	Snyder (2008, 93); Spector, 65	Volhynia
Młynów	Kruglov (2004, 11)	Volhynia
Monasteryzyska	Kruglov (2010, 337)	Tarnopol
Mościska	Żbikowski (1992, 12–13); Kruglov (2000, 47); Kruglov (2010, 336)	Lwów
Mosty Wielkie	Struve (2015, 670); Kruglov (2004, 11); Kruglov (2000, 109)	Lwów
Motol	Żbikowski (2006, 223)	Polesie
Nadorożna	Kruglov (2010, 339)	Stanisławów
Nahujowice	Struve (2015, 487); Kruglov (2000, 47)	Lwów
Nadwórna	Kruglov (2010, 339)	Stanisławów
Niemirów	AŻIH 301-4950; Kruglov (2010, 336)	Lwów
Niezwiska	AŻIH 301-5775; Kruglov (2010, 339)	Stanisławów
Niżniów	Kruglov (2010, 339)	Stanisławów
Nowe Miasto	Kruglov (2004, 49)	Lwów
Nowosielica	Kruglov (2010, 340)	Stanisławów
Obertyn	AŻIH 301-1072; Struve (2015, 660)	Stanisławów
Oleszów	Kruglov (2010, 339)	Stanisławów
Ołyka	Snyder (2008, 93); Kruglov (2004, 10)	Volhynia
Oryszkowce	Kruglov (2010, 338)	Tarnopol
Ostapie	Kruglov (2010, 338)	Tarnopol
Ostróg	http://yizkor.nypl.org/index.php?id=2501	Volhynia
Ottynia	AŻIH 301-2153	Stanisławów
Pauszkówka	Kruglov (2010, 338)	Tarnopol
Petlikowce Stare	Struve (2015, 555); AŻIH 301-3770; Kruglov (2010, 337)	Tarnopol
Petranka	Kruglov (2010, 339)	Stanisławów
Pilatkowce	Kruglov (2010, 338); Żbikowski (1992, 12–13)	Tarnopol
Pinsk	Żbikowski (2006, 221)	Polesie
Podhajce	AŻIH 302-227; Kruglov (2010, 338)	Tarnopol
Podwołoczynska	Kruglov (2010, 337); AŻIH 301-1745	Tarnopol
Polowce	Struve (2015, 544); Kruglov (2010, 338)	Tarnopol
Potok złoty	Kruglov (2010, 338); Struve (2015, 533)	Tarnopol
Prużana	Żbikowski (2006, 223)	Polesie
Radziłów	Żbikowski (2006, 223); AŻIH 301-974, 301-1284, 301-1994	Białystok
Radziwiłłów	https://www.jewishvirtuallibrary.org/jsource/judaica/ejud_0002_0017_0_16341.html	Lwów
Rafałówka	Snyder (2008, 93); Spector, 65	Volhynia
Rajgród	Żbikowski (2006, 224)	Białystok
Rakowiec	Kruglov (2010, 340)	Stanisławów

LOCALITY	SOURCE	VOIVODSHIP
Ratno	Snyder (2008, 93); Spector, 65	Volhynia
Rawa Ruska	Żbikowski (1992, 12–13); Kruglov (2010, 335)	Lwów
Rokitno	AŻIH 301-3179	Polesie
Rożanka	Kruglov (2010, 336)	Lwów
Równe	AŻIH 301-2886; Żbikowski (1992, 12–13)	Volhynia
Rożana	Żbikowski (2006, 224)	Polesie
Rożniatów	Kruglov (2010, 339)	Stanisławów
Rożyszcze	Spector, 65	Volhynia
Rudki	AŻIH 302-215, Struve (2015, 444)	Lwów
Rutki-Kossaki	Żbikowski (2006, 223)	Białystok
Rydoduby	Kruglov (2010, 338)	Tarnopol
Sambor	AŻIH 301-3768; Struve (2015, 47, 675)	Lwów Sarny
Sarny	Brendan and Lower, 93; Spector, 74	Volhynia
Sasów	AŻIH 301-1403, 301-1200, 301-3701	Tarnopol
Schodnica	AŻIH 301-2931; Struve (2015, 484); Kruglov (2010, 336)	Lwów
Serniki	Spector, 73; Snyder (2008, 93)	Polesie
Siemiatycze	Żbikowski (2006, 223); AŻIH 301-1463, 301-973	Białystok
Skała	Kruglov (2010, 337)	Tarnopol
Skałat	Struve (2015, 622); Kruglov (2010, 337)	Tarnopol
Skorodynce	Struve (2015, 544); Kruglov (2010, 338)	Tarnopol
Śniatyn	AŻIH 301-2153; Kruglov (2010, 339)	Stanisławów
Sokal	Kruglov (2010, 336); Żbikowski (1992, 12–13)	Lwów
Sokołów	Kruglov (2010, 339)	Tarnopol
Sokoły	Żbikowski (2006, 229)	Białystok
Stanisławów	AŻIH 301-1734, 301-2514, 302-135, 302-175	Stanisławów
Stary Sambor	Manor, 37; Struve (2015, 438, 442–444)	Lwów
Stawiski	AŻIH 301-1958; Żbikowski (2006, 223–224)	Białystok
Stepań	Snyder (2008, 93); Spector, 78	Volhynia
Stolin	https://sites.google. com/site/stolinshtetl/stolin-the-holocaust; https://drive.google.com/file/d/0B-v1Xj6GQGltMjIyMmZhODQtNzkwYS00YzJiLWFkOTUtZTJkMTA2MDd view?num=50\&sort=name\&layout=list\&pli=1	Polesie
Strusów	Kruglov (2010, 337)	Tarnopol
Stryj	AŻIH 301-2570	Stanisławów
Suchowola	Żbikowski (2006, 225)	Białystok
Swidowa	AŻIH 301-4976; Kruglov (2010, 338)	Tarnopol
Swie ta Wola	Żbikowski (2006, 225)	Polesie
Szczerzec	http://kehilalinks.jewishgen.org/Shchirets/	Lwów
Szczuczyn	Żbikowski (2006, 223); AŻIH 301-1958; http://www.szczuczyn.com/yizkorbook2a.htm#golding	Białystok
Szumsk	Snyder (2008, 93)	Volhynia

(continued)

(continued)

LOCALITY	SOURCE	VOIVODSHIP
Targowica	Spector, 87	Volhynia
Tarnopol	Mec dykowski, 250–259; AŻIH 301-1036, 301-20, 301-367, 301-2165, 301-3774, 302-158, 302-295, 301-1038	Tarnopol
Telechany	Żbikowski (2006, 346)	Polesie
Tłumacz	http://kehilalinks.jewishgen.org/tlumach/tlumach.html; Struve (2015, 653); Kruglov (2010, 339)	Stanisławów
Tłuste	AŻIH 301-3337, 301-3459, 301-4976; Kruglov (2010, 339)	Tarnopol
Toporów	Dacbrowska and Wein, 253; Struve (2015, 670)	Tarnopol
Tremblowa	AŻIH 301-4973; Kruglov (2010, 338)	Tarnopol
Truskawiec	AŻIH 301-3119; Kruglov (2010, 336)	Lwów
Trybuchowce	Kruglov (2010, 337)	Tarnopol
Trzcianne	Żbikowski (2006, 223)	Białystok
Tuczyn	AŻIH 301-3178; Snyder (2008, 93)	Volhynia
Turka	AŻIH 301-4974, 301-2931; Struve (2015, 486)	Lwów
Turówka	Kruglov (2010, 338)	Tarnopol
Tykocin	Żbikowski (2007, 346)	Białystok
Ułaszkowce	AŻIH 301-3337	Tarnopol
Uroż	Jüdisches Komitee Drohobycz	Lwów
Wasilkow	Machcewicz and Persak, 356–358; AŻIH 301-1266	Białystok
Wacsosz	AŻIH 301-1846, 301-1933, 301-1955; Machcewicz and Persak, 169–172	Białystok
Wielkie Oczy	Kruglov (2010, 337)	Lwów
Wiśniowiec	Spector, 65, Kruglov (2000, 157)	Volhynia
Wizna	AŻIH 301-4391; Żbikowski (2006, 223)	Białystok
Włodzimierzec	Spector, 92; Snyder (2008, 93)	Volhynia
Wołkowysk	Żbikowski (2006, 356)	Białystok
Wołosianka	Kruglov (2010, x)	Stanisławów
Woronow	Żbikowski (1992, 12–13); AŻIH 302-105	Lwów
Wysokie Mazowieckie	Żbikowski (2006, 223)	Białystok
Zabłudów	AŻIH 301-3604, 301-1266; Żbikowski (2006, 223)	Białystok
Zaborów	Żbikowski (1992, 12–13)	Lwów
Załolkieć	Jüdisches Komitee Drohobycz	Lwów
Załośce	Kruglov (2010, 337)	Tarnopol
Zambrów	Jasiewicz (2000)	Białystok
Zarecby Kosciełne	AŻIH 301-1998; Żbikowski (2006, 223)	Białystok
Zbaraż	AŻIH 301-2571	Tarnopol
Zborów	AŻIH 301-2520; Golczewski (2008, 137)	Tarnopol
Zdołbunów	AŻIH 301-1266; Spector, 238	Volhynia
Zelwa	Żbikowski (2006, 223)	Białystok
Zielince	Struve (2015, 555)	Tarnopol
Złoczów	AŻIH 301-1403, 301-87, 301-2850	Tarnopol
Żołkiew	AŻIH 301-1892, 302-141	Lwów

Notes

1. WHY NEIGHBORS KILL NEIGHBORS

1. The testimonies of the Jewish Historical Institute in Warsaw are filled with such descriptions. The atrocities described in this sentence occurred in a single pogrom, in Stawiski. See Faygl Golombek's testimony AŻIH 301-1858. See also Yizkor book testimony of Chaim Wilamowski: http://www.jewishgen.org/Yizkor/stawiski/ sta299.html, p. 301.
2. Żbikowski 2007, 334–335, 334n61, 335n65.
3. Ibid., 335n67.
4. Ibid., 335n64, 335n66.
5. Ibid., 347–348.
6. Żbikowski 2007, 334n61.
7. Ibid., 335n64.
8. Ibid., 335n 67.
9. "You know, if you had something with the Jews, you killed them. I'll give you an example. After the Soviets retreated, that summer of 'forty-one, a lot of Jewish boys who'd been conscripted by the Russians had made their way home to Bolechów–they'd been drafted into the Russian army and were returning home. So the Ukrainians were standing on the bridge looking into the returning soldiers' eyes as they came back, and if they thought someone was a Jew, they threw him down from the bridge into the river. And it was a river with big boulders and so forth, you can imagine what happened" (Mendelsohn 2006, 195).
10. Cited in Melzer 1997, 21.
11. Cited in Rudnicki 2005, 160.
12. We borrow the label "pessimistic" from Polonsky 1997, which provides a balanced overview of the debate on how much anti-Semitism there was in interwar Poland. See also Mendelsohn 1986.
13. The literature on racial threat is enormous. A good place to start is the selections in Wang and Todak (2016). Because we conceive of the "threat" in power-threat theory primarily in political terms (and measure it that way), we also refer to this approach as "political threat."
14. We actually expect the relationship between the perceived minority threat and the incidence of antiminority violence to be nonlinear over the full range of the relevant demographic and political variables. Thus, there should be a positive relationship between the proportion of Jews/support for parties advocating Jewish equality and the probability of a pogrom, but only up to a point. As those proportions become overwhelming the probability of a pogrom should drop. In the limit, where all non-Jews support Jewish equality, no pogrom should occur. As we discuss in chapter 3, however, the overwhelming number of our observations have low or moderate proportions of Jews and political support for Jewish equality, where the expected relationship should be positive.

2. ETHNIC POLITICS IN THE BORDERLANDS

1. Scholars disagree on whether much of the Białystok district should be designated as part of the kresy. For simplicity we do so.

2. Those with the least established sense of national identity were the Slavic-speaking peasants of the Russian partition who would later be Belarusians and Ukrainians. See Snyder 2003, 144–145.

3. Within the Habsburg partition, however, many Jews did acculturate along Polish lines, as seen in the Polish census of 1921 when a large portion of respondents in Galicia who declared themselves Jewish by religion opted to classify themselves Polish by nationality. On changing Jewish identities in the interwar shtetl, see Kassow 1989.

4. Assimilation was, in any case, largely a phenomenon of the larger cities of central Poland and, to some extent, Lwów. Even there, fully assimilated Jews found themselves received as "amateur Poles" (Krzemiński 1998, 74).

5. Boycotts and violence occurred in Warsaw in 1912 after the city's Jewish population supported the Socialists rather than the National Democrats in the election to the Russian Duma.

6. National Democrats dominated the Constituent Sejm because the 1919 elections were held only in western and central Poland, the traditional Endecja strongholds.

7. Unless otherwise indicated, the party descriptions follow the platforms and narratives laid out in Bełcikowski 1925.

8. The Piast opposed any radical land reform touching on the large estates of the kresy primarily because the beneficiaries would have been primarily Ukrainian and Belarusian peasants.

9. A further indication of the complexity of relations between Zionists and their non-Jewish neighbors in eastern Galicia comes through in the account of strategic voting in the Reichsrat election of Vasyl Kuchabsky, who served in the Sich Riflemen during the Ukrainian struggle for independence: "In 1907 the Ukrainian political leaders, to the great surprise of the Poles, were in a position, in those electoral districts where Ukrainians did not have a majority, to direct tens of thousands of Ukrainian votes, almost at will, toward the Zionists, for example, in order to prevent the Poles from winning the mandate" (Kuchabsky 2009, 11). This, despite the fact that by 1919 the Galician Zionists had a reputation for being polonophile or at least highly polonized.

10. This was true until the late 1930s, when the Bund took voters from the Zionists in many locations, although not primarily in the kresy, once the Zionists proved incapable of defending Jewish rights and communal interests.

11. Our analysis of more than one thousand settlements in eastern Galicia shows that 89 percent of Ukrainians did not vote. On the methods for this estimate, see chapter 3. Communists in eastern Galicia split on the boycott primarily along ethnic lines (Radziejowski 1983, 16).

12. During 1920, as Poland asserted control over the East, followers of Dmowski and Piłsudski disagreed on just how far east Poland's borders should extend. National Democrats favored incorporating eastern Galicia with its large urban Polish enclaves, especially in Lwów, but worried that a potential Piłsudskiite "push to Kiev" would bring in an unassimilable mass of Ukrainians and lead to a federative arrangement, an updated version of the premodern Polish-Lithuanian Commonwealth, rather than a national state. The National Democrats prevented a "push to Kiev" by dominating Polish diplomatic representation to the Entente powers (Krzemiński 1998, 60).

13. In the run-up to the election in 1928, Kazimierz Świtalski, a Piłsudskiite and the chief of the Political Department in the Ministry of the Interior (and later prime minister of Poland), was dispatched to eastern Poland to negotiate especially with the Ukrainian and Jewish minorities. His diary of these machinations, frequently involving threats and bribery, show just how intractable the problem was from Warsaw's standpoint. Consider one entry, that of November 10, 1927. Świtalski records that he had spent several hours with Dmytro Levytsky (cofounder of the UNDO and editor of its newspaper) discussing

the possibility of a common Polish-Ukrainian-Jewish list. Seats would be distributed according to demographic proportion in individual constituencies. Levytsky refused to sign on, believing that the idea was "premature" for both Poles and Ukrainians. He also worried about the accusations of betrayal from other Ukrainian parties, especially the Socialist Radical Party and the Communist Party of Western Ukraine. The same day Świtalski met with Leon Reich, leader of the east Galician General Zionists, who complained about the pressure he was under to join the Bloc of National Minorities, which he understood the government viewed as a subversive organization. Świtalski argued that the Jews would be best served by being part of a state list, and "the fate of the Jews did not depend as much on the number of their seats in the Sejm as on the configuration of Polish political forces. The BNM might offer tactical success and more seats, but, strategically, joining the bloc would also give the impression that the Jews supported anti-state elements." Świtalski believed that if the elections were carried out along ethnic lines (by which he meant ethnic lists for individual minorities), ethnic conflicts would worsen, which would in turn "prevent the process of negotiating a modus vivendi in Eastern Galicia" (Świtalski 1992, 214–215).

14. Without these rights, school diplomas would not be recognized by institutions of higher education.

15. Apart from invalidating ballots, the regime kept some parties off voting lists. It put the BBWR in the first place among the state lists and changed the Bloc of National Minorities from list number 16 (it was known as "the sixteen") to 18 in an attempt to reduce its total.

16. The BBWR and its allied parties won 24 percent of the vote.

17. Archiwum Akt Nowych [AAN], MSW 1186, "Udział wywrotowych w wyborach do ciał w Polsce w roku 1928 [Participation in the Elections of 1928 in Poland]," 1–37. This report drawn up by the Ministry of the Interior provides a district (*powiat*) by district breakdown of the "subversive" (mostly Communist) votes invalidated.

18. For methods of calculation, see chapter 3.

19. Violence against Jews reached a zenith from 1935 to 1937 but continued until the German invasion. See Polish police reports by voivodship in March, April, and May 1939 in AAN, KG PP Wydział IV Referat Kryminalny, Miesieczne wykazy przestec pczości wedlug województw [Monthly List of Crime by Province], 1222, 1224, 1226 (dopływ).

20. Ibid.

3. MEASURING THREAT AND VIOLENCE

1. Beissinger (2002) provides an extended discussion of these issues.

2. The main collection documenting the pogroms from the German point of view are published in Klein 1997 and the abridged English version of the same collection; Arad, Krakowski, and Spector 1989. The main witness testimony for the pogroms comes from two sources, which partially overlap. The Yad Vashem Archives has three record groups, O.3, O.33, and M.1.E. These testimonies partially overlap with the extensive and by far the best collection of survivor accounts, located in the Jewish Historical Institute in Warsaw, Archiwum Żydowskiego Instytutu Historycznego [AŻIH], Record Groups 301 and 302. The 301 record group accounts are relatively brief (ten typewritten pages, on average) but highly informative depictions of what occurred in individual towns before the Germans arrived, during their presence, and following their departure. They were recorded primarily in the four years following the war and are therefore extremely valuable because they are less subject to flaws in memory attributable to delay or cultural pressure. They are primarily in Polish but also in German, Russian, and Yiddish. The 302 record accounts are much longer but were accumulated in the decades after the war. Our narratives draw

extensively on these accounts. Sometimes pogroms receive no more than a sentence of mention in an individual account; other times the descriptions are thorough and packed full of context and detail. We draw less on reports from the Soviet Extraordinary State Commissions (led by the NKVD) that were compiled to deal with local collaborators, not because they were inaccurate but primarily because they focused less on pogroms than on other atrocities. A further source are the memorial books for individual towns put together in the decades following the war by survivor associations primarily in Israel but also in other countries. All of these sources have also been used in previous studies that discuss the pogroms we analyze here. One source we do not evaluate but which is referenced in some of the secondary literature (e.g., Himka 2011) is the USC Shoah Foundation Institute for Visual History and Education video testimonies. The occurrence of pogroms during summer 1941 has long been known, and some scholars have already drawn on these collections. For pioneering work, see Friedman 1980; Spector 1990; Gross 2001; Kruglov 2004; Machcewicz and Persak 2002; Żbikowski 1993, 2006.

3. For the contours of this debate, see the discussion in Gross 2001, the responses in Polonsky and Michlic 2004, and the general issue of testimony of survivors in Greenspan 2010.

4. The controversy over the use of Soviet versus Nazi sources is especially pronounced in the Ukrainian and Ukrainian diaspora historiography.

5. We tested for spatial autocorrelation using Moran's I for Białystok and Polesie together, and then separately for the Galician voivodships. We find no evidence of it.

6. Our analysis includes only localities where at least some Jews resided. Remarkably, of the 2,365 observations in our data set, only 49 had no Jews (based on religion) according to the 1921 census.

7. Kubijovyč (1983) provides 1939 local-level demographic data for Ukrainian areas, but reports the numbers in multiples of five. We therefore opted not to employ these numbers in statistical analyses.

8. These data come from the YIVO archive (RG 585), papers of Jacques Rieur, Folder 1.

9. Among the large parties, only Piłsudski's BBWR truly appealed to both Poles and non-Poles (Kopstein and Wittenberg 2011).

10. See Kopstein and Wittenberg 2011 for a more detailed discussion of the application of these methods to interwar Polish voting behavior.

11. Highly unlikely exceptions would be if the pattern of emigration had resulted in a relatively uniform distribution of nationalist Jews, leaving too little variance to detect an effect; or if all the nationalist Jews emigrated, which is manifestly untrue.

12. Wittenberg (2015) provides further examples.

4. BEYOND JEDWABNE

1. "Gruenbaum's most notorious disservice to Polish Jewish-relations," according to Strachura, "came in 1922 when, with the assistance of the German senator and subsequent Nazi Erwin Hasbach, he masterminded the organization of the Bloc of National minorities to fight the parliamentary elections in November" (Stachura 1998, 75).

2. We computed these according to the logic laid out in chapter 3, by making two assumptions. The first is that voter turnout was uniform across localities (though not across nationalities). The second is that Endecja support came exclusively from Poles, and BNM support came exclusively from non-Poles. Given the profiles of the two parties, this assumption is quite reasonable.

3. Indeed the risks to the perpetrators would have been lower where there were fewer Jews (who would presumably have less capacity to resist). On the calculation of these risks

and the propensity to target individuals in locations with low risk to the perpetrators, see Horowitz 2001, 527.

4. Shuster-Rozenblum's 1946 testimony on Jasionówka: "It is a quiet life there, the market in the middle of the shtetl is peaceful with its church and several little Jewish shops, no markets or fairs, the village survived on hard, honest work. . . . The Jewish and Polish workers live in harmony. Everyone has the same joys and sadness" (AŻIH 301-1274).

5. Although we have chosen to present the results from models employing the aggregate popularity of Jewish and Polish nationalist parties rather than the proportions of Jews and Poles supporting their respective nationalist parties, our explanation holds when we include these other variables.

6. Note that some of the confidence intervals exceed one, which is an artifact of the estimation process. Any predicted probability exceeding one should be considered equal to one. Note also that although all predicted probabilities are computed for Minorities Bloc support equal to 0, .1, .2, and .3, to increase readability the vertical lines are slightly offset from one another.

7. https://www.jewishgen.org/yizkor/szczuczyn/szc003.html.

8. http://www.szczuczyn.com/yizkorbook2a.htm#destruction.

9. According to Moyshe Farbarovits's contribution to Szczuczyn's *yizkor* (memorial) book, even before the Germans left, it was clear that "the Russians are coming—not a total consolation for us. It was known under what type of conditions people lived in the land of the Soviets, persecuted for no reason at all; but as it is said: 'A drowning man will grab even for a piece of burning straw.' Moreover us Jews, as an afflicted people, lived constantly with the hopes for better—but mediocre good was a respite nonetheless" (Former Residents of Szczuczyn [1954] 1987, 21).

10. Yad Vashem Archives (Israel) M.41, 2888, "Spisok chlenov i kandidatov BKP(b) prisutstvuyushchikh na partiinom sobranii ot 10 ianvarya 1940g [List of members and candidate members of the Communist Party present at the party meeting on January 10, 1940]."

11. Ironically, despite the hardships facing those Jews deported to the deep interior of the Soviet Union, they had a much better chance of surviving the war than those who remained in Szczuczyn.

12. For a similar narrative on Szczyczyn, see that of Bashe Katsper in AŻIH 301-1958.

13. The allusion to sexual slavery here is intentional. Although we cannot be certain, it would not have been unusual. In a different letter, Soika-Golding writes of her own service to the Germans: "Yes, I washed and cleaned floors, I sewed and quilted often. The most beautiful daughters polished and scrubbed, cleaned for them, cooked for them—for our bloody enemies." "Chaye Golding Letters, 1945," http://www.szczuczyn.com/golding.htm.

14. In a not untypical case of gerrymandering, authorities in Warsaw widened Białystok's administrative boundaries several times to increase the size of the Polish population for electoral purposes.

15. We assess resentment caused by external support with more systematic data in chapter 5.

16. According to Zalman Kaleshnik, a survivor of the Białystok ghetto, "It is interesting to note that the cottage next to the Shul, and in which the Polish watchman lived, was not set on fire by the Germans, since they knew that Poles lived there" (AŻIH 301-546). Although one may doubt Kaleshnik's ability to estimate the state of German knowledge, his observation does point to the importance of local Polish assistance in identifying Jews and Jewish property during the Białystok massacre.

17. On this project, see Snyder 2005. Even though the BBWR was a party of elites, it spawned a large number of pro-Piłsudskiite, nonelite associations and publications in the years after 1928 to promote civic activism and "moral regeneration." See also Plach 2006.

5. UKRAINIAN GALICIA AND VOLHYNIA

1. Pinchuk 1990, 121–122.
2. Golczewski 2008, 131.
3. Wildner also mentions the presence of Poles among the perpetrators, though makes clear that the lead was taken by the Ukrainians. The same can be said for Erna Klinger's account of the pogrom in Borysław. She maintains in her testimony that the bodies left by the retreating Soviets were mutilated by the Ukrainian militia. "Poles and Ukrainians burst into the apartments of Jews. . . . They beat them and threw their belongings through windows. This gave impetus to the Polish and Ukrainian population to murder Jews. On the street there were scattered brains, torn out tongues, the picked out eyes of Jews" (AŻIH 301-1096). In Lwów, Tadeusz Jelenski spoke of being beaten with clubs by both Poles and Ukrainians (AŻIH 301-4943). The question of mutilation of the bodies is contentious—Struve (2015) in multiple places notes that what locals may have perceived as mutilation was mostly likely the result of decomposition following a shot to the back of the head administered by the NKVD.
4. The OUN-B arrived in Lwów hours after the Germans on June 30 and quickly proclaimed a "sovereign and united" Ukrainian state to have come into existence. The Germans demanded a withdrawal of the proclamation but the OUN-B leadership refused. In the weeks thereafter its leadership, including Stetsko and Bandera, were arrested and spent the remainder of the war in various forms of detention. Both survived the war. Even with the arrest of its leadership, however, the OUN openly continued its activities in German-occupied Ukraine, only later to be driven underground and into opposition to Nazi rule (Berkhoff and Carynnyk 1999, 151–152).
5. After being captured in 1944, Volodymyr Logvinovich described his recruitment to deputy chief of the local Ukrainian nationalist militia in Dąbrowica in 1941. "On July 14 or 15, while walking by a church . . . I was hailed by my acquaintance Ivan Gavrilchik who was standing around with a group of people. Greeting me, Gavrilchik introduced me to a middle aged man standing there, who it turned out was head of the local administration, Luzik. From the resulting conversation I understood that Luzik was in Dąbrowica to organize the local administration in cooperation with the Ukrainian nationalists. In the course of the conversation Luzik, who seemed to be very well informed about me, asked me: 'Mr Logvinovich, the local inhabitants recommend you for the post of deputy chief of the regional police. I hope that you will give us your agreement and that now that the soil has been freed by the German army, organs of self-administration will be created, headed by the temporary Ukrainian government in Lwów under the guidance of our leader Stepan Bandera.' I answered Luzik that I was ready to accept the offer. Soon, after the conversation with Luzik, a prayer service was held in the church in honor of the creation of 'Independent and United Ukraine.' Upon completion of the service, Luzik spoke before the people of the church and read a manifesto of the 'temporary government'—Bandera with the declaration of an 'independent Ukraine. . . .' That same day I showed up for duty. The police complement included about 50 people, impatiently waiting for 'dirty work'" (Haluzevyi Derzhavnyi Arkhiv Sluzhby Bezpeky Ukrainy [State Archives of Ukraine, Security Service], fond 13, sprava 372, tom 1, arkushi 4–16). After this point in his testimony, Logvinovich proceeds to describe his unit's participation in a massacre of Jews together with elements of the Einsatzgruppen.

6. Ukrainians had earlier cooperated with the Zionists in the 1907 Reichsrat elections to reduce Polish parliamentary representation by voting for the Zionist candidates in those eastern Galicia areas where Ukrainians did have a majority (Kuchabsky 2009, 11).

7. *Dilo*, October 2, 1927, cited in Honigsman 2001, 67.

8. In one NKVD interrogation conducted immediately after the Soviet reconquest of Ukraine in 1944, an OUN operative sent from Skalat (in western Ukraine) to the shtetl Kupin to set up the new Ukrainian state claimed that the reason for the pogrom was that the local Jews opposed the pronouncement of an independent Ukraine. Haluzevyi Derzhavnyi Arkhiv Sluzhby Bezpeky Ukrainy [HAD-SBU], DASBU, F-1, vol. 96, Delo 372, Kyiv.

9. In the first days of Operation Barbarossa, in Volhynia, the OUN claimed seven thousand members spread over one thousand villages (Grelka 2005, 256). See also Ukrainska Presova Sluzhba, Materiali-Informatsii, June 30, 1941, Prolog Archive of OUN Documents [UPA Archive], New York, 3059, p. 3. We thank Serhiy Kudelia for sharing these documents.

10. Informativni listok Pivdennoi i Pokhidnoi Hrupy dlia Uchasnika pokhodu (Tarnopol) Ternopil [Informational leaflet of the southern expeditionary groups for participation in the Tarnopol campaign]," July 13, 1941, UPA Archive.

11. We do not use the 1922 election turnout as an indicator because its average values in the pogrom and nonpogrom subsamples (table 5.1) do not accord with theoretical expectation.

12. Avrom Venitser from Równo describes the murder of fourteen Jews by a small group of Ukrainan boys whom he identifies by name: Mitra Strakhartsuk, Arazip Drazdyuk, and Ivan Bunyak (AŻIH 301-662).

13. In Drohobycz, Jan Kulbinger reports that his neighbor hid him during the pogrom but "then she became a Volksdeutsche" (AŻIH 301-344).

14. Isak Weiser's testimony from Lwów (AŻIH 301-1584).

15. Most famously the main representative of the city's Jews, Alfred Nossig, renounced assimilation in favor of Zionism (see Amar 2015, 27). Less known at the time but subsequently more famous, both Hersch Lauterpacht and Raphael Lemkin—the former would introduce "crimes against humanity" and latter "genocide" into international law (see Sands 2016)—emerged from their legal studies in Lwów as Zionists. The failure of Poland's assimilationist project among Lwów's Jews is intimately connected to the violence of 1918 carried out primarily by Polish military units against the city's Jews who had attempted to remain neutral in the armed conflict between Poles and Ukrainians.

16. Jewish and Polish corpses were also found in the prisons, but this fact remained unpublicized by the Germans and Ukrainians.

17. Of course, not all bystanders did nothing and testimonies show some bystanders helped. Miles Lerman reports that during the pogrom as one Ukrainian attempted to take him off to Brygidki NKVD prison, the scene of some of the most horrific anti-Jewish violence, another Ukrainian intervened saying, "These people have a—a document—that they are employed by the Wehrmacht, you have no right to touch them," and he was permitted to go (United States Holocaust Memorial Museum Archives [USHMM], RG-50.030*0413).

18. Among the perpetrators in Lwów on July 1, 1941, were both Ukrainians and Poles (Amar 2015, 97; Himka 2011, 232; Struve 2015, 306).

19. According to Rita Harmelin's testimony, "I had only Ukrainian girls with me in primary school. . . . But I also had friends, Ukrainian girls, single. I wouldn't say a lot, but, I can't say who were, that I had trouble with anybody, really personally." Rita Harmelin, testimony, Collections USHMM. According to her husband, Raoul Harmelin, in answering

the question of whether there was anti-Semitism, "To a lesser degree, yes, mainly from Poles, who [were], where from some, sometimes for fun, kicking or hitting Jews. But generally the atmosphere was quite friendly" (USHMM testimony, April 26, 1992).

20. In testimony given in 1946, Sonia Armel put the total at 370 dead (AŻIH 301-2575).

21. The owners of Borysław's oil industry were mostly Polish, and the workers primarily Polish and Jewish, with some Ukrainians. Jews also dominated the local small-business sector, and Ukrainians tended to live in the villages surrounding the city (some of which were annexed to the municipality after 1929). For an extended treatment of oil in the region, see Frank 2005.

22. Raoul Harmelin describes the plethora of competing Zionist youth organizations in Borysław: "There was the HaShomer Hatzair. There was Akiba. There were many, many other organizations. There was a Jewish sports club, Kadima. There . . . were religious organizations, like Bnai Akiba, and so on, and Beit Y'akov, and the Jews were very active in their social life. . . . I joined a Jewish club, Kadima, which was perhaps the backbone of the Jewish Zionist movement" (USHMM testimony, December 26, 1992).

23. Cited in Aleksiun 2016, 248.

24. In her account, Irene Horowitz flees from two Ukrainian boys intent on violence and almost knocks over a Ukrainian policeman, "Misko," who turns out to have been a friend from school. "Irene, go home. Lock the doors and don't let anyone in. You people are in trouble." Later, when she is hauled down to the NKVD prison to clean corpses, Misko again rescues her and takes her home (Horowitz 1992, 88–89). See also the account in AŻIH 301-1737.

25. The 1921 census lists eighteen Jews, so this probably represents all Jews in the community.

26. According to Spector (1990, 243), "Against this depressing background only one small Ukrainian denomination stood apart in its attitude to the Jews—the Baptists. . . . Jewish testimonies contain details about individuals and groups from twenty-five cities and small towns throughout Volhynia who had been rescued by the Baptists. . . . In several cases Baptists were executed for giving refuge to Jews." According to Friedman (1980, 182), Seventh Day Adventists played a similar role in eastern Galicia. In addition, "Assistance rendered by Polish peasants [in Volhynia] was more frequent" (250). In the villages of Novino (near Luck) approximate sixty Jews from nearby villages were sheltered by Czechs. "Twelve Jewish children who wandered in the area of Ostrozhets (southeast of Luck) were collected by Czech villagers who saved their lives" (Friedman 1980, 253).

27. In 1935 for Poland as a whole, only a third of Jewish children attended Jewish schools. In Volhynia, by contrast, more than half of Jewish children attended Jewish grade schools, "and of those, two-thirds went to Zionist schools" (Bauer 2009, 24).

28. McBride offers a similar interpretation when we writes, "Thus, whether Poles left on their own accord as a result of nationalist violence or they died at the hands of the OUN-UPA, the goal remained the same for Ukrainian nationalists: to create a 'nationally pure space' in western Ukraine through cleansing policies. This, as many scholars on the subject have noted, distinguishes the case from one of genocide as the OUN-UPA did not intend to kill every Pole as a goal in and of itself—they only wanted to cleanse the territory of them" (McBride 2016, 632).

6. POGROMS OUTSIDE THE EASTERN BORDERLANDS

1. As in western Ukraine, in Lithuania the NKVD murdered approximately one thousand prisoners before their departure. Some historians have characterized the Kaunas pogrom as a reaction to this massacre. Dieckmann notes, however, that it is difficult to do so, since the Kaunas events occurred from June 25 to June 27, 1941, but news of the massacre only reached the city on June 28 and 29 (Dieckmann 2007, 362).

2. On this same pogrom, see the testimony in Geissbühler (2013, 67), "In early morning of July 7, 1941, 86 Jews, men, women, and children were ripped from their beds half naked and taken to the town hall. From there they were led in the morning darkness to a part of the woods on a nearby hill. There they stood before a pre-prepared pit. Then they were shot. 73 people died. The rest managed to flee. Present at the massacre were 50 Romanians and Ukrainians who lived in Sadagura. The next day the Rusu gang dragged the rest of the Jews from their houses and brought them to the city hall. The Jewish houses were completely plundered."

3. Solonari (2007, 783) finds this for the town of Rezina.

4. Solonari continues, "Had this part of the population protested the persecution and murder of their Jewish neighbors, nothing of the kind would have happened" (2007, 787).

5. Although the sixty thousand Jews of Salonica could not control the government, the divisions of the country were stark enough that the theme of "alien as arbiter" remained persistent throughout the interwar republic.

6. Rogger notes sixty communities affected by violence in Alsace during spring 1848 (1992, 320).

7. According to Weinberg, for example, apart from economic competition between Jewish and non-Jewish workers, the most immediate factors in the Odessa pogrom of 1905 included "the visible position of Jews in the opposition movement against the autocracy" (1992, 250).

8. A narrative from the massacre of four thousand Jews in Proskurov in February 1919 indicates a common pattern: "On February 13, 1919 the first ranks of *ataman* Semiesenko's cavalry entered the town. Two days passed in expectation, then, after a night of unlimited licentiousness and drinking, the war trumpet sounded as a sign that the pogrom had begun and that soldiers might rob and murder as they pleased. . . . Nobody was spared; women, old people and children fell under the bayonets of the soldiers and toward evening one could see the soldiers holding up on their lances the still convulsively moving bodies of Jewish babies. Here and there on the streets lay human bodies with amputated hands and feet, or corpses of women who had been violated before being cruelly murdered. A trumpet signal closed the pogrom." In the case of Felstyn after the massacre, "Jewish property was plundered and what the Ukrainians could not carry off they gave the peasants 'as a memento'" (Batchinsky 1919, 6–7).

9. Approximately ten thousand people died and thirty thousand were injured in Hindu-Muslim riots between 1950 and 1995 (Wilkinson 2004, 12).

10. Brass (2003) makes a broadly similar argument in his study of the city of Aligarh.

11. Frazier reports that 78 percent of lynching victims in Kansas between the 1850s and 1932 were white (2015, 6).

12. See Bailey et al. 2008, 48–49; and esp. Bailey and Tolnay 2015, 1–31 for summaries of the literature.

13. Blalock (1989) makes the same point.

7. INTIMATE VIOLENCE AND ETHNIC DIVERSITY

1. On Ukrainian debate, see Rossolinski-Liebe 2014, x; and relatedly Carrynyk 2007; Himka 2013. For the Polish nationalist view, see Chodakiewicz 2003.

2. Germany is the paradigmatic case. On this point, see Arendt 2007, 53.

References

ARCHIVAL SOURCES

AAN: Archiwum Akt Nowych (Warsaw)
AŻIH: Archiwum Żydowskiego Instytutu Historycznego (Warsaw)
DALO: Derzhavnyi Arkhiv Lvivskoi Oblasti (Lviv)
GARF: Gosudarstvenyi Arkhiv Rossiskoi Federatsii (Moscow)
HAD-SBU: Haluzevyi Derzhavnyi Arkhiv Sluzhby Bezpeky Ukrainy (Kyiv)
USHMM: United States Holocaust Memorial Museum Archives (Washington, DC) Yad Vashem Archives (Jerusalem)
YIVO: Institute for Jewish Research (New York)

SECONDARY SOURCES

Abramson, Henry. 1999. *A Prayer for the Government: Ukrainians and Jews in Revolutionary Times, 1917–1920*. Cambridge, MA: Harvard University Press.
Achen, Christopher H., and W. Phillips Shively. 1995. *Cross-Level Inference*. Chicago: University of Chicago Press.
Ainsztein, Reuben. 1974. *Jewish Resistance in Nazi-Occupied Eastern Europe*. New York: Barnes and Noble Books.
Aleksiun, Natalia. 2016. "Neighbours in Borysław: Jewish Perceptions of Collaboration and Rescue in Eastern Galicia." In *The Holocaust and European Societies: Social Processes and Social Dynamics*, edited by Frank Bajohr and Andrea Low. London: Palgrave Macmillan.
Amar, Tarik Cyril. 2015. *The Paradox of Lviv: A Borderland City between Nazis, Stalinists, and Nationalists*. Ithaca, NY: Cornell University Press.
Arad, Yitzhak. 1976. *The "Final Solution" in Lithuania in the Light of German Documentation*. Jerusalem: Yad Vashem.
Arad, Yitzhak, Shmuel Krakowski, and Shmuel Spector. 1989. *The Einsatzgruppen Reports: Selections from the Dispatches of the Nazi Death Squads*. New York: Holocaust Library.
Arendt, Hannah. 1963. *Eichmann in Jerusalem: A Report on the Banality of Evil*. New York: Viking.
———. 2007. *The Jewish Writings*. Edited by Jerome Kohn and Ron H. Feldman. New York: Schoken.
Aronson, I. Michael. 1990. *Troubled Waters: The Origins of the 1881 Anti-Jewish Pogroms in Russia*. Pittsburgh: University of Pittsburgh Press.
Asher, Abraham. 2008. "Interpreting 1905." In *The Revolution of 1905 and Russia's Jews*, edited by Sefani Hoffman and Ezra Mendelsohn, 15–30. Philadelphia: University of Pennsylvania Press.
Aster, Howard, and Peter J. Potichnyj. 1983. *Jewish-Ukrainian Relations: Two Solitudes*. Oakville, ON, CAN: Mosaic Press.
Avineri, Shlomo. 2014. *Herzl's Vision: Theodore Herzl and the Foundation of the Jewish State*. Katonah, NY: BlueBridge.
Bacon, Gershon. 1996. *The Politics of Tradition: Agudat Yisrael in Poland, 1916–1939*. Jerusalem: Magnes Press.

Bailey, Amy Kate, and Stewart E. Tolnay. 2015. *Lynched: The Victims of Southern Mob Violence*. Chapel Hill: University of North Carolina Press.

Bailey, Amy Kate, Stewart E. Tolnay, E. M. Beck, Alison Renee Roberts, and Nicholas H. Wong. 2008. "Personalizing Lynch Victims: A New Database to Support the Study of Mob Violence." *Historical Methods* 41 (1): 47–61.

Barkan, Elazar, Elizabeth A. Cole, and Kai Struve, eds. 2007. *Shared History—Divided Memory: Jews and Others in Soviet-Occupied Poland, 1939–1941*. Leipzig: Leipziger Universitatsverlag.

Bartov, Omer. 2017. *Erased: Vanishing Traces of Jewish Galicia in Present-Day Ukraine*. Princeton, NJ: Princeton University Press.

Batchinsky, Julian. 1919. *The Jewish Pogroms in Ukraine*. Washington, DC: Friends of Ukraine.

Bauer, Yehuda. 2007. "Sarny and Rokitno in the Holocaust: A Case Study of Two Townships in Wolyn (Volhynia)." In *The Shtetl: New Evaluations*, edited by Steven T. Katz, 253–289. New York: New York University Press.

———. 2009. *The Death of the Shtetl*. New Haven, CT: Yale University Press.

Bauman, Zygmunt. 1989. *Modernity and the Holocaust*. Cambridge, UK: Polity Press.

Beissinger, Mark. 2002. *Nationalist Mobilization and the Collapse of the Soviet State*. Princeton, NJ: Princeton University Press.

Bełcikowski, Jan. 1925. *Stronnictwa i związki polityczne w Polsce: Charakterystyki, dane historyczne, programy, rezolucje, organizacje partyjnje, prasa, przywódcy*. Warsaw: Dom Książki Polskiej.

Bender, Sara. 2008. *The Jews of Bialystok during World War II and the Holocaust*. Waltham, MA: Brandeis University Press.

Berenbaum, Michael, ed. 1990. *A Mosaic of Victims: Non-Jews Persecuted and Murdered by the Nazis*. New York: New York University Press.

Bergen, Doris. 2009. *War and Genocide: A Concise History of the Holocaust*. Lanham, MD: Rowman and Littlefield.

Berkhoff, Karel C., and Marco Carynnyk. 1999. "The Organization of Ukrainian Nationalists and Its Attitudes towards Germans and Jew: Iaroslav Stets'ko's Zhyttiepys." *Harvard Ukrainian Studies* 23 (3–4): 149–184.

Bernhard, Michael. 2005. *Institutions and the Fate of Democracy: Germany and Poland in the Twentieth Century*. Pittsburgh: University of Pittsburgh Press.

Blalock, Hubert M. 1967. *Toward a Theory of Minority-Group Relations*. New York: John Wiley.

———. 1989. "Percent Black and Lynchings Revisited." *Social Forces* 67 (3): 631–633.

Blobaum, Robert, ed. 2005. *Anti-Semitism and Its Opponents in Modern Poland*. Ithaca, NY: Cornell University Press.

Boćkowski, Daniel. 2005. *Na zawse razem: Białostocczyzna i Łomżyńskie w polityce radzieckiej w czasie II woyjny światowej (IX 1939–VIII 1944)*. Warsaw: Instytut Historii Polska Akademia Nauk.

Bonacich, Edna. 1972. "A Theory of Ethnic Antagonism: The Split Labor Market." *American Sociological Review* 37 (5): 547–559.

Brakel, Alexander. 2007. "Was There a 'Jewish Collaboration' under Soviet Occupation?" In Barkan, Cole, and Struve 2007, 225–244.

Brandon, Ray, and Wendy Lower. 2008. *The Shoah in Ukraine: History, Testimony, Memorialization*. Bloomington: Indiana University Press.

Brass, Paul R. 2003. *The Production of Hindu-Muslim Violence in Contemporary India*. Seattle: University of Washington Press.

———. 2006. *Forms of Collective Violence: Riots, Pogroms, and Genocide in Modern India*. Haryana, India: Three Essays Collective.

Braun, Robert. 2016. "Religious Minorities and Resistance to Genocide: The Collective Rescue of Jews in the Netherlands during the Holocaust." *American Political Science Review*, 110 (1): 127–147.
Bronsztejn, Szyja. 1994. "Polish-Jewish Relations in Memoirs." *Polin: Studies in Polish Jewry* 8: 66–88.
Brown, Kate. 2004. *A Biography of No Place: From Ethnic Borderland to Soviet Heartland.* Cambridge, MA: Harvard University Press.
Brubaker, Rogers. 1993. *Nationalism Reframed: Nationhood and the National Question in the New Europe.* Cambridge: Cambridge University Press.
———. 2001. "The Return of Assimilation? Changing Perspectives on Immigration and Its Sequels in France, Germany, and the United States." *Ethnic and Racial Studies* 24 (4): 531–548.
Brubaker, Rogers, and David Laitin. 1998. "Ethnic and Nationalist Violence." *Annual Review of Sociology* 24: 423–452.
Bruder, Franziska. 2007. *"Den ukrainischen Staat erkämpfen oder sterben!" Die Organisation Ukrainischer Nationalisten (OUN), 1929–1948.* Berlin: Metropol Verlag.
Brumberg, Abraham. 1989. "The Bund and the Polish Socialist Party." In Gutman 1989, 75–94.
———. 2002. "Poles and Jews." *Foreign Affairs* 81 (5): 174–186.
Brundage, W. Fitzhugh. 1993. *Lynching in the New South: Georgia and Virginia, 1880–1930.* Urbana: University of Illinois Press.
Brustein, William I. 2003. *Roots of Hate: Anti-Semitism in Europe before the Holocaust.* Cambridge: Cambridge University Press.
Byman, Daniel. 2000. "Forever Enemies? The Manipulation of Ethnic Identities to End Ethnic Wars." *Security Studies* 9 (3): 149–190.
Cała, Alina. 1989. *Asymilacja Żydów w Królestwie Polskim, 1864–1897: postawy, konflikty, stereotypy.* Warsaw: Państwowy Instytut Wydawniczy.
Cang, Joel. 1939. "The Opposition Parties and Their Attitude towards the Jews and the Jewish Problem." *Jewish Social Studies* 1 (2): 241–256.
Carey, John M., and Matthew S. Shugart. 1995. "Incentives to Cultivate a Personal Vote: A Rank Ordering of Electoral Formulas." *Electoral Studies* 14 (4): 417–439.
Carynnyk, Marco. 2005. "Zolochiv Movchit." *Krytyka* 9 (10): 14–17.
———. 2007. "The Palace on the Ikva–Dubne, September 18th, 1939, and June 24, 1941." In Barkan, Cole, and Struve 2007, 263–304
———. 2011. "Foes of Our Rebirth: Ukrainian Nationalist Discussions about Jews, 1929–1947. *Nationalities Papers* 39 (3): 315–352.
Charnysh, Volha. 2015. "Historical Legacies of Interethnic Competition: Anti-Semitism and the EU Referendum in Poland." *Comparative Political Studies*, 48 (13): 1711–1745.
Chodakiewicz, Jan Marek. 2003. *After the Holocaust: Polish-Jewish Conflict in the Wake of World War II.* Boulder, CO: East European Monographs.
———. 2005. *The Massacre in Jedwabne, July 10, 1941: Before, During, After.* Boulder, CO: East European Monographs.
Chojnowski, Andrzej. 1979. *Koncepcje polityki narodowościowej rządów polskich w latach, 1921–1939.* Wrocław: Zakład Narodowy im. Ossolińskich.
———. 1986. *Piłsudczycy u władzy: Dzieje Bezpartyjnego Bloku Współpracy z Rządem.* Wrocław: Zakład Narodowy im. Ossolińskich.
Connelly, John. 2002. "Poles and Jews in the Second World War: The Revisions of Jan T. Gross." *Central European History* 11 (4): 641–658.
Corzine, Jay, James Creech, and Lin Corzine. 1983. "Black Concentration and Lynchings in the South: Testing Blalock's Power-Threat Hypothesis." *Social Forces* 61 (3): 774–796.

Creech, James C., Jay Corzine, and Lin Huff-Corzine. 1989. "Theory Testing and Lynching: Another Look at the Power Threat Hypothesis." *Social Forces* 67 (3): 626–630.
Cutler, James Elbert. (1905) 1969. *Lynch-Law: An Investigation in the History of Lynching in the United States*. Montclair, NJ: Patterson Smith.
Dabrowska, Danuta, and Abraham Wein. 1976. *Pinkas ha-kehillot: Polin*. Jerusalem: Yad Vashem.
Darden, Keith. Forthcoming. *Resisting Occupation: Mass Literacy and the Creation of Durable National Loyalties*. Cambridge: Cambridge University Press.
Dhattiwala, Raheel, and Michael Biggs. 2012. "The Political Logic of Ethnic Violence: The Anti-Muslim Pogrom in Gujarat, 2002." *Politics and Society* 40 (4): 483–516.
Dieckmann, Christoph. 2007. "Lithuania in Summer 1941—The German Invasion and the Kaunas Pogrom." In Barkan, Cole, and Struve 2007, 355–385.
———. 2011. *Deutsche Besatzungspolitik in Litauen, 1941–1944*. Göttingen: Wallstein Verlag.
Dieckmann, Christoph, and Saulius Suziedelis. 2006. *The Persecution and Mass Murder of Lithuanian Jews during Summer and Fall of 1941*. Vilnius, LT: Margi raštai.
Dmitrów, Edmund. 2004. "Die Einsatzgruppen der deutschen Sicherheitspolitzei und des Sicherheitsdienstes zu Beginn der Judenvernichtung im Gebiet von Łomża und Białystok im Sommer 1941." In *Der Beginn der Vernichtung: Zum Mord an den Juden in Jedwabne und Umgebung im Sommer 1941*, edited by Edmund Dmitrów, Paweł Machcewicz, and Tomasz Sarota, 95–208. Osnabrück, DE: fibre Verlag.
Drugi Powszechny Spis Ludności [Second General Population Census] z dn. 9.XII 1931r. 1934–1938. Warsaw: Główny Urząd Statystyczny Rzeczypospolitej Polskiej.
Dumitru, Diana, and Carter Johnson. 2011. "Constructing Interethnic Conflict and Cooperation: Why Some People Harmed Jews and Others Helped Them during the Holocaust in Romania." *World Politics* 63 (1): 1–42.
Duverger, Marice. 1972. *Party Politics and Pressure Groups: A Comparative Introduction*. New York: Crowell.
Dziewankowski, M. K. 1959. *The Communist Party of Poland: An Outline of History*. Cambridge, MA: Harvard University Press.
Ehrenreich, Robert M., and Timothy Cole. 2005. "The Perpetrator-Bystander-Victim Constellation: Rethinking Genocidal Relationships." *Human Organization* 64 (3): 213–224.
Eidintas, Alfonsas. 2003. *Jews, Lithuanians, and the Holocaust*. Vilnius, LT: Versus Aureus.
Finkel, Evgeny. 2015. "The Phoenix Effect of State Repression: Jewish Resistance during the Holocaust." *American Political Science Review* 109 (2): 339–353.
Forbes, H. D. 1997. *Ethnic Conflict: Commerce, Culture, and the Contact Hypothesis*. New Haven, CT: Yale University Press.
Former Residents of Szczuczyn. (1954) 1987. *Destruction of the Jewish Community of Szczuczyn*. Tel Aviv: Former Residents of Szczuczyn.
Frank, Alison Fleig. 2005. *Oil Empire: Visions of Prosperity in Austrian Galicia*. Cambridge, MA: Harvard University Press.
Frazier, Harriet C. 2015. *Lynchings in Kansas: 1850s–1932*. Jefferson, NC: McFarland.
Friedländer, Saul. 2007. *Nazi Germany and the Jews, 1939–1945*. New York: Harper.
Friedman, Philip. 1980. *Roads to Extinction: Essays on the Holocaust*. New York: Jewish Publication Society of America.
Fujii, Lee Ann. 2009. *Killing Neighbors: Webs of Violence in Rwanda*. Ithaca, NY: Cornell University Press.
Gagnon, V. P., Jr. 2004. *The Myth of Ethnic War: Serbia and Croatia in the 1990s*. Ithaca, NY: Cornell University Press.

Geissbühler, Simon. 2013. *Blutiger Juli: Rumä niens Vernichtungskrieg und der vergessene Massenmord an den Juden, 1941*. Paderborn: Ferdinand Schöningh.
Gergel, N. 1951. "The Pogroms in the Ukraine, 1918–1920." *YIVO Annual of Jewish Social Science* 6: 237–252.
Gilbert, Martin. 1985. *The Holocaust: A History of the Jews during the Second World War*. New York: Henry Holt.
Główny Urząd Statystyczny. 1925. Various volumes. *Skorowidz Miejscowości Rzeczypospolitej Polskiej*. Warszawa: Nakładem Głównego Urzędu Statystycznego.
Główny Urząd Statystyczny Rzeczypospolitej Polskiej. 1926. *Statistique des Élections a la Diét et au Sénat: Effectuées le 5 et le 12 Novembre 1922*. Warsaw: L'Office Central de Statistique.
———. 1930. *Statystyka wyborów do Sejmu i Senatu odbytych w dniu 4 i 11 marca 1928 roku*. Warsaw: Główny Urząd Statystyczny.
Golczewski, Frank. 1981. *Polnisch-jüdische Beziehungen, 1881–1922: Eine Studie zur Geschichte des Antisemitismus in Osteuropa*. Wiesbaden: Steiner.
———. 2008. "Shades of Grey: Reflections on Jewish-Ukrainian and German-Ukrainian Relations in Galicia." In Brandon and Lower 2008, 114–155.
———. 2010. *Deutsche und Ukrainer, 1914–1939*. Paderborn, DE: Ferdinand Schöningh.
Goldhagen, Daniel Jonah. 1996. *Hitler's Willing Executioners: Ordinary Germans and the Holocaust*. New York: Vintage.
Grachova, Sofiya. 2009. "Wartime Diaries of Ukrainians as an Insight into Ukrainian-Jewish Relations during the Holocaust." Paper delivered to Annual Meeting of American Association for the Advancement of Slavic Studies, Boston, November.
Greenspan, Henry. 2010. *On Listening to Holocaust Survivors: Beyond Testimony*. St. Paul, MN: Paragon House.
Grelka, Frank. 2005. *Die ukrainische Nationalbewegung unter deutscher Besatzungsherrshaft, 1918 und 1941–42*. Wiesbaden: Harrassowitz Verlag.
Gross, Jan T. 2001. *Neighbors: The Destruction of the Jewish Community in Jedwabne, Poland*. Princeton, NJ: Princeton University Press.
———. 2002. *Revolution from Abroad: The Soviet Conquest of Poland's Western Ukraine and Western Belorussia*. Princeton, NJ: Princeton University Press.
———. 2006. *Fear: Anti-Semitism in Poland after Auschwitz*. New York: Random House.
Groth, Alexander J. 1960. "Parliament and the Electoral System in Poland, 1918–1935." PhD diss., Columbia University.
Gutman, Yisrael, Ezra Mendelsohn, Jehuda Reinharz, and Chone Shmeruk, eds. 1989. *The Jews of Poland between Two World Wars*. Hanover, NH: University Press of New England.
Hagen, William H. 2005. "The Moral Economy of Popular Violence: The Pogrom in Lwów, November 1918." In Blobaum 2005, 124–147.
Heschel, Abraham Joshua. 1946. "The Eastern European Era in Jewish History." *YIVO Annual of Jewish Social Science* 1: 86–106.
Hilberg, Raoul. 1961. *The Destruction of the European Jews*. New Haven, CT: Yale University Press.
———. 1992. *Perpetrators, Victims, Bystanders: The Jewish Catastrophe, 1933–1945*. New York: Harper Perennial.
Himka, John-Paul. 1997. "Ukrainian Collaboration in the Extermination of the Jews during the Second World War: Sorting Out the Long-Term and Conjunctural Factors." In *The Fate of the European Jews, 1939–1945: Continuity of Contingency?*, edited by Jonathan Frankel, 170–189. Oxford: Oxford University Press.

———. 2011. "The Lviv Pogrom of 1941: The Germans, Ukrainian Nationalists, and the Carnival Crowd." *Canadian Slavonic Papers* 53 (2–4): 209–243.

———. 2013. "The Reception of the Holocaust in Postcommunist Ukraine." In *Bringing the Dark Past to Light: The Reception of the Holocaust in Postcommunist Europe*, edited by John-Paul Himka and Joanna Beata Michlic, 626–662. Lincoln: University of Nebraska Press.

Hoffman, Stefani, and Ezra Mendelsohn, eds. 2008. *The Revolution of 1905 and Russia's Jews*. Philadelphia: University of Pennsylvania Press.

Hoffmann, Christhard, Werner Bergmann, and Helmut Walser Smith. 2002. *Exclusionary Violence: Antisemitic Riots in Modern German History*. Ann Arbor: University of Michigan Press.

Hollander, Ethan J. 2008. "The Final Solution in Bulgaria and Romania: A Comparative Perspective." *East European Politics and Societies* 22 (2): 203–248.

Holzer, Jerzy. 1994. "Polish Political Parties and Antisemitism." *Polin: Studies in Polish Jewry* 8: 194–205.

Honigsman, Jakob. 2001. *Juden in der Westukraine: Jüdisches Leben und Leiden in Ostgalizien, Wolhynien, der Bukowina und Transkarpatien, 1933–1945*. Konstanz, DE: Hartung-Gorre Verlag.

Horowitz, Donald. 2001. *The Deadly Ethnic Riot*. Berkeley: University of California Press.

Horowitz, Donald L. 1985. *Ethnic Groups in Conflict*. Berkeley: University of California Press.

Horowitz, Irene, and Carl Horowitz. 1992. *Of Human Agony*. New York: Sheingold.

Hryciuk, Grzegorz. 2007. "Victims 1939–1941: The Soviet Repressions in Eastern Poland." In Barkan, Cole, and Struve 2007, 173–200.

Hundert, Gershon David. 2008. *The Yivo Encyclopedia of Jews in Eastern Europe*. Vol. 2. New Haven and London: Yale University Press.

Idan, Y., et al. 1957. *Sefer zikaron Davidgrodek*. Tel Aviv: Former Residents of Dawidgrodek in Israel.

Iwry, Samuel. 2004. *To Wear the Dust of War: From Bialystok to Shanghai to the Promised Land*. New York: Palgrave Macmillan.

Jacobson, Gary C., and Samuel Kernell. 1981. *Strategy and Choice in Congressional Elections*. New Haven, CT: Yale University Press.

Jasiewicz, Krzysztof. 2000. "Unerforschte Nachbarn." In *Gazeta Wyborcza*, December 9–10. Excerpted in German translation in *Transodra*, no. 23: 271–285.

———. 2001. *Pierwsi po diable: Elity sowieckie w okupowanej Polsce, 1939–1941* (Białostocczyzna, Nowogródczyzna, Polesie, Wileńszczyzna). Warsaw: Instytut Studiów Politycznych Polska Akademia Nauk Oficyna Wydawnicza Rytm.

———. 2009. "'The Past Is Never Dead': Identity, Class, and Voting Behavior in Contemporary Poland." *East European Politics and Societies* 23 (4): 491–508.

Johnpoll, Bernard K. 1967. *The Politics of Futility: The General Jewish Workers Bund of Poland, 1917–1943*. Ithaca, NY: Cornell University Press.

Jolluck, Katherine R. 2005. "Gender and Antisemitism in Wartime Soviet Exile." In Blobaum 2005, 210–232.

Jüdisches Komitee Drohobycz. 1941. *Zusammenstellung der Vorfälle, betreffend die jüdische Bevölkerung in der Umgebung von Drohobycz*. DALO R-1928/1/4.

Kalyvas, Stathis N. 2006. *The Logic of Violence in Civil War*. Cambridge: Cambridge University Press.

Kassow, Samuel D. 1989. "Community and Identity in the Interwar Shtetl." In Gutman 1989, 198–220.

Kenez, Peter. 1992. "Pogroms and White Ideology in the Russian Civil War." In Klier and Lambroza 1992, 293–313.

Keys, Kerry Shawn, and Geoffrey Vasil, eds. 2011. *Lithuanian Holocaust Atlas*. Vilnius, LT: Vilna Gaon Jewish State Museum.
King, Charles. 2012. "Can There Be a Political Science of the Holocaust?" *Perspectives on Politics* 10 (2): 323–341.
King, Gary. 1997. *A Solution to the Ecological Inference Problem*. Princeton, NJ: Princeton University Press.
Klee, Ernst, Willi Dressen, and Volker Riess. 1988. *'The Good Old Days': The Holocaust as Seen by Its Perpetrators and Bystanders*. Old Saybrook, CT: Konecky and Konecky.
Klein Peter, ed. 1997. *Die Einsatzgruppen in der besetzten Sowjetunion 1941–42*. Berlin: Edition Hentrich.
Klier, John. 2000. "What Exactly Was a Shtetl?" In *The Shtetl: Image and Reality*, edited by Gennady Estraikh and Mikhail Krutikov, 18–30. Oxford: Legenda.
Klier, John, and Shlomo Lambroza, eds. 1992. *Pogroms: Anti-Jewish Violence in Modern Russian History*. Cambridge: Cambridge University Press.
Kobrin, Rebecca. 2010. *Jewish Bialystok and Its Diaspora*. Bloomington: Indiana University Press.
Kopstein, Jeffrey S., and Jason Wittenberg. 2003. "Who Voted Communist? Reconsidering the Social Bases of Radicalism in Interwar Poland." *Slavic Review* 62 (1): 87–109.
———. 2010. "Beyond Dictatorship and Democracy: Rethinking National Minority Inclusion and Regime Type in Interwar Eastern Europe." *Comparative Political Studies* 43 (8): 1089–1118.
———. 2011. "Between State Loyalty and National Identity: Electoral Behavior in Interwar Poland." *Polin: Studies in Polish Jewry* 24 (November): 171–185.
Korzec, Pawel. 1980. *Juif en Pologne: La question juive pendent l'entre deux guerres*. Paris: Presses de la Fondation nationale des sciences politiques.
Kruglov, Aleksandr. 2000. *Entsyklopedia Kholokosta*. Kiev: Evreiskii Soviet Ukraina.
———. 2004. *Khronika Kholokosta v Ukraine, 1941–1944 gg*. Dnepropetrovsk: Tsentr Tkuma.
———. 2010. "Pogromy v Vostochnoi Galitsii letom 1941 g.: Organizatori, Uchstniki, Masshabi i Posledstviya." In *Voina na Unichtozhenie: Natsistskaia Politika Genotsida na Territorii Vostochnoi Evropi*, edited by A. R. Diukov and O. E. Orlenko, 324–341. Moscow: Fond Istoricheskaia Pamiat, 2010.
———. 2012. "Brody." In *Encyclopedia of Camps and Ghettos, 1933-1945*, edited by Martin Dean, vol. 2. Washington, DC: United States Holocaust Memorial Museum/ Bloomington: Indiana University Press.
Krzemiński, Adam. 1998. *Polen im 20. Jahrhundert: Ein Historischer Essay*. Munich: Beck.
Kubijovyč, Volodymyr. 1983. *Ethnic Groups of the South-Western Ukraine (Halyčyna-Galicia), 1.1.1939*. Wiesbaden: Otto Harassowitz.
Kuchabsky, Vasyl. 2009. *Western Ukraine in Conflict with Poland and Bolshevism, 1918–1923*. Edmonton, AB: Canadian Institute of Ukrainian Studies Press.
Kymlicka, Will, and Magda Opalski, eds. 2001. *Can Liberal Pluralism Be Exported? Western Political Theory and Ethnic Relations in Eastern Europe*. Oxford. Oxford University Press.
Lambroza, Shlomo. 1992. "The Pogroms of 1903–1906." In Klier and Lambroza 1992, 195–247.
Landau-Czajka, Anna. 1994. "The Image of the Jew in the Catholic Press during the Second Republic." *Polin: Studies in Polish Jewry* 8: 146–175.
Langmuir, Gavin. 1990. *Toward a Definition of Antisemitism*. Berkeley: University of California Press.
Levin, Dov. 1990. "Lithuania." In *Encyclopedia of the Holocaust Vol.3*, edited by Israel Gutman, 895–899. New York: Macmillan.

———. 1995. *The Lesser of Two Evils: Eastern European Jewry under Soviet Rule, 1939–1941*. Lincoln: University of Nebraska Press.
Levine, Louis D., ed. 2002. *Lives Remembered: A Shtetl through a Photographer's Eye*. New York: Museum of Jewish Heritage.
Levinson, Joseph, ed. 2006. *The Shoah (Holocaust) in Lithuania*. Vilnius, LT: Vilna Gaon Jewish State Museum.
Libionka, Dariusz. 2005. "Antisemitism and the Polish Catholic Clergy." In Blobaum 2005, 233–264.
Lijphart, Arend. 1968. *The Politics of Accommodation: Pluralism and Democracy in the Netherlands*. Berkeley: University of California Press.
Lipset, Seymour Martin. 1959. "Some Social Requisites of Democracy: Economic Development and Political Legitimacy." *American Political Science Review* 53 (1): 69–105.
Lower, Wendy. 2011. *The Diary of Samuel Goldfard and the Holocaust in Galicia*. Lanham, MD: AltaMira Press.
Luebbert, Gregory M. 1991. *Liberalism, Fascism, or Social Democracy: Social Classes and the Political Origins of Regimes in Interwar Europe*. Oxford: Oxford University Press.
Machcewicz, Paweł, and Krzysztof Persak, eds. 2002. *Wokół Jedwabnego*. Warsaw: Instytut Pamięci Narodowej.
Magocsi, Robert Paul. 2010. *A History of Ukraine: The Land and Its Peoples*. Toronto: University of Toronto Press.
Mann, Michael. 2005. *The Dark Side of Democracy: Explaining Ethnic Cleansing*. Cambridge. Cambridge University Press.
Manor, Alexander, ed. 1980. *Sefer Sambor, Stary Sambor*. Tel Aviv: Former Residents of Sambor and Stary Sambor in Israel.
Marcus, Joseph. 1983. *Social and Political History of the Jews in Poland, 1919–1939*. Berlin, New York: Mouton.
Mavrogordatos, George. 1983. *Stillborn Republic: Social Coalitions and Party Strategies in Greece, 1922–1936*. Berkeley: University of California Press.
———. 2008. "The Greek Case: A Vindication of Assimilation?" Paper presented at The Holocaust as Local History Conference, Thessaloniki, Greece.
McBride, Jared. 2016. "Peasants into Perpetrators: The OUN-UPA and the Ethnic Cleansing of Volhynia, 1943–1944." *Slavic Review* 75 (3): 630–654.
McGovern, James R. 1982. *Anatomy of a Lynching: The Killing of Claude Neal*. Baton Rouge: Louisiana State University Press.
Mędykowski, Witold. 2012. *W cieniu gigantów: pogromy 1941 r. w byłej sowieckiej strefie okupacyjnej: kontekst historyczny, społeczny i kulturowy*. Warsaw: Instytut Studiów Politycznych Polskiej Adademii Nauk.
Meir-Glitzenstein, Esther. 2004. *Zionism in an Arab Country: Jews in Iraq in the 1940s*. London: Routledge.
Melamed, Vladimir. 2007. "Organized and Unsolicited Collaboration in the Holocaust: The Multifaceted Ukrainian Context." *East European Jewish Affairs* 37 (2): 217–248.
Melson, Robert. 1996. *Revolution and Genocide: On the Origins of the Armenian Genocide and the Holocaust*. Chicago. University of Chicago Press.
Melzer, Emanuel. 1997. *No Way Out: The Politics of Polish Jewry, 1935–1939*. Pittsburgh: Hebrew Union College Press.
Mendelsohn, Daniel. 2006. *The Lost: A Search for Six of Six Million*. New York: Harper Collins.
Mendelsohn, Ezra. 1974. "The Dilemma of Jewish Politics in Poland: Four Responses." In *Jews and Non-Jews in Eastern Europe, 1918–1945*, edited by Bela Vago and George Mosse, 203–220. Israel: Israel Universities Press.
———. 1981. *Zionism in Poland: The Formative Years, 1915–1926*. New Haven, CT: Yale University Press.

———. 1983. *The Jews of East-Central Europe between the World Wars*. Bloomington: Indiana University Press.
———. 1986. "Interwar Poland: good or bad for the Jews?" In *The Jews of Poland*, edited by Chimen Abramsky, Maciej Jachimczyk, and Antony Polonsky, 130–139. Oxford: Basil Blackwell.
Michlic-Coren, Joanna. 2000. "Anti-Jewish Violence in Poland, 1918–1939 and 1945–1947." *Polin: Studies in Polish Jewry* 13: 34–61.
———. 2006. *Poland's Threatening Other: The Image of the Jew from 1880 to the Present*. Lincoln: University of Nebraska Press.
Mick, Christoph. 2007. "'Only the Jews do not Waver' . . . : L'viv under Soviet Occupation." In Barkan, Cole, and Struve 2007, 245–262
———. 2010. *Kriegserfahrungen in einer mutliethnischen Stadt: Lemberg, 1914–1947*. Wiesbaden: Harassowitz Verlag.
Motyl, Alexander J. 1980. *The Turn to the Right: The Ideological Origins and Development of Ukrainian Nationalism, 1919–1929*. East European Monographs, no. 65. Boulder, CO: East European Quarterly.
Musiał, Bogdan. 2004. "The Pogrom in Jedwabne: Critical Remarks about Jan T. Gross's *Neighbors*." In Polansky and Michlic 2004, 304–343.
Olzak, Susan. 1992. *The Dynamics of Ethnic Competition and Conflict*. Stanford, CA: Stanford University Press.
Petersen, Roger D. 2002. *Understanding Ethnic Violence: Fear, Hatred, and Resentment in Twentieth Century Eastern Europe*. Cambridge: Cambridge University Press.
Pettigrew, Thomas F., and Linda R. Tropp. 2006. "A Meta-Analytic Test of Intergroup Contact Theory." *Journal of Personality and Social Psychology* 80 (5): 751–783.
Pinchuk, Ben-Cion. 1990. *Shtetl Jews under Soviet Rule*. Oxford: Blackwell Publishers.
Plach, Eva. 2006. *The Clash of Moral Nations: Cultural Politics in Piłsudski's Poland, 1926–1935*. Athens: Ohio University Press.
Pohl, Dieter. 1996. *Nationalsozialistische Judenverfolgung in Ostgalizien, 1941–1944: Organisation under Durchführung eines staatlichen Massenverbrechens*. Munich: Oldenbourg.
———. 2007. "Anti-Jewish Pogroms in Western Ukraine: A Research Agenda." In Barkan, Cole, and Struve 2007, 305–314.
Polonsky, Antony. 1972. *Politics in Independent Poland, 1921–1939: The Crisis of Constitutional Government*. Oxford: Clarendon.
———. 1997. "Beyond Condemnation, Apologetics, and Apologies." In *The Fate of the European Jews, 1939–1945: Continuity or Contingency*, edited by Jonathan Frankel, 190–224. Oxford: Oxford University Press.
Polonsky, Antony, and Joanna B. Michlic, eds. 2004. *The Neighbors Respond: The Controversy over the Jedwabne Debate in Poland*. Princeton, NJ: Princeton University Press.
Porter, Brian. 2000. *When Nationalism Began to Hate: Imagining Modern Politics in Nineteenth Century Poland*. New York: Oxford University Press.
Potichnyj, Peter. 1986. "Ukrainians in World War II Military Formations: An Overview." In *Ukraine during World War II*, edited by Yury Boshyk. 54–65, Edmonton, AB: Canadian Institute of Ukrainian Studies.
Radu, Ioanid. 2000. *The Holocaust in Romania: The Destruction of the Jews and Gypsies under the Antonescu Regime, 1940–1944*. Chicago: Ivan Dee.
Radziejowski, Janusz. 1983. *The Communist Party of Western Ukraine, 1919–1929*. Edmonton. AB: Canadian Institute of Ukrainian Studies.
Redlich, Shimon. 2002. *Together and Apart in Brzezany: Poles, Jews, and Ukrainians, 1919–1945*. Bloomington: Indiana University Press.

Reed, John Shelton. 1972. "Percent Black and Lynching: A Test of Blalock's Theory." *Social Forces* 50 (3): 356–360.
Rogger, Hans. 1992. "Conclusion and Overview." In Klier and Lambroza 1992, 314–372.
Rohrbacher, Stefan. 1993. *Gewalt im Biedermeier: Antijüdische Ausschreitungen in Vormärz und Revolution (1815–1848/49)*. Frankfurt: Campus Verlag.
———. 1999. "Deutsche Revolution un antijüdische Gewalt (1815–1848/49)." In *Die Konstruktion der Nation gegen die Juden*, edited by Petere Alter, Claus-Ekkehard Bärsch, and Peter Berghoff, 30–47. Munich: W. Fink.
———. 2002. "The 'Hep-Hep' Riots of 1819: Anti-Jewish Ideology, Agitation, and Violence." In Hoffmann, Bergmann, and Smith 2002, 23–42.
Rosen, Anda Meisels. 2005. *Middle Andzia: A Memoir*. Charleston, SC: BookSurge.
Rosen, O., W. Jiang, G. King, and M. A. Tanner. 2001. "Bayesian and Frequentist Inference for Ecological Inference: The R x C Case." *Statistica Neerlandica* 55: 134–156.
Rosman, Moshe. 2003. "Dubno in the Wake of Khmel'nytskyi." *Jewish History* 17 (2): 239–255.
Rossoliński-Liebe, Grzegorz. 2014. *Stepan Bandera: The Life and Afterlife of a Ukrainian Nationalist; Fascism, Genocide, and Cult*. Stuttgart: ibidem.
Rothschild, Joseph. 1974. *East Central Europe between the Two World Wars*. Seattle: University of Washington Press.
Rubin, Arnon. 2006. *The Rise and Fall of the Jewish Communities in Poland and Their Relics Today*. Vol. 1, *District Bialystok*. Tel-Aviv: Tel Aviv University Press.
Rudnicki, Szymon. 2005. "Anti-Jewish Legislation in Interwar Poland." In *Antisemitism and Its Opponents in Modern Poland*, edited by Robert Blobaum, 148–170. Ithaca, NY: Cornell University Press.
Sands, Philippe. 2016. *East West Street: On the Origins of "Genocide" and "Crimes Against Humanity."* New York: Knopf.
Scacco, Alexandra. 2008. "Who Riots? Explaining Individual Participation in Ethnic Violence." PhD diss., Columbia University.
Schenke, Cornelia. 2004. *Nationalstaat und nationale Frage: Polen und die Ukrainer, 1921–1939*. Hamburg: Dölling und Galitz Verlag.
Schrodt, Philip A. 2013. "Seven Deadly Sins of Contemporary Quantitative Political Analysis." *Journal of Peace Research* 51 (2): 287–300.
Segal, Simon. 1938. *The New Poland and the Jews*. New York: Lee Furman.
Snyder, Timothy. 2003a. "The Causes of Ukrainian-Polish Ethnic Cleansing 1943." *Past and Present* 179 (1): 197–234.
———. 2003b. *The Reconstruction of Nations: Poland, Ukraine, Lithuania, and Belarus, 1569–1999*. New Haven, CT: Yale University Press.
———. 2005. *Sketches from a Secret War: A Polish Artist's Mission to Liberate Soviet Ukraine*. New Haven, CT: Yale University Press.
———. 2008. "The Life and Death of Western Volhynian Jewry, 1921–1945." In Brandon and Lower 2008, 77–113.
———. 2010. *Bloodlands: Europe between Hitler and Stalin*. New York: Basic Books.
———. 2015. *Black Earth: The Holocaust as History and Warning*. New York: Random House.
Solonari, Vladimir. 2007. "Patterns of Violence: The Local Population and the Mass Murder of Jews in Bessarabia and Northern Bukovina, July/August 1941." *Kritika: Explorations in Russian and Eurasian History* 8 (4): 749–787.
Spector, Shmuel. 1990. *The Holocaust of the Volhynian Jews, 1941–1944*. Jerusalem: Yad Vashem.
Spilerman, Seymour. 1970a. "The Causes of Racial Disturbances: A Comparison of Alternative Explanations." *American Sociological Review* 35 (4): 627–648.

———. 1970b. "The Causes of Racial Disturbances: Tests of an Explanation." *American Sociological Review* 36 (3): 427–442.
———. 1976. "Structural Characteristics of Cities and the Severity of Racial Disorders." *American Sociological Review* 41 (5): 771–793.
Spulber, Nicholas. 1966. *The State and Economic Development in Eastern Europe.* New York: Random House.
Stachura, Peter D. 1998. "National Identity and Ethnic Minorities in Early Interwar Poland." In *Poland between the Wars 1918–1939*, 60–86. London: Macmillan.
Stauter-Halsted, Keely. 2001. *The Nation in the Village: The Genesis of Peasant National Identity in Austrian Poland, 1848–1914.* Ithaca, NY: Cornell University Press.
———. 2005. "Jews as Middleman Minorities in Rural Poland: Understanding the Galician Pogroms of 1898." In Blobaum 2005, 39–59.
Stebel'ski, Ivan. 1999. *Shliakhami, Molodosti, i Borotb'y.* Kiev: Smoloskiy.
Stola, Dariusz. 2001. "Ein Denkmal aus Worten." *Transodra*, no. 23: 271–285.
———. 2004. "Jedwabne: How Was It Possible?" In Polonsky and Michlic 2004, 386–402.
Straus, Scott. 2006. *The Order of Genocide: Race, Power, and War in Rwanda.* Ithaca, NY: Cornell University Press.
———. 2010. "Genocide Studies and Political Science." In *Oxford Handbook on Genocide*, edited by Donald Bloxham, 163–181. Oxford: Oxford University Press.
Struve, Kai. 2005. "Ritual und Gewalt: Die Pogrome des Sommers 1941." In *Synchrone Welten: Zeiträume jüdischer Geschichte*, edited by Dan Diner. 225–250. Göttingen: Vandenhoeck und Rupprecht.
———. 2012. "Rites of Violence? The Pogroms of Summer 1941." *Polin: Studies in Polish Jewry* 24: 257–274.
———. 2015. *Deutsche Herrschaft, ukrainischer Nationalismus, antijüdische Gewalt: Der Sommer 1941 in Westukraine.* Oldenbourg: De Gruyter.
Subtelny, Orest. 1989. *Ukraine: A History.* Toronto: University of Toronto Press.
Świtalski, Kazimierz. 1992. *Diariusz, 1919–1935.* Warsaw: Czytelnik.
Sysyn, Frank E. 2003. "The Kheml'nytskyi Uprising: A Characterization of the Ukrainian Revolt." *Jewish History* 17 (3): 115–139.
Szarota, Tomasz. 2004. "Mord in Jedwabne–Dokumente, Publikationen und Interpretationen aus den Jahren 1941–2000: Ein Kalendarium." In *Der Beginn der Vernichtung*, edited by Paweł Machcewicz, Edmund Dmitrów and Tomasz Szarota. 209–250. Osnabrück: fibre Verlag.
Tec, Nechama. 1986. *When Light Pierced Darkness: Christian Rescue of Jews in Nazi-Occupied Poland.* Oxford. Oxford University Press.
Tilly, Charles. 1984. *Big Structures, Large Processes, Huge Comparisons.* New York. Russell Sage Foundation.
Tolisch, Otto. 1937. "Jews Face Crisis in Eastern Europe." *New York Times*, February 7.
Tolnay, Stewart E., and E. M. Beck. 1995. *A Festival of Violence: An Analysis of Southern Lynchings, 1882–1930.* Urbana: University of Illinois Press.
Tolnay, Stewart E., E. M. Beck, and James L. Massey. 1989a. "Black Lynchings: The Power Threat Hypothesis Revisited." *Social Forces* 67 (3): 605–623.
———. 1989b. "The Power Threat Hypothesis and Black Lynching: 'Wither' the Evidence." *Social Forces* 67 (3): 634–640.
Tomaszewski, Jerzy. 1985. *Rzeczpospolita wielu narodów* [Republic of many nations]. Warsaw: Czytelnik.
———. 1989. "The Role of the Jews in Polish Commerce, 1918–1939." In Gutman 1989, 141–157.
———. 1994. "The Civil Rights of Jews in Poland, 1918–1939." In *Polin: Studies in Polish Jewry* 8: 115–128.

REFERENCES

———. 2002. *Auftakt zur Vernichtung*. Osnabrück: fibre Verlag.
Tryczyk, Mirosław. 2015. *Miasta śmerci: sąsiedzkie pogromy Żydów*. Warsaw: Wydawnictwo RM.
Valentino, Benjamin A. 2004. *Final Solutions: Mass Killing and Genocide in the 20th Century*. Ithaca, NY: Cornell University Press.
van der Linden-Wolanski, Sabina. 2010. *Drang Nach Leben: Erringerungen*. Berlin: Stiftung Denkmal fr den Juden Europas.
Varshney, Ashutosh. 2002. *Ethnic Conflict and Civic Life: Hindus and Muslims in India*. New Haven, CT: Yale University Press.
Varshney, Ashutosh, and Joshua R. Gubler. 2012. "Does the State Promote Communal Violence for Electoral Reasons?" *India Review* 11 (3): 191–199.
———. 2013. "The State and Civil Society in Communal Violence: Sparks and Fires." In *Routledge Handbook of Indian Politics*, edited by Atul Kohli and Prerna Singh, 155–166. New York: Routledge.
Vital, David. 1999. *A People Apart: A Political History of the Jews in Europe, 1789–1939*. Oxford: Oxford University Press.
Wang, Xia, and Natalie Todak. 2016. "Racial Threat Hypothesis." *Oxford Bibliographies*. Oxford: Oxford University Press. Accessed July, 2017. DOI: 10.1093/obo/9780195396607-0204.
Weeks, Theodore R. 2005. "Assimilation, Nationalism, Modernization, Antisemitism: Notes on Polish-Jewish Relations, 1855–1905." In Blobaum 2005, 20–38.
Weinberg, Robert. 1992. "The Pogrom of 1905 in Odessa: A Case Study." In Klier and Lambroza 1992, 248–290.
Weiser, Kalman. 2011. *Jewish People, Yiddish Nation: Noah Prylucki and the Folkists in Poland*. Toronto: University of Toronto Press.
Weiss, Aharon. 1990. "The Holocaust and the Ukrainian Victims." In Berenbaum 1990, 109–115.
Western, Bruce, and Simon Jackman. 2004. "Bayesian Inference for Comparative Research." *American Political Science Review* 88 (2): 412–423.
Wierzbiecki, Marek. 2000. *Polacy i Białorusini w zaborze sowieckim: stosunki polsko-białoruskie na ziemach północno-wschodnich II Rzeczypospolitej pod okupacją sowiecką 1939–1941*. Warsaw: Oficyna Wydawnicza Wolumen.
———. 2007. "Western Belarus in September 1939: Revisiting Polish-Jewish Relations in the Kresy." In Barkan, Cole, and Struve 2007, 135–146.
Wilkinson, Steven I. 2004. *Votes and Violence: Electoral Competition and Ethnic Riots in India*. Cambridge: Cambridge University Press.
———. 2013. "Electoral Competition, the State, and Communal Violence: A Reply." *India Review* 12 (2): 92–107.
Williams, Robin M. 1994. "The Sociology of Ethnic Conflicts: Comparative International Perspectives." *Annual Review of Sociology* 2: 49–79.
Wittenberg, Jason. 2015. "Conceptualizing Historical Legacies." *East European Politics and Societies* 29 (2): 366–378.
Wittenberg, Jason, Ferdinand Alimadhi, Badri Narayan Bhaskar, and Olivia Lau. 2007. "ei. RxC: Hierarchical Multinomial-Dirichlet Ecological Inference Model." In Kosuke Imai, Gary King, and Olivia Lau, "Zelig: Everyone's Statistical Software." http://gking.harvard.edu/zelig.
Wolsza, Tadeusz. 1992. *Narodowa Demokracja wobec chłopów w latach, 1887–1914: programy, polityka, działalność*. Warsaw: Ludowa Spółdzielnia Wydawnicza.
Wright, George C. 1990. *Racial Violence in Kentucky, 1865–1940*. Baton Rouge: Louisiana State University Press.

Wróbel, Piotr. 2012. "Polish-Ukrainian Relations during World War II: The Boryslav Case Study: A Polish Perspective." *East European Politics and Societies* 26 (1): 215–235.

Wynot, Edward D. 1971. "'A Necessary Cruelty': The Emergence of Official Anti-Semitism in Poland, 1936–1939." *American Historical Review* 74 (4): 1035–1058.

Yones, Eliyahu. 2004. *Smoke in the Sand: The Jews of Lvov in the War Years, 1939–1944.* Jerusalem: Geffen.

Yurkevich, Myroslav. 1986. "Galician Ukrainians in German Military Formations and the German Administration." In *Ukraine during World War II*, edited by Yury Boshyk, 67–88. Edmonton, AB: Canadian Institute of Ukrainian Studies.

Zabuski, Charles. 1996. *Needle and Thread: A Tale of Survival from Bialystok to Paris.* Oakland: Popincourt Press.

Żbikowski, Andrzej. 1992. "Lokalne pogromy Żydów w czerwcu i lipcu 1941 roku na wschodnich rubieżach II Rzeczypospolitej." *Biuletyn Żydowskiego Instytutu Historycznego*, nos. 2–3: 3–18.

———. 1993. "Local Anti-Jewish Pogroms in the Occupied Territories of Eastern Poland, June–July 1941." In *The Holocaust in the Soviet Union: Studies and Sources on the Destruction of the Jews in the Nazi-Occupied Territories of the USSR, 1941–1945*, edited by Lucjan Dobroszycki and Jeffrey S. Gurock, 173–179. Armonk, NY: M. E. Sharpe.

———. 2006. *U genezy Jedwabnego: Żydzi na Kresach północno-wschodnich II Rzeczypospolitej, wrzesień 1939–lipiec 1941.* Warsaw: Żydowski Instytut Historyczny.

———. 2007. "Pogroms in Northeastern Poland—Spontaneous Reactions and German Instigations." In Barkan, Cole, and Struve 2007, 315–354.

Zloch, Stephanie. 2010. *Polnischer Nationalismus: Politik und Gesellschaft zwischen den beiden Weltkriegen.* Cologne: Bölau Verlag.

Żyndul, Jolanta. 1994. *Zajścia antyżydowskie w Polsce w latach, 1935–1937.* Warsaw: Fundacja Im. K. Kelles-Krauza.

Index

Abramson, Henry, 27
Agudas Yisrael, 33–34, 63, 66, 96, 131
Aleksiun, Natalia, 107
Alter, Avraham Mordechai, 33
Amar, Tarik, 105
American Jewish Joint Distribution Committee, 13, 40, 98
arrests, 5, 42, 59–60, 62, 74–75, 80, 87–90, 105
Asher, Abraham, 120
Austria, 26, 109, 122

Bailey, Amy, 124–25
Bandera, Stepan, 91
Baranowicze, 4, 6
Bauer, Yehuda, 48, 110, 129
Bauman, Zygmunt, 127–28
beatings, 1, 4, 77, 89, 103, 105, 116, 118
Beck, E. M., 2, 125
Belarus, 6, 11, 30, 39, 57, 59–60, 63–65, 68–69, 80, 88, 111–13
Bender, Sara, 79
Bessarabia, 117–18
Białystok (city), 46, 78–81, 105
Białystok voivodship
   Białystok Pedagogical Institute, 60
   Bloc of National Minorities (BNM), role of, 51–52, 64–67, 69–72
   Communist Party, role of, 52, 58, 66–67, 69–70, 80, 100
   demographic patterns, 6, 27, 47, 51–52, 57, 64–67, 100
   educational environment, 60
   free loan associations, 52, 69, 71
   German occupation, 58, 60, 80–81
   Jewish population density, 6, 27, 51–52, 57, 61, 64–67, 69–70
   National Democrats' party, role of, 52, 61–62, 64–67, 70
   Non-Party Bloc for Cooperation with the Government (BBWR), role of, 52, 81
   pogrom frequency, 2, 7, 13, 45, 61, 64–70
   public administration ethnic composition, 60
   religious environment, 64–65
   retail shop ownership, 61
   shtetls, 52, 70
   Soviet Union occupation, 57–60, 65, 80–81
   See also Jedwabne pogrom
Biggs, Michael, 123
Blalock, Hubert, 124, 129
Blobaum, Robert, 11
Bloc of National Minorities (BNM), 15, 33–36, 52, 62–72, 83, 93, 95–97, 99–101, 110–11
Boćkowski, Daniel, 60
Bolechów, 6, 103–4
Bolshevism, 25–26, 75, 86, 89, 121
Borysław, 86, 91, 103–4, 107–9, 112
boycotts, 7, 9–11, 13, 26, 34–35, 38, 40, 61, 74, 90, 93, 96–97, 105, 107
Brakel, Alexander, 4, 6–7, 67–68
Branicki Palace, 81
Brass, Paul, 17
Bronsztejn, Szyja, 10
Brundage, W. Fitzhugh, 124–25
Brzezany, 88
Bukovina, 117–18
Bund organization, 10, 33–34, 41, 50, 55, 66, 79, 94–96, 117
Butrimonys, 116
Byman, Daniel, 135

Camp of National Unity, 40
Catholicism, 8–9, 31, 35, 38, 61, 73, 77, 80, 103
Chjena, 29
Chliboroby, 34
Christian Alliance of National Unity, 29
Christian Democrats, 29, 36
Christianity, 8, 11, 23–24, 26, 29, 35–36, 73, 79, 118
communism
   Belarus, role in, 30, 39, 66
   Białystok voivodship, role in, 52, 58, 66–67, 69–70, 80, 100
   equality ideal, 26, 68
   Galicia, role in, 52, 95, 98–100, 113
   Jewish sympathy, 3, 5–6, 11, 15, 66, 98
   Lwów voivodship, role in, 99–100
   Polesie voivodship, role in, 52, 66–67, 69–70, 100
   Stanisławów voivodship, role in, 99–100
   Szczuczyn, role in, 74

167

communism *(continued)*
  Tarnopol voivodship, role in, 99–100
  Ukraine, role in, 30–31, 39, 41
  universalism form, 30, 100, 134
  Volhynia voivodship, role in, 52, 85, 98, 110–13
Constituent Sejm, 28–29, 31, 33–38, 40, 83, 90
Corzine, Jay, 125
Creech, James, 125
Czechoslovakia, 109, 133, 135

Dagalevski, Aleksander, 77
Datner, Szymon, 61, 77–78
Democratic Party (U.S.), 14, 125
deportations, 4, 10, 42, 55, 59–60, 74–75, 89, 105, 128
Dhattiwala, Raheel, 123
Dieckmann, Christoph, 116
Dilo, 93
Dmitrów, Edmund, 59
Dmowski, Roman, 26
Dobroszklanaka, Sewerwyn, 91
Dontsov, Dmytro, 105
Draganówka, 104, 109
Drohobycz, 86, 103, 107
Dumitru, Diana, 87, 118

Eichmann, Adolf, 127
Einsatzgruppen, 57, 59, 85–86, 97, 121. *See also* Nazis
El-Livnot, 93
Endecja. *See* National Democrats' party

fascism, 19, 40–41, 55, 61, 90–91, 117
Feder, Szaje, 89, 91
Folkism, 33–34, 117
free loan associations, 13, 17, 40, 48, 52, 69, 71, 94, 98, 101
French Revolution, 119
Fujii, Lee Ann, 16

Galicia
  Bloc of National Minorities (BNM), role of, 52, 95–97, 99–101
  Communist Party, role of, 52, 95, 98–100, 113
  demographic patterns, 14, 27, 47, 51–52, 92, 94–95, 99–100
  election boycotts, 34–35, 38
  free loan associations, 52, 94, 98, 101
  Habsburg rule, 24–26, 90, 112
  Jewish population density, 51–52, 92, 95, 99
  Nazi occupation, 91

Non-Party Bloc for Cooperation with the Government (BBWR), role of, 52, 95, 99–100
oil industry, 107–8
Organization of Ukrainian Nationalists (OUN), role of, 41, 90–92, 97, 110
pogrom frequency, 2, 7, 13, 45, 86–87, 94–104
religious environment, 47, 49, 52
shtetls, 52, 94, 97–99, 101
Soviet Union occupation, 87–89, 102, 104–7
Ukrainian majority, 14, 25, 94–98, 101, 132
Zionism, role of, 15–16, 33–34, 36, 51–52, 93–96, 99–102, 105
See also individual voivodships
genocide, 16, 127–28
Gergel, N., 27
Germany
  Białystok voivodship occupation, 58, 60, 80–81
  emancipation-related riots, 119–20
  German Army Group Center, 58
  Lithuania invasion, 116–17
  Lwów voivodship occupation, 86
  Operation Barbarossa, 75, 116
  pogroms, role in, 2, 74, 92, 119–20
  Poland occupation, 2–3, 9, 41–42, 58–60, 80–81
  Polesie voivodship occupation, 58–59
  Soviet Union, conflicts with, 2, 17, 19, 41–42, 58, 60, 75, 85, 117
  Stanisławów voivodship occupation, 86
  Szczuczyn occupation, 74
  Tarnopol voivodship occupation, 86
  Ukraine invasion, 85–87, 91
  Volhynia voivodship occupation, 85
  See also Nazis
Ginzburg, Asher, 31
Glerntner, Matylda, 103
Golczewski, Frank, 87
Goldhagen, Daniel, 130
Great Powers, 132–33
Greece, 31, 118–19
Grodzinski, Chaim Ozer, 33
Gross, Jan, 8, 18, 129
Grünbaum, Yitzhak, 32–34, 62–63
Gubler, Joshua, 123
Gurianov, Alexander, 59

Habsburg dynasty, 24–26, 90, 112
Hamerman, Blima, 108
Hasebach, Edwin, 34
Hasidism, 10, 33, 51, 55, 96, 117, 131

INDEX 169

Haskalah, 117
Hebrew culture, 10, 15, 32–33, 63, 73, 79, 92, 94, 117
Herzl, Theodor, 31–32
Heydrich, Reinhard, 46, 85
Himka, John-Paul, 8, 106
Hindu-Muslim conflict, 3, 122–24, 126
Hitler, Adolf, 59
Hlond, August, 9
Hollander, Ethan, 118
Holocaust, 1, 44–45, 77, 109, 127–31, 134
Horowitz, Donald, 16, 44, 133–34
Horowitz, Irene, 108
Hovevei Zion, 79
humiliations, 1, 4–5, 7, 11, 33, 42, 81, 89, 103–6, 124

Iași, 117
India, 2–3, 17, 20, 122–24, 126
Israel, 5
Iwry, Samuel, 79

Jabotinsky, Vladimir (Zev), 41
Jasiewicz, Krzysztof, 6, 67–68
Jasionówka, 69
Jedwabne pogrom
　brutality, 1, 4, 64–65, 130
　civilian participation, 1, 20
　German approval, 1
　Jan Gross analysis, 8, 18, 64
　Lenin statue removal, 4
　looting, 13
　Nazi collaboration, 18
　political polarization, role of, 64–65
　scholarly research, 45
　stereotypes, impact of, 8
　symbolic role, 57, 64
Jim Crow legislation, 14
Johnson, Carter, 87, 118
Jolluck, Katherine, 10
Jordan River, 41
Józewski, Henryk, 39

Kales, Yehoshua, 58–59
Kalyvas, Stathis, 2, 17
Kenez, Peter, 121
King, Charles, 127–28
Kishinev, 120
Klier, John, 24
Klinger, Erna, 91
Kobrin, Rebecca, 80
Kolno, 4–5, 61
Kolomyja, 89, 91

Komsomol, 6
Konovalets, Ievhen, 90
Kopelman, Bolesław, 102–3
Korczynski, Janislaw, 91
Korzec, Pawel, 36
Kościelne, 5
kosher animal slaughter, 8, 40
Kostopol, 85
Kovno, 116
Kulików, 91

Lambroza, Shlomo, 120
Lanckorona Pact, 36
Lenin, Vladimir, 4–5, 89
Levin, Moshe, 4, 87
Levkanskyj, Stepan, 91
Levkovitch, Basia, 86, 108
Levytsky, Dmytro, 31, 93
Lewin, Israel, 61
Liberation party, 30
Lithuania, 20, 24–26, 42, 79, 115–18
Lithuanian Activist Front, 117
Łomża, 61
looting, 1, 13, 77, 85–86, 94, 98, 108, 118, 121
Lviv, 81
Lwów (city) pogrom, 6–7, 11, 91, 93, 103–8
Lwów voivodship
　Bloc of National Minorities (BNM), role of, 99–101
　Communist Party, role of, 99–100
　demographic patterns, 6, 27, 47, 84
　German occupation, 86
　Jewish population density, 6, 27, 84, 99
　Non-Party Bloc for Cooperation with the Government (BBWR), role of, 99–100
　pogrom frequency, 2, 7, 13, 45, 86
　reintegration efforts, 39
　shtetls, 84, 99
　Zionism, role of, 99–102
lynching, 2, 14, 18, 20, 122, 124–26

Magocsi, Robert Paul, 86
Mann, Michael, 130–32
Marcus, Joseph, 10
Massey, James, 125
Mavrogordatos, George, 118–19
McGovern, James, 124
Melnyk, Andrei, 91
Mendelsohn, Ezra, 10, 31–32, 62–63, 117
Michlic, Johanna, 9–10
Mick, Christopher, 6–7
Ministry of Education, 8

INDEX

Ministry of Religious Affairs and Public Education, 37
Ministry of the Interior, 64, 78, 80
Minorities Treaty, 28, 133
Minsk, 58–60
Mizrachi, 79
Mohilever, Samuel, 78–79
Molotov-Ribbentrop Pact, 3, 41, 74, 116
Mudry, Vasyl, 31, 90
murders, 1, 11, 16, 44, 58, 64, 75, 77, 81, 86, 89, 103–5, 108, 118, 121, 124

Nagler, Schulem, 89
Narutowicz, Gabriel, 36, 62
National Democrats' party, 11, 14, 26, 29, 35–38, 40, 52, 61–62, 64–70, 78, 81–82, 93, 96
National Party, 74
National Workers Party, 29
Nazis
  Einsatzgruppen (death squads), 57, 59, 85–86, 97, 121
  Galicia occupation, 91
  Greece invasion, 119
  Holocaust exterminations, 1
  Jedwabne pogrom, role in, 18
  Lithuania invasion, 116–17
  Organization of Ukrainian Nationalists (OUN), relations with, 90
  Poland invasion, 4, 12, 15, 83
  Polish collaboration, 18
  power seizure, 40, 59
  Schutzstaffel (SS) units, 46, 59
  Soviet Union invasion, 2–3, 16
  Wehrmacht, 59, 85
Nebe, Arthur, 59
Neighbors, 129
Niemerów, 87
Niezwisk, 104
NKVD (Soviet secret police), 5, 42, 74, 89, 92, 103, 105–6, 108
Non-Party Bloc for Cooperation with the Government (BBWR), 14–15, 37–39, 52, 57, 68–69, 81–83, 95, 99–100, 110–11, 134

Olzak, Susan, 12
On Repealing Special Regulations Related to Origin, Nationality, Race, or Religion of the Republic of Poland, 37
Operation Barbarossa, 75, 116
Organization of Ukrainian Nationalists (OUN), 31, 41, 88, 90–92, 97, 104–6, 108, 109
Ostryn, 60

Pale of Settlement, 120
Palestine, 41, 63, 73
Peasant Party (Ukraine), 34
Petersen, Roger, 2, 4, 115
Petlura, Szymon, 121
Piast, 38
Piast. *See* Polish Peasant Party (Piast)
Pieracki, Bronisław, 90
Piłsudski, Marshal Józef, 14, 19, 26–28, 37–40, 61, 68, 74, 81–82, 95, 100, 134–35
Pinchuk, Ben-Cion, 42
Plehve, Vyacheslav von, 32
Pohl, Dieter, 91
Poalei Zion, 34, 39, 79, 94
Poland
  Agudas Yisrael, role of, 33–34, 63, 66, 131
  Bloc of National Minorities (BNM), 15, 33–36, 52, 62–72, 83, 93, 96
  Bund organization, 10, 33–34, 41, 50, 55, 66, 79, 94–96
  Camp of National Unity, 40
  Christian Alliance of National Unity, 29
  Christian Democrats, 29, 36
  Constituent Sejm, 28–29, 31, 33–38, 40, 83, 90
  demographic patterns, 12, 23–24, 27
  educational environment, 8, 10, 12, 37, 39–40, 42, 63, 90
  Folkism, 33–34, 117
  free loan associations, 13, 17, 40, 48, 52, 69, 71
  German occupation, 2–3, 9, 41–42, 58–60, 80–81
  Liberation party, 30
  Ministry of Education, 8
  Ministry of Religious Affairs and Public Education, 37
  Ministry of the Interior, 64, 78, 80
  National Democrats' party, 11, 14, 26, 28–29, 35–38, 40, 52, 61–62, 64–70, 78, 81–82, 93, 96
  National Workers Party, 29
  Nazi invasion, 4, 12, 15, 83
  Non-Party Bloc for Cooperation with the Government (BBWR), 14–15, 37–39, 52, 57, 68–69, 81–83, 134
  Polish Center, 29
  Polish Peasant Party (Piast), 29, 36–38, 64
  Polish Socialist Party (PPS), 10, 30, 33, 35, 38, 83, 107
  Soviet Union occupation, 2–4, 7, 10–11, 17, 19, 41–42, 57–60, 65, 74–77, 80–83, 130

INDEX 171

Ukraine, relations with, 4, 7, 13, 26–27, 90–96
Versailles Peace Agreement impact, 27–28
Yiddishist autonomy, 33
Zionism, role of, 31–36, 41, 62–63, 79, 119
See also individual voivodships
Polesie voivodship
 Bloc of National Minorities (BNM), role of, 51–52, 66–67, 69–72
 Communist Party, role of, 52, 66–67, 69–70, 100
 demographic patterns, 27, 47, 51–52, 57, 65–67, 100
 free loan associations, 52, 69, 71
 German occupation, 58–59
 Jewish population density, 27, 51–52, 57, 65–67, 69–70
 National Democrats' party, role of, 52, 61–62, 66–67, 70
 Non-Party Bloc for Cooperation with the Government (BBWR), role of, 52, 82
 pogrom frequency, 2, 13, 45, 65–70
 Rokitno pogrom, 58–59
 shtetls, 52, 70
 Soviet Union occupation, 57–60
Polish Center, 29
Polish-Lithuanian Commonwealth, 24, 26
Polish Peasant Party (Piast), 29, 36–38, 64
Polish Socialist Party (PPS), 10, 30, 33, 35, 38, 83, 107
Ponomarenko, Panteleimon, 82
power-threat theory, 13–15, 57, 83, 85, 107–8, 111–12, 118, 120, 122, 124, 129, 134
Pripet marshes, 58
Progressive Party (U.S.), 14, 124–25
Pryłucki, Noah, 33

Radziłow, 4–5, 8, 77–78
rapes, 1–2, 118
Red Army, 3, 6, 27, 58, 60, 69, 85, 117
Redlich, Shimon, 88, 129
Reed, John, 125
Reich, Leon, 33, 93
Republican Party (U.S.), 14, 124–25
Ridna-Khata, 39
rioting, 17, 20, 44, 62, 75, 119–23, 126, 134
robberies, 11, 13, 58, 69, 106, 108
Rohrbacher, Stefan, 119–20
Rokitno, 58–59
Romania, 1, 20, 104, 117
Równo, 91
Rudnicki, Szymon, 7

Russia, 7, 20, 24–28, 31–34, 39, 60, 73, 78–80, 89, 94, 106, 109–12, 120–22, 135
Ryndner, Richard, 91

Sadagura, 117–18
Salonica, 118–19
Sambor, 104
Sanacja, 37–38, 40
Sapieha, Adam, 9
Scholl, Abraham, 87
Schutzstaffel (SS) units, 46, 59
Sheptytsky, Anrdrey, 103
shtetls, 12–13, 17, 23–25, 30, 52, 61, 69, 84, 97–99, 101, 110
Shuster-Rozenblum, Petseye, 69
Siberia, 74
Siemiatycze, 4–5, 58
Skubelski, Yeshiah, 73
Sławoj-Składkowski, Felicjan, 9, 62
Snyder, Timothy, 38, 110, 112
Social Democratic Party, 28
socialism, 10, 30–36, 41, 50, 55–56, 66, 96, 107
Soika-Golding, Chaya, 75
Solonari, Vladimir, 118
Soviet Union
 Białystok voivodship occupation, 57–60, 65, 80–81
 Galicia occupation, 87–89, 102, 104–7
 Germany, conflicts with, 2–3, 16–17, 19, 41–42, 58, 60, 75, 85, 117
 Jewish administrative representation, 4–6, 67–68, 74
 NKVD (Soviet secret police), 5, 42, 74, 89, 92, 103, 105–6, 108
 Poland occupation, 2–2, 7, 10–11, 17, 19, 41–42, 57–60, 65, 74–77, 80–83, 130
 Polesie voivodship occupation, 57–60
 Red Army, 3, 6, 27, 58, 60, 69, 85, 117
 Romania occupation, 117–18
 Szczuczyn occupation, 74–77
 Ukraine, relations with, 4, 6, 42, 85–92, 97–98
Społem, 39
Stachura, Peter, 63
Stalin, Joseph, 82, 89
Stanisławów voivodship
 Bloc of National Minorities (BNM), role of, 99–101
 Communist Party, role of, 99–100
 demographic patterns, 27, 47, 84
 German occupation, 86
 Jewish population density, 27, 84, 99

Stanisławów voivodship *(continued)*
  Non-Party Bloc for Cooperation with the Government (BBWR), role of, 99–100
  pogrom frequency, 2, 13, 45, 86
  shtetls, 84, 99
  Zionism, role of, 99–102
Stetsko, Iaroslav, 91
Stola, Dariusz, 71–72
Struve, Kai, 106
Świtalski, Kazimierz, 64
Szczuczyn pogrom, 72–80
Szyper, Henryk, 4, 6, 97

Tarnopol voivodship
  Bloc of National Minorities (BNM), role of, 99–101
  Communist Party, role of, 99–100
  demographic patterns, 27, 47, 84
  German occupation, 86
  Jewish population density, 27, 84, 99
  Non-Party Bloc for Cooperation with the Government (BBWR), role of, 99–100
  pogrom frequency, 2, 13, 45, 86, 97
  shtetls, 84, 99
  Zionism, role of, 99–102
Tarnów, 59
Terletski, Mikolaj, 108
Thoughts of a Modern Pole, 26
Tolnay, Stewart, 2, 124–25
tortures, 1, 89, 105
Transnistria, 87
Transylvania, 118
Tryczyk, Mirosław, 73
Tuczyn, 103
Turka, 89

Ugoda agreement, 36
Ukraine
  Chliboroby, 34
  Communist Party, role of, 30–31, 39, 41
  educational environment, 15, 88, 90, 94, 103
  election boycotts, 34–35, 38, 93, 96–97, 105, 107
  German invasion, 85–87, 91
  nationalist aspirations, 4, 14–16, 19, 25, 88, 90–94, 96–101
  Organization of Ukrainian Nationalists (OUN), 31, 41, 88, 90–92, 97, 104–6, 108, 110
  Peasant Party, 34
  pogrom frequency, 9, 15, 89
  Poland, relations with, 4, 7, 13, 26–27, 90–96

  religious environment, 88, 90, 94, 103–4
  Russia, relations with, 26–27, 39
  Soviet Union, relations with, 4, 6, 42, 85–92, 97–98
  Ukrainian Greek Catholic Church, 31, 47, 103, 109
  Ukrainian Military Organization, 90
  Ukrainian National Democratic Alliance (UNDO), 31, 41, 90–91, 96–97, 105
  Ukrainian Party of Labor, 93–94
  Ukrainian Social Democratic Party, 93–94
  Ukrainian Socialist Radical Party, 31
  Zionism, role of, 32–33, 93–94
  See also individual voivodships
Ukrainian Greek Catholic Church, 31, 47, 103, 109
Ukrainian Military Organization, 90
Ukrainian National Democratic Alliance (UNDO), 31, 41, 90–91, 96–97, 105
Ukrainian Party of Labor, 93–94
Ukrainian Social Democratic Party, 93–94
Ukrainian Socialist Radical Party, 31
United States, 2, 13–14, 17–18, 20, 124–26, 129

Varshney, Ashutosh, 2–3, 83, 115, 123
Versailles Peace Agreement, 27–28, 37
Volhynia voivodship
  Bloc of National Minorities (BNM), role of, 110–11
  Communist Party, role of, 52, 85, 98, 110–13
  demographic patterns, 27, 39, 47, 52, 84, 109–11
  election fraud, 38
  free loan associations, 52
  German occupation, 85
  Jewish population density, 27, 52, 84, 110–11
  Non-Party Bloc for Cooperation with the Government (BBWR), role of, 52, 110–11
  Organization of Ukrainian Nationalists (OUN), role of, 106, 110
  Peasant Party, 34
  pogrom frequency, 2, 13, 45, 110–13
  reintegration efforts, 39
  religious environment, 47, 52
  Russian partition origins, 109–10
  shtetls, 52, 84, 110
  Timothy Snyder research, 38, 110, 112
  Ukrainian majority, 109–10
  Zionism, role of, 52, 110
Von Rundstedt, Gerd, 85

Weeks, Theodore, 10
Wehrmacht, 59, 85
Wierzbiecki, Marek, 100
Wildner, Regina, 86
Wilkinson, Steven, 44, 123
Wilno, 117
Witos, Wincenty, 29, 38
Wizna, 61
Wołyn. *See* Volhynia voivodship
Wróbel, Piotr, 107
Wysoki Mazowiecki, 62
Wyszatycki, Michał, 108

Yiddish culture, 10, 15, 32–33, 63, 73, 79–80, 92, 94, 131
Yugoslavia, 135

Zabuski, Charles, 79
Zajd, Jakub, 109
Żbikowski, Andrzej, 4, 6
Zeml, Boruch Fishl, 73
Zionism, 5, 15–16, 31–36, 41, 51–52, 62–63, 73, 79, 93–96, 99–102, 105, 110, 119, 131
Złoczów, 102–3
Żółkiew, 104

www.ingramcontent.com/pod-product-compliance
Lightning Source LLC
Chambersburg PA
CBHW031441160426
43195CB00010BB/812